CAMBRIDGE LIBRARY COLLECTION

Books of enduring scholarly value

Education

This series focuses on educational theory and practice, particularly in the context of eighteenth- and nineteenth-century Europe and its colonies, and America. During this period, the questions of who should be educated, to what age, to what standard and using what curriculum, were widely debated. The reform of schools and universities, the drive towards improving women's education, and the movement for free (or at least low-cost) schools for the poor were all major concerns both for governments and for society at large. The books selected for reissue in this series discuss key issues of their time, including the 'appropriate' levels of instruction for the children of the working classes, the emergence of adult education movements, and proposals for the higher education of women. They also cover topics that still resonate today, such as the nature of education, the role of universities in the diffusion of knowledge, and the involvement of religious groups in establishing and running schools.

Schools for Girls and Colleges for Women

The author of handbooks that reflected the Victorian emphasis on bettering one's prospects, Charles Eyre Pascoe (1842–1912) addressed the topic of female education in this work of 1879, at a time when the Cambridge colleges of Girton and Newnham were in their infancy. 'Chiefly designed for the use of persons of the upper middle class', the guide aims to assist parents in making informed choices about their daughters' education. The coverage extends from kindergarten through to university, before focusing on career options for women in the late nineteenth century, in fields such as teaching, the arts and medicine. Throughout, Pascoe's recommendations are based on consideration of the breadth of the curriculum, the qualifications of the teaching staff and the results achieved in examinations. For higher education, details of entrance examinations are provided, together with information on the subjects and lectures that were open to women at that time.

Cambridge University Press has long been a pioneer in the reissuing of out-of-print titles from its own backlist, producing digital reprints of books that are still sought after by scholars and students but could not be reprinted economically using traditional technology. The Cambridge Library Collection extends this activity to a wider range of books which are still of importance to researchers and professionals, either for the source material they contain, or as landmarks in the history of their academic discipline.

Drawing from the world-renowned collections in the Cambridge University Library and other partner libraries, and guided by the advice of experts in each subject area, Cambridge University Press is using state-of-the-art scanning machines in its own Printing House to capture the content of each book selected for inclusion. The files are processed to give a consistently clear, crisp image, and the books finished to the high quality standard for which the Press is recognised around the world. The latest print-on-demand technology ensures that the books will remain available indefinitely, and that orders for single or multiple copies can quickly be supplied.

The Cambridge Library Collection brings back to life books of enduring scholarly value (including out-of-copyright works originally issued by other publishers) across a wide range of disciplines in the humanities and social sciences and in science and technology.

Schools for Girls and Colleges for Women

A Handbook of Female Education Chiefly Designed for the Use of Persons of the Upper Middle Class

CHARLES EYRE PASCOE

CAMBRIDGE
UNIVERSITY PRESS

University Printing House, Cambridge, CB2 8BS, United Kingdom

Published in the United States of America by Cambridge University Press, New York

Cambridge University Press is part of the University of Cambridge.
It furthers the University's mission by disseminating knowledge in the pursuit of education, learning and research at the highest international levels of excellence.

www.cambridge.org
Information on this title: www.cambridge.org/9781108066358

This edition first published 1879
This digitally printed version 2013

ISBN 978-1-108-06635-8 Paperback

SCHOOLS FOR GIRLS

AND

COLLEGES FOR WOMEN.

SCHOOLS FOR GIRLS
AND
COLLEGES FOR WOMEN.

A HANDBOOK OF FEMALE EDUCATION

CHIEFLY DESIGNED FOR THE USE OF PERSONS OF THE UPPER MIDDLE CLASS.

TOGETHER WITH SOME CHAPTERS ON

THE HIGHER EMPLOYMENT OF WOMEN.

BY

CHARLES EYRE PASCOE

AUTHOR OF 'A PRACTICAL HANDBOOK TO THE PRINCIPAL SCHOOLS OF ENGLAND'; 'A PRACTICAL HANDBOOK TO THE PROFESSIONS,' ETC.

LONDON:
HARDWICKE AND BOGUE, 192, PICCADILLY, W.
1879.

CONTENTS.

CHAPTER I.

CHAPTER II.

CHAPTER III.

CHAPTER IV.

CHAPTER V.

CHAPTER VI.

CHAPTER VII.

CHAPTER VIII.

CHAPTER IX.

CHAPTER X.

CHAPTER XI.

CHAPTER XII.

CHAPTER XIII.

CHAPTER XIV.

CHAPTER XV.

CHAPTER XVI.

SCHOOLS FOR GIRLS

AND

COLLEGES FOR WOMEN.

CHAPTER I.

INTRODUCTORY.

THE purpose with which I have undertaken the preparation of this little work has not been altogether devoid of self-interest. Like many other parents of limited means, I have reason to know, that not the least anxious moments of a father's life are those when the time has come for making choice of schools for the children. The word "children" I use advisedly, believing, in common with others, elementary education to be the common basis of intelligence and culture, and demanding, therefore, as earnest consideration from heads of families as education in the higher form, when the children have grown to be young men and women. In a book recently published, I ventured to direct attention to the Foundation benefits within reach of boys at our greater Public Schools. The attempt was therein made to point the way by which a clever boy, conscientious, painstaking, and apt to learn, might both become a present help to his parents by relieving them, in a measure, of his school expenses, and afterwards advance himself to, and at, the University. It has not been without some mistrust of my ability to deal satisfactorily with the subject of Girls' Schools that I have entered upon the present work. In the case of the boys, I had the irreproachable testimony of centuries of splendid tradition to guide me to the selection I made of schools which were entitled to the confidence of parents. In the present instance no such ample authority was at my command; and I have had to rely, almost wholly, upon personal inquiry and research to establish the claim of each school to its place in the following pages. If such an attestation of the value of the facts herein collected be worth anything, I may be permitted to say, that this handbook will be my own trusty counsellor and guide in planning and furthering the education of my own children. Already—while, indeed, I was engaged in writing its first chapter—the book has proved of service; for it has led me to discover that the Primary Schools of the State, with their numerous appliances, trained teachers, and system of independent inspection, offer to the children of the humbler ranks advantages which those above them in the social scale cannot command. What the precise result of this will be as regards the coming generation it would be venturesome to predict; but one effect must surely be—unless, at least, new vigour can be infused into our voluntary educational machinery—that the foremost places in the battle of life will no longer belong to those whose birth used to be supposed to ensure their position. The recognition of this in the case of the girls is less general, perhaps, than in that of the boys; but happily there is a livelier and increasing interest being shown in the whole matter of female education by women themselves, which indicates that they are awakening to wants which must be attended to and supplied.

How immediate and pressing is the necessity for some

well-devised and comprehensive scheme of Elementary and Secondary education for the daughters of persons "to middle fortune born," may possibly be gathered from a statement of my own experiences in searching for primary instruction for a little girl. I happen to reside in a populous western suburb of London, whose inhabitants, for the purposes of my story, may be classified as follows:—(1) the wealthy, who live in very noticeable mansions on the hill-side; (2) the well-to-do, consisting of prosperous professional men, merchants, and others, occupying comfortable villa residences on the plain; (3) a subordinate class—in point of numbers far exceeding the other two classes put together—composed of thrifty tradesfolk, clerks, and their fellows, striving hard, and mostly with gratifying success, to pay their way, and, we may surmise, looking forward hopefully to promotion to the hill-side by and by. Occasionally, while strolling about the thoroughfares of this outskirt of London, I have ventured an opinion with myself as to where the younger members of the families of these people are educated. At holiday seasons I have not unfrequently noticed the natty hat and well-cut jacket of Eton and Harrow in the neighbourhood of the mansions, and, therefore, conjecture that their owners, so far as their sons are concerned, support the Great Schools of England. At times I have thought that I could trace something of the youthful athleticism and sturdy independence of Rugby and Marlborough in the aspect of the lads whom I meet in the vicinity of the villa residences of the plain. And from a daily experience of some years in travelling to and from town, I can testify to the countenance given by my neighbours, the thrifty clerks and liberal-minded tradesfolk, to the excellent public day-schools of London, whereof King's and University College Schools offer very sufficient examples. So far, I feel able to give fair account of the place of education of the boys of my neighbourhood; but when I turn to the girls I am, figuratively speaking, nowhere. I take it for granted, however, that the mansions on the hill-side shelter competent governesses, and therefore pass them by. The owners of the villa residences, doubtless, also find suitable means for the daily instruction of their daughters. My curiosity, not to say wonder, is excited to know where the girls of the less prosperous inhabitants of this populous western London suburb procure their education. If the experiences of these good people in seeking for an eligible school has been anywise like my own, then I fear my curiosity is destined to remain unsatisfied, until such time as public opinion shall have pronounced in favour of systematized education for girls of the Middle classes, and a public school shall have been founded in my neighbourhood as the natural outcome of this beneficent and much-to-be-desired action.

Statistics being wearisome to the generality of readers, I guard myself against employing them here. In their place, I must ask the reader to accept of the assurance that I have been at all needful pains to confirm the truth of the following statement. In the suburb where I reside there are not less than a thousand persons, able, and doubtless willing to pay for a good Day-school for Girls, who are at present without one. Under existing circumstances, all these good people are thrown upon the resources of the neighbourhood for their daughters' education; and these failing are driven to seek for instruction for them elsewhere. An opinion of the nature and extent of the available means for female education within reach of the Middle-class inhabitants of my district, may be formed from a consideration of the following few particulars gleaned from prospectuses of existing day-schools within its boundaries. At present there are eight such schools offering education to persons of the Middle classes. Their respective proprietors (with one exception) claim, each one for her school, first, that it is "Select," and therefore of special value or excellence in the true meaning of the term; and next that it is an "Establishment" set apart for the education and bringing-up of "Young Ladies." Let us show no disposition to quibble about words, but at once admit these expressions to mean, in a scholastic sense, that only the children of persons of reasonable propriety are acceptable to the several Head-mistresses of these—I may be pardoned for using the phrase—elegant receptacles of learning. We will now proceed to consider the advantages the schools offer to girls in the way of education.

School A "provides a sound English education." It gives instruction in "English literature, with special attention to composition, and reading, ancient and modern history, physical geography with mapping, English grammar and analysis," to day-scholars for eight guineas the school year. Drawing, music, Latin, German, and calisthenic exercises are charged for extra; and a parent who indulges in these subjects of study for his daughter must pay an additional six guineas a year, and some ten guineas more if she venture upon the luxury of "Finishing Masters."

School B "bestows the utmost care on the cultivation of the minds of its pupils," and to this end finds it desirable to divide its scholastic year into four terms. It asks the scarce remunerative sum, one would think, of four guineas per annum for the instruction of day-scholars, and charges extra for "pianoforte," singing, drawing, "use of the globes," German, French, painting, and (very properly) for instruction in "the art of moulding flowers out of wax." A matter of 10*l.* per annum would, however, cover the expenses of instruction in all these desirable accomplishments.

School C desires "to render the acquirement of knowledge as attractive as possible; also to ensure a thorough understanding of the same." Its course of general study comprises "all the essentials requisite to the formation of a superior English education, including Biblical knowledge, mediæval and modern history, geography, grammar, arithmetic, drawing, French, German," &c. Ancient history, it may be noted, finds no place in the curriculum of School C, whose pupils may be supposed, therefore, to be *au fait* with the history of the world prior to the period of the Middle Ages. All subjects but English are charged for in this "School for Young Ladies" as "extras."

School D exhibits, as its ordinary course of study, "scripture history, the grammar, analysis, composition, and literature of the English language, political and physical geography, map-drawing, history, and arithmetic." It devotes special attention to instrumental music, singing, drawing, French, and German; and for the whole course of instruction, both ordinary and special, asks but the modest fee of 18*l.* per school year.

School E makes every effort to ensure a thorough knowledge of the subjects it proposes to teach, and "as far as possible to excite in the pupils themselves a sense of pleasure in their work, regard being had to their individual capacity and state of health." Its course of study is comprehensive, not to say solid, ranging from the three R's in elementary instruction to Physical Science and Political Economy in the higher parts of education. Only music is set down as an extra at this school, whose fees, in the aggregate, amount to 20*l.* per annum.

Schools F, G, and H offer no less tempting inducements to parents of moderate means, with the additional privilege that they may pay, if they are so disposed, some 50 per cent.

in addition to the ordinary school fees for tuition by "Finishing Masters." As a matter of fact, in neither of the school prospectuses under notice are the names of these "Finishing Masters" given, so that it is impossible to determine whether their instruction is worth paying for or not. Probably, however, few parents would begrudge this increased outlay if, in return for it, they could but see the end of their daughters' education.

Being in the position of a generous contributor to the rates of my district, I cannot conscientiously ask for the admission of my child to the School Board school. In this respect, it may be remarked in passing, the tradesman who supplies me with my morning's newspapers has a considerable advantage over me. He is a fairly prosperous, thrifty, and civil shopkeeper, deriving a present competence from the pleasant, and, we may trust, profitable callings of news-agent and tobacconist, with an income in addition arising from the wholesome occupation of rural postman. He would seem to have claims on the sympathy of the School Board, and his children, young and old, I am pleased to be able to say, are being educated under its admirable control. I will not weary the reader, nor make confession of my own helplessness and poverty, by setting forth the many ways in which I find the little fellow in high-lows and corduroy, who daily knocks at my door to deliver newspapers, is out-distancing my little girl in grappling with the intricacies of Elementary education. This, however, merely by the way. Not having the right of entry to the School Board schools of my neighbourhood, I am, perforce, obliged to select one from among those eight "Establishments for Young Ladies" whose prospectuses have been brought under review. At one of these schools, then—it matters not at which—my little daughter, aged six and a half years, is at present receiving

Elementary instruction. Her schoolfellows range in age from seven to sixteen years, and, in point of the social standing of their parents, are, in the true democratic meaning, her equals. In fact, the "Young Ladies' School" at which my child attends, is a distinct, and I was about to add triumphant, refutation of the oft-repeated assertion that the children of, let us say, for example, Mrs. Smith, wife of Captain Smith, retired officer of the army, have no sympathies or pursuits in common with the children of Mrs. Brown, whose husband supplies Mrs. Smith with groceries. I make mention of this matter only to show that in my neighbourhood, at least, we have practically overcome one of the great objections ordinarily urged against Public Day-schools for Girls—to wit, that class prejudices would thwart their usefulness. In our Establishments for Young Ladies, we have, in reality, no class distinctions, the word "Select" printed on the school circulars being used simply as a serviceable, and, I am bound to add, very taking decoy in the general interests of education. So far, then, it may be said that the Middle-class Private schools which I and my less prosperous neighbours support, are in alliance with those of the School Board. Both merge their claims to social pre-eminence in a common effort to distribute instruction among the million. When, however, I turn to the quality of the education that each class of school provides, and examine the methods followed by each in imparting it, I am obliged to confess—as far as my experience allows me to form an opinion—that the Middle-class Day-schools of my neighbourhood and those of the School Board are greatly at variance. I find, in the one case, no satisfactory guarantee as to the qualifications of teachers; unsuitable accommodation provided for scholars; a tendency towards showy superficiality as regards results; a neglect of proper rudimentary instruction according to approved methods; an absence of thoroughness and foundation in the subjects taught; a general lack of system from end to end of the school course; and no independent examination of pupils. In the case of the other, I notice very sufficient guarantees afforded as to the competency of teachers; admirable school buildings; great care bestowed on elementary education from the beginning; systematized instruction given to children according to their age, capabilities, and needs; due attention paid to such matters as drawing, singing, and physical exercise as part of the school curriculum; healthy emulation encouraged among the scholars; and last, not least, independent inspection by well-qualified examiners. One illustration must suffice as to the method of instruction followed in the school at which my little daughter attends. Fifteen or twenty girls, of ages varying as already stated, are herded in one small room, and taught "the various branches of an English education" to the tune of a piano! The reader may smile; but I can assure him that I am guilty of no exaggeration. The jingle of a practising piano, thrummed upon incessantly through the hours of school-work, has accompanied my child's lispings of the vowels and consonants. And, for aught I know, she may have engaged daily in the twofold occupation of keeping time with her feet to a polka-mazurka, while spluttering out the harmonious parts of ab, eb, ib, ob, and ub.

"But have you no redress?" I am asked; "surely you can remove your child to another school?" My reply to these questions is that the educational resources of my neighbourhood at present afford me no prospect of redress. I have been at some pains to inquire into the management and efficiency of the other Day-schools for girls within reach, and, on the whole, I may safely say there is not a pin's choice lying between them. There is, in fact, no alternative between the School Board schools and a school whose charges amount in the aggregate to something in excess of one hundred pounds a year. To the former I am precluded from sending my child, because, providentially in one sense, unfortunately in another, I am not quite poor enough; and for the present I am all too poor to be able to avail myself of the advantages offered by the latter. Then what is the remedy to be proposed? I confess that I should like to see established, in every town of a certain population, say of 4000 inhabitants and upwards, a Public Day-school for Middle-class Girls, under proper authority and supervision. I am not quite sure but that, in any scheme proposed for the founding of such schools, I would substitute for "proper" the word public. Considering that "there are nearly a million more females than males in Great Britain and Ireland"—as the *Times*,* in a very able leading article, discussing the subject of women's employment, the other day, pointed out—there does not seem to be any reason why the State, or the action of local bodies, should not do for Girls whatever it is desirable to do for Boys. I would create, then, in every large town a school for girls the counterpart of the excellent "City of London School" for boys, whose object is (I quote from its prospectus) "to furnish a liberal and useful education for the sons of respectable persons who are engaged in professional, commercial, or trading pursuits, without the necessity of removing them from the care and control of their parents." The cost of this "liberal and useful education" is set down in the school's prospectus at 10*l.* 10*s.* per annum, and the only extra fee is for instruction in drawing, which is charged for at the rate of "14*s.* per term." It might savour of snobbishness to dwell upon the several

* *Times*, November 13, 1878.

occupations of the parents of the boys attending this school; but it may be permitted me to say, that their social standing varies in degree just as the social position of the parents of candidates for commissions in the Queen's services, and for places in other honourable professions, varies. If it is allowed to be reputable in a brother to win a scholarship at a school such as this, the excellence of whose teaching is guaranteed by a governing body composed of some of the ablest men in the City of London, why should it be deemed unbefitting in a sister to seek admission to a similar school, the efficacy of whose instruction is attested in a like satisfactory manner? Surely the education of a daughter should be no less an object of solicitude with parents than the education of a son. Both may find it necessary to work for their living; and why, in the name of all that is reasonable, a girl should be placed at a greater disadvantage in the struggle for existence than a boy, passes comprehension. In all other respects save in the matter of education we yield protection to women; in this one matter—the most important, perhaps, of all—we leave them comparatively defenceless. Probably no life is more intensely wretched than that of the girl brought up in the sunshine of a happy home, who suddenly finds herself, as many do, reduced by the death or illness of the head of the family to the hard life of one toiling for her daily bread. Unless qualified by special education, nothing but the event, most unlikely under those circumstances, of a fortunate marriage, can save her from such a life. We should be spared the experience of much misery if women were educated so as to be independent of others if necessary, and were taught to regard as a duty the acquisition of this power of independence.

I have said that I should like to see established in all

large towns Public Day-schools for Middle-class Girls* on the model just discussed. While waiting for these, however, what existing schools, it may be asked, are deserving the attention and consideration of parents? I have endeavoured to reply to that question in the following pages. It seems to me that one of the most satisfactory guarantees of a school's efficiency that can be offered the public, is the fact that it voluntarily submits the work of its pupils to the periodical inspection of examiners appointed by the Universities. Holding this opinion, I have pursued the following plan in regard to the compilation of a principal portion of this handbook. Having carefully considered the Class Lists published by the Delegates for Local and other Examinations, appointed by the several Universities and other educational bodies, I noted the degree of proficiency exhibited by the candidates from various schools, as published in the tabular statements of the Examiners. Thereupon, I applied to the Head-mistresses or other principal authorities of such schools, for detailed information respecting the curriculum of studies and school fees. This application was in every case readily granted; and with such facts as I had succeeded in collecting before me, I proceeded to make selection of the schools whose whereabouts will be found published in the following pages.

* The reader will notice that I have given proper consideration to the excellent High Schools of the "Girls' Public Day School Company," and other associations, further on. Of the former schools, however, there are only seventeen yet established, and of these nine are within the Metropolitan district.

CHAPTER II.

PRIMARY EDUCATION: KINDERGARTENS—KINDERGARTEN TEACHING—KINDERGARTEN TRAINING.

It has been frequently remarked that the main deficiencies of boys and girls in Middle-class schools are, not so much in the advanced branches of instruction, as in the grounding that lies at the base of them all. If this be admitted, it is difficult to understand why no systematic efforts have yet been made to establish for the children of Middle-class parents, Elementary Schools on the plan of those existing under public authority. As a matter of fact, there are no such schools separate from the higher-class educational establishments and Training colleges. And, in the case only of a very few, out of a large number of Girls' Schools of the higher grade that have fallen under my notice in the course of inquiries made for the purposes of this handbook, have I found any special provision made for the systematic instruction of young children. In the "Code of Regulations" published by the School Board for London, the following are set down as the authorized subjects to be taught the youngest classes: viz. (*a*) The Bible and the Principles of Religion and Morality; (*b*) Reading, Writing, and Arithmetic; (*c*) Object lessons of a simple character, with some such exercise of the hands and eyes as is given in the Kindergarten system; (*d*) Singing and Physical exercises; (*e*) Sewing. Compare this simple and judicious course of preparatory training with that ordinarily followed in Middle-class schools. The Board School in dealing with a child takes nothing for granted; it receives her in the rough, so to speak, and educates her from the beginning. The Middle-class school, on the contrary, presupposes that the child has been taught many things at home in the nursery, and at once launches her into what are vaguely termed "the usual branches of English." It makes no systematic attempt to promote the simultaneous development of the moral, intellectual, and physical powers of the little one, who is mostly jerked from spelling to English grammar, from English grammar to outlines of geography, before, perhaps, she can read without misgiving the words pronoun and promontory. One result of this want of method is that the High Schools, now growing into favour with the Middle classes, are burdened with girls who from age belong to the upper forms, but who have not learned to use their faculties. So, at least, writes Miss Beale, Principal of Cheltenham Ladies' College, no mean authority in such a matter. "A brighter prospect, however, is before us, and our greatest hope is in our youngest classes. Still, these are not yet what they may, and will be, when the supreme importance is duly recognized of the first years of life. Then, these little ones will come to us from the intermediate class of the Kindergarten, with a physical frame well developed by daily exercises and active games; with healthy lungs and voice accustomed to singing and shouting; with a clear and accurate pronunciation; with fingers well under control; with a taste for order and symmetry in sound, form, number, and colour; with habits of attention, a lively imagination, and a delight in learning which has always been associated with brightness and happy companionship. The temper will not have been soured and made obstinate and sullen, and we may hope to find children's dispositions generally responsive, docile, and reverent." * These are the qualities

* 'On a Curriculum for Higher Schools.' A paper read at the Teachers' Conference, January 9, 1878. By Miss Beale.

which Miss Beale herself hopes to find in children who have been brought under the influence of the Kindergarten system of training. The Council of the Ladies' College over which she presides, so far share her views in regard to this interesting branch of elementary education, that they have lately added to the other departments of that excellent school a Kindergarten. It is satisfactory to learn from a recently published report that "already there are as many children attending it as can be conveniently received, until an additional room is ready." With such sufficient testimony to the advantages of the Kindergarten system at hand, I need offer no words of apology for the introduction here of such facts, explanatory of its principles, as I have thought may prove useful to parents. I have no particulars to give respecting ordinary Elementary instruction, for I regret to have to say, that all my inquiries after a well-organized Middle-class Primary School for girls, apart from the Secondary School, have for the present proved futile.

The idea that true education consists in the judicious guidance of self-education was used by Fröbel, the inventor of the system, as the basis of his Kindergarten teaching. "To take the supervision of the child before he is ready for school-life; to exert an influence over the whole being in correspondence with its nature; to strengthen the bodily powers; to exercise the senses; to employ the awakening mind; to make the child thoroughly acquainted with the world of nature and of man; to guide his heart and soul in a right direction, and lead him to the Origin of all life and to union with Him," was, as he himself has left on record, the comprehensive purpose of his new method of education. In his earlier experiences as an instructor of youth, the kindly German had noticed that boys came to him to be taught, with defects in their ways of thinking, and of feeling, which he could never satisfactorily overcome. Searching for the cause, Fröbel came to the conclusion that there was a good deal that was radically wrong in the early training of children. They were left too much, he felt, to the chance influences of the nursery, without any judicious attempts being made by parents to connect the undesigned education received there with the more deliberately planned instruction afterwards to be given at school. He, therefore, looked about for some plan by which nursery teaching might attain a permanent value in the general system of education, by making it the beginning of the same work to be continued through childhood and youth. In all his thoughts on education the illustration constantly present to Fröbel's mind was that of the growth of plants. He was wont to remark, that the tree was his teacher; and he held the work of the gardener to be very similar to that of the educator. "In an often-quoted passage he expresses himself thus: 'As the farmer and gardener treat their seeds in accordance with Nature, and in harmony with her laws, so we should educate the child and man according to their being, according to the inherent laws of life, in harmony and unity with Nature and with the Supreme Being, Source of all life.' The gardener imparts no force, establishes no laws, but after making himself acquainted with the nature of the plants under his care, secures for them, by his watchful toil, plenty of light, air, water, and space, sure that the leaves, flowers, and fruit will appear in due time. And so in the case of children, the teacher first acquires a true ideal of what they may become, and afterwards simply gives scope for the quickening and strengthening of their varied capacities. When, then, Fröbel had planned a training place for infants, he called it a *Children's Garden*, expressing thus his educational principle, and conveying a beautiful idea of the kind of influences to be exerted there, such influences as may reasonably be compared to the sunshine, rain, and good soil, by means of which plants thrive and grow." *

It was observed by Fröbel that the play of children had often a high meaning, and that it was to them as much real and earnest work as the more advanced occupation of their parents. He found, in fact, that play constituted the child's world, and wielded a certain amount of power over his after-life; that while engaged in it he was liable to childish errors of temper, lack of obedience and self-control, evils which had to be repressed; but that he was also full of activity, sociability and playfulness, and, generally, observing, constructive and appreciative, qualities that were to be encouraged. To give a child full scope for its inventive, constructive and productive faculties, writes Fräulein Heerwart (Principal of the Kindergarten College at Stockwell), and to meet its active restlessness, he provided a number of occupations, all taken from the kind of occupation which he observed in the play of children. These he formed into a system, beginning at the most easy, and advancing gradually to the more difficult—from the simple to the complicated, from the known to the unknown, but always connecting each step with the previous one, and always aiming to instruct as well as to please, to develope some faculty, and to prepare for some future subject of study. These occupations are so varied and so manifold, that even to those of riper years, they afford new sources of pleasure and occupation. The materials required for executing them are of the simplest and least expensive kind. A finished toy soon loses its charm, because nothing can be done to it; what a child delights in is to undo it, and for this he often receives undeserved punishment. He

* 'Kindergarten Training.' A paper read at the Social Science Congress at Glasgow, 1874. By E. A. Manning.

should rather have been supplied with rude materials from which he could make his own toy.*

Like other philosophical systems, that of the Kindergarten is often misunderstood, owing to the indifferent carrying out of the inventor's principles. One of the chief and most frequent accusations urged against it is, that it is simply a kind of systematized play, rather destroying than promoting the individuality of children, and, by the predominance it gives to play, tending to unfit them for the serious work of school. Wherever this accusation seems to be well founded, it may, in general, be traced to incompetence, or want of sympathy on the part of the teacher. Upon her it mainly depends whether a Kindergarten accomplishes its true intention or not. The important thing is that she should be thoroughly imbued with Fröbel's principle. As Miss Manning points out in the interesting paper already quoted:—No doubt the teacher requires special training in the use of the Gifts and in the Games and Occupations, &c. "But she will have studied these to little avail if she treats them as unrelated mechanical arts, instead of as helps to the carrying out of a whole ideal. For Fröbel's system is, after all, *not* a system. It is life acting on life. It is the calling forth of the emotions, the intellect, the physical powers, and the conscience, by one in whom all good faculties are already developed. The teacher must keep her principles constantly in view, and must test every portion of her practice by its conformity to those principles. Through a wise and loving influence she must prepare her impressible little pupils for further progress, and if she has trained them as Fröbel meant them to be trained, they will begin their school life with a happy and regulated consciousness of possessing force—physical, intellectual, and moral."

* 'Short Explanation of Fröbel's Principles of the Kindergarten System of Education.' By Eleonore Heerwart.

It is not my purpose to describe at length the method of instruction employed in Kindergartens. The reader will find much information of an interesting and useful kind on this branch of the subject in the works published for the Fröbel Society, of which I shall have something to say presently.

To ascertain the practical results to be looked for from a judicious course of training by Fröbel's system, I may be permitted once more to refer to the authority of Miss Manning, a lady who has devoted much time and study to mastering its details, and whose opinion upon this point is, therefore, of great weight. She considers that in a good Kindergarten the following processes are at work:—The children are gaining new ideas every day, and in the manner most suited to their young nature, through *handling* and *doing*. Experimentally they are taking in accurate notions of form and number, learning, in fact, the elements of geometry and arithmetic, and as great keenness of observation is cultivated, they will afterwards find reading easy of attainment. Their stock of knowledge about the world in which they are so lately come to live is increasing through the teacher's talk with them, and their intercourse with Nature. Their fondness for construction finds scope; the little fingers become deft and nimble, and thus the way is paved for writing, needlework, and other manual operations. Their inventive powers are also greatly developed, and in presenting the little objects that they make to some one at home, their affections find a healthy gratification. Order, industry, perseverance, and respect for the rights of others, are among the qualities which are quietly growing. The games, too, have a special educational value, being carefully adapted to secure bodily development. The child is moreover learning in the Kindergarten the power of language. Day by day it is adding to its limited vocabulary, and, through habit, finding it more easy to convey its thoughts to others. By the stories it hears related, and by the teacher's approval of all good tendencies, a moral enthusiasm is kindled, the child's vista of life is widened, and true judgments of right and wrong are instinctively formed. These are the beneficial effects which, in Miss Manning's opinion, should ensue upon a proper application of the methods of Fröbel.

It has been remarked, that, in cases where Kindergartens fail to accomplish the purpose at which their founder intended they should aim, in general, the teaching is somewhere at fault. Unless a competent instructor be chosen thoroughly acquainted with the characteristics of Fröbel's system, its toys and games will be but toys and games, instead of proving, as intended, stepping-stones to that which is higher, the gradual and harmonious development of all the senses, faculties, and virtues of the child. The inquiry then naturally arises, how may parents, anxious to take advantage of Kindergarten for their children's elementary training, be assured of the qualifications of *Kindergärtnerinnen* (children-gardeners). The most practical answer, probably, that I can give to such inquiry is to set before the reader the sources whence I have collected the material which has enabled me to write this chapter. I am indebted, then, chiefly to the "Fröbel Society," an association of ladies and gentlemen "formed with the objects of promoting co-operation among those engaged in Kindergarten work, of spreading the knowledge and practice of the system, and of maintaining a high standard of efficiency among Kindergarten teachers." Among the practical aims of this Society, the following are to be noticed, viz.:—

(*a*) The Examination of Students and the granting of Certificates of their qualification to become Kindergarten Teachers.

(*b*) The Inspection and Registration of Kindergartens.

(*c*) The establishment of a Central Kindergarten and a Training College in London.

The annual examinations of the Fröbel Society have been well attended by candidates from all parts of the country anxious to secure its certificate, which may now be looked upon as a sort of diploma of competency in the art of Kindergarten teaching. In the report of the British and Foreign School Society for 1878, the Committee, referring to their "Kindergarten College and Practising School" at Stockwell, remark, that "the demand for Kindergarten teachers is far greater than the supply." The Committee, therefore, feel it right to give every possible facility to young women who wish to qualify themselves as teachers of little children on Fröbel's principles. To this end they make public the antecedent qualifications for pupils desirous of entering their college classes. I reproduce them here, in order that the reader may estimate for himself, first the value of the certificate of the Fröbel Society, whose examinations the Stockwell students take; and next the degree of proficiency which is essential in a Kindergarten teacher.

"It is presumed," write the Committee, "that those who apply for training have already received a good English education, and have passed, or are prepared to pass, an examination in reading, writing, arithmetic, grammar and composition, history, and geography. For those, however, who have had no early advantages, an opportunity is given of attending evening classes in English language, arithmetic, geography, history, domestic economy and needlework, French, singing, and school management. Candidates must be over seventeen years of age, and be able to furnish evidence of good character and love for children. The training occupies two years (six terms). In the first year the students attend classes, and are chiefly engaged in study and observation. During the second year they have, in addition, to take part in the management and teaching of the classes of the model kindergarten, and thus obtain the requisite practice." The course comprises the following:—

1. The Theory of education, embracing the principles of physical, mental, moral, and religious training of children, and, specially, the method of managing a kindergarten and transition class.
2. The History of education in ancient and modern times, and the biography of celebrated teachers.
3. Fröbel's life and principles, with special reference to the kindergarten system.
4. Children's games and the art of story-telling.
5. Singing and the elements of harmony.
6. Geometry as applied to the kindergarten occupations.
7. The elements of natural science—botany, zoology, physics.
8. School hygiene.
9. Practical lessons in all the kindergarten occupations, viz.:—

Group I.—SOLIDS: balls, cubes, and cylinders.

Group II.—PLANES of wood, planes of paper; folding, cutting, and plaiting.

Group III.—LINES: paper-twisting, stick-plaiting, stick-laying, peas work; curved lines, metal rings and thread-laying, drawing.

Group IV.—POINTS: pricking and sewing.

Group V.—PAINTING and MODELLING.

10. Practice in teaching and the management of children in classes.
11. Gardening.

This curriculum will serve to show that a Kindergarten teacher requires, in practice, to know something more than the mere art of amusing children, which some suppose alone to be sufficient. It may be mentioned, that the Fröbel Society, in addition to undertaking the examination of students, helps in other ways to promote the efficiency of Kindergartens, and those who profess to teach in them. At the request of head-mistresses it arranges for periodical inspection of Kindergartens by competent inspectors who give special attention to the following among other points: —(1) The manner and method of teaching of the staff; (2) The course of lessons carried out, and specimens of the children's work; (3) General arrangements, such as suitability of rooms, ventilation, furniture, &c. A list of Kindergartens which have conformed to the inspection rules is kept for reference by the Society. At Easter, 1879, a Kindergarten Training College under its auspices will be opened in a central district of London. On the whole, I think, I cannot do better than advise parents seeking to establish Kindergartens in their neighbourhood, or wishing to select such schools for their children, or desiring to secure the services of efficient teachers, to take counsel with the Fröbel Society, the address of whose Honorary Secretary is 27, Upper Bedford Place, London, W.C. I also recommend to the attention of parents the following books and papers which among others have afforded me much useful information, viz. :—

'The Kindergarten, Principles of Fröbel's System.' By Miss Shirreff.

'Life of Fröbel.' The same author.

'The Kindergarten in Relation to Family Life.' Paper read at the monthly meeting of the Fröbel Society, March 12, 1878. By the same.

'Kindergarten Training.' Paper read at the Social Science Congress at Glasgow, 1874. By E. A. Manning.

'Fröbel and Infant Education.' Pamphlet by the same author.

'The Kindergarten Explained.' By Ethel Ridley.

'Address Delivered by Mrs. William Grey at the Annual Meeting of the Fröbel Society, December 5, 1876."

'Short Explanation of Fröbel's Principles of the Kindergarten System of Education.' By Fräulein Heerwart.

'The New Education.' By Miss Shirreff.

'The Kindergarten in Relation to Schools.' By the same author.

All these publications may be procured for a few shillings.

The following list of existing Kindergartens of well-ascertained efficiency will afford parents a means of examining Fröbel's methods of teaching in practice.

LONDON.—The Kindergarten College and Practising School (*under the auspices of the British and Foreign School Society*), 21, Stockwell Road, S.W.

Miss Roth's Kindergarten, 54, Kensington Gardens Square, W.

Miss Emily Lord's, 9, Norland Place, Notting Hill, W.

Miss Frank's, 143, Camden Road, N.

Miss Bishop's, 10, Fitzroy Square, W.C.

Miss Chapman's (The School of Art), Croydon.

The City of London College for Ladies, 8, City Road, Finsbury Square.

The Chelsea High School, Durham House, Smith Street, Chelsea, S.W.

The Home and Colonial Training College Kindergarten, Gray's Inn Road, W.C.

CHELTENHAM.—The Ladies' College. Kindergarten for children under seven.

GRAVESEND.—The Laurels, Overcliffe. Kindergarten for children under seven.

NORWICH.—The High School for Girls, Theatre Street, Norwich.

OXFORD.—The High School, 16, St. Giles's.

SOUTHAMPTON.—The Girls' College.

CHAPTER III.

SECONDARY EDUCATION: THE PRESENT STANDARD OF FEMALE MIDDLE-CLASS EDUCATION CONSIDERED WITH REFERENCE TO THE JUNIOR LOCAL EXAMINATIONS OF THE UNIVERSITIES.

THE phrase "Higher Culture of Women," common among those engaged in the beneficent task of improving and raising the condition of Middle-class female education, is calculated to mislead. Moreover, it too frequently proves an offence to those old-fashioned but, doubtless, very worthy people who still cherish the notion, that well-educated young ladies must needs be pedants and blue-stockings, and that marriage being the goal at which all true women should aim, high attainments on their part are to be discouraged. A great deal of prevalent misapprehension in regard to this all-important question of female education might be removed, and not a little hostility to its purpose be averted, if, for the above, the expression Proper Culture of Women were to be substituted. A Cambridge student might, we will say, to suit his inclination, enter on the higher cultivation of mathematical knowledge after appearing senior on the list of wranglers. If his means were scanty, most persons would consider that he might be more profitably engaged in earning his living. Few, however, would venture the opinion that he had displayed lack of wisdom in competing, during his college course, for the highest honour in the mathematical tripos, the attainment of which might very well serve to denote the acme of proper culture among Englishmen. To make my meaning more clear, may I be allowed to consider, in company of the reader, a few of the questions from the examination papers set to Junior candidates (Girls) at the Local Examinations held in 1878 under the auspices of the Universities of Oxford and Cambridge?

These examinations, it should be remarked, are of two parts, (1) Compulsory, (2) Optional. Every candidate for the certificate of the examiners is required to satisfy them in: —(*a*) Reading aloud a passage from some English author; (*b*) Writing from dictation; (*c*) English Grammar, including the parsing and analysis of sentences, generally selected from a portion of some well-known English author read beforehand; (*d*) Arithmetic. In addition to the foregoing, the candidate is required to satisfy the examiners in three at least of nine "optional" subjects which she has studied at school. These are as follows:—(*a*) Religious Knowledge (which must be one of the three selected); (*b*) English; (*c*) Latin; (*d*) Greek; (*e*) French; (*f*) German; (*g*) Mathematics; (*h*) Mechanics and Mechanism; (*i*) Chemistry. In the case of the Cambridge examination, Zoology and Botany may be taken up.

At the first glance this is a somewhat solid array of work for a girl of sixteen to undertake, and, may be, is calculated to frighten timid parents who have not dissected the regulations and papers of the Universities' examiners. But in the first place, the questions set are only of an elementary character; and in the next, it may be assumed that no girl will ask to be examined in a given subject who has not devoted some special attention to it at school. Thus, knowledge of Latin and Greek is not commonly met with among girls; still, a girl may have read both languages and learned to appreciate their educational value. In such case she will naturally elect to be examined in these, instead of in French or German, of which perchance she may know but little. And so in regard to Mathematics, Mechanics, and Chemistry. Personally I may know very little of Mechanics, and as a matter of fact, unfortunately do know very little of that science; but I suppose, that were I to give ordinary attention to the study of it, I might hope to master its principles in time. What I might do in my leisure moments at home, a girl might very well do at school; and, probably, at the end of our course of reading she would pass quite as satisfactory an examination as I. If parents would but look at these matters fairly, the "Higher Culture of Women" spectre would soon vanish. Let us now consider a few of the questions (and I will select those of average difficulty) proposed to girls of sixteen years of age at the last Local Examinations of the Universities mentioned.

OXFORD.

In "'Reading aloud," a passage from Scott's 'Waverley' was selected. In "Dictation" a passage from English history. In "English Grammar" the candidate (having already read the selected work, be it borne in mind, during the preceding school year) was asked to parse the words printed in italics in the following passage from Milton's 'L'Allegro':—

"Hard by, a *cottage chimney* smokes
From betwixt two aged oaks;
Where Corydon and Thyrsis *met*,
Are at their savoury dinner set
Of herbs, and other *country* messes,
Which the neat-handed Phyllis dresses:
And then in haste her bower she leaves,
With Thestylis *to bind* the sheaves:
Or if the earlier season *lead*,
To the tanned haycock in the mead."

Here is another question in Grammar :—

" Explain the following terms, and give examples of each: (1) Auxiliary verb, (2) Infinitive mood, (3) Participle, (4) Passive voice, (5) Tense."

In " English Composition " the candidate was asked to describe either " A Journey taken," " An Event witnessed," or " A Battle read of."

In " Arithmetic " the following examples of the questions proposed are of average difficulty :—

" Thirty-three telegraph posts, placed at equal distances, extend a mile ; how far apart are the posts ? "

" If 159 articles cost 19*s.* 10½*d.*, find the cost of 161 such articles."

The above examples are selected from the examination papers set in the Compulsory, or, as it is called, " Preliminary " part of the examination. Now we come to the Optional subjects, whereof Religious Knowledge stands first as essential. Here again the books on which questions were proposed were supposed to have been specially read in the school course by candidates during the previous year. These books in 1878 happened to be Joshua, Judges i.–xviii., and the Gospel of St. John, and here are one or two of the questions asked upon them :—

" Explain the following, with reference to the context in which they occur :

(1) 'Loose thy shoe from off thy foot ; for the place whereon thou standest is holy.'

(2) 'Out of the eater came forth meat, and out of the strong came forth sweetness.'

(3) 'Give an outline of the conversation of our Lord with the woman of Samaria, mentioning the circumstances under which it was spoken.' "

In " Outlines of English History " (a given period had been already set by the examiners in the previous year) such questions as these were put:—"Who were the leading Saxon nobles or clergy left in England after the battle of Hastings, and what became of them?"

"What circumstances caused Charles the First's want of money? By what unconstitutional measures did he try to obtain money, and on what legal grounds did he defend those measures?"

In "Geography," a candidate was asked, among other questions, to point out:—"What parts of Europe are peopled chiefly by Slavonian races?—What places in the United Kingdom are the chief seats of the manufacture of (1) woollen, (2) cotton, (3) linen goods; and from what countries are the raw materials of those goods chiefly derived?"

In "Latin," an easy piece from Cæsar and Virgil was set; in "Greek," from Xenophon and Homer; in "French," a passage from Souvestre's 'Un Philosophe sous les toits'; in "German," from Schiller's 'Wilhelm Tell.' The passages from each of the above-named works, set in the 1878 examination, were selected in 1877. In "Mathematics," the examples set were purely elementary, and the same may be said of the other "Optional" subjects, in which Oxford last year examined girls not above the age of sixteen.

CAMBRIDGE.

In "Dictation," a passage from one of Mr. Ruskin's works was selected. In "English Grammar," a candidate was asked, among other things, to parse:—

"No fire had we but the seal-oil lamp,
Nor other light did know."

"To write down the plurals of *motto*, *die*, *staff*, *chimney*, *soliloquy*, *brief*, *pea*, *phenomenon*, *penny*."

To analyse the following sentence:—

"When the men who were exploring the pit ascertained that

the water had reached a certain level, they knew that the imprisoned colliers could not be rescued without great difficulty."

In "Arithmetic," such questions as the following were in the paper:—

"Find by *Practice* the cost of 2 cwt. 1 qr. 20 lbs. 4 oz. at 1*l.* 17*s.* 4*d.* per quarter.

"Find the greatest common measure of 40457 and 420325.

"Resolve the numbers 18, 16, 36, 44, 45, 48, 63, 121 into their simplest possible factors, and find their least common multiple."

In "Old Testament History" and "Scripture," candidates were examined in Kings (II.) and the Gospel of St. Luke. Here is a specimen question on the latter:—

"What message was borne by the disciples of St. John the Baptist to our Lord, and what was the reply?

"Explain the phrase, 'and much more than a prophet.'"

In "English History" and "Geography," the examiners asked for answers to such questions as these:—

"What charges were brought against the Seven Bishops?

"When, and under what circumstances, did the following become part of the British Empire—*Ireland*, *Scotland*, *Jamaica*, *Gibraltar*, *Bombay*, *Canada*, *Guernsey*?

"State the events which were the immediate cause of the revolt of the North American colonies.

"Give in order of their size:—

(1) The six largest seaports of England, naming the rivers they are on.
(2) The three highest mountains of Scotland.
(3) The three largest lakes of Ireland.

"What are the principal exports of India, Russia in Europe, Spain, and Turkey in Asia."

In "Latin," "Greek," "French," "German," "Mathematics," &c., the papers set by the examiners for Cambridge were not in any degree more difficult than those placed before candidates by the examiners acting for the University of Oxford. Here are some specimen questions in Latin, for instance:—

"Translate into Latin:

(*a*) Your father and I are here.
(*b*) He lived ten years.
(*c*) He is worthy to die.
(*d*) If I had known I would have told you.
(*e*) Tell me if you have been at Rome.

"(8) Translate into Latin:

insilio
The signal for battle being given, the King leapt upon his horse. The enemy were already close to the walls,
intercipio
and were preparing to cut off some of the Romans, and to
occupo
take possession of the heights."

And, here, in French:—

Translate:

"Loin de me rassurer, en voyant Bonaparte plus souvent, il m'intimidait toujours davantage. Je sentais confusément qu'aucune émotion du cœur ne pouvait agir sur lui. Il regarde une créature humaine comme un fait ou comme une chose, mais non comme un semblable. Il ne hait pas plus qu'il n'aime; il n'y a que lui pour lui: tout le reste des créatures sont des chiffres. La force de sa volonté consiste dans l'imperturbable calcul de son égoïsme; c'est un habile joueur d'échecs dont le genre humain est la partie adverse, qu'il se propose de faire échec et mat.

"What is the gender of *histoire*, *permanence*, *position*, *main*?

"Give the plurals of *arc-en-ciel*, *sauf-conduit*, with reasons for your answers: also the plural and feminine of *nouveau-marié*, *aigre-doux*.

"Write in French: *these generous qualities*, *a pretty peasant woman* ('*paysan*' = peasant *man*), *his long white hair* (plural)."

Now, is it possible for anyone to say, after glancing at these examples from the papers set to Junior candidates at the Oxford and Cambridge Local Examinations, that they represent too high a standard of knowledge for a girl of sixteen? Do they not, on the contrary, seem to propose a standard so moderate, that one would at once say that the school-years of a girl from nine to sixteen must have been very grossly misspent if, at the latter age, she were unable to pass it? And yet in many of the prospectuses of Girls' Schools that have come under my notice, it is advertised to parents, that "Pupils are prepared for the Oxford and Cambridge Local Examinations," positively, as if a *special* preparation were necessary to reply to such questions as I have selected! With shame it must be admitted that, in some cases, "special" preparation is necessary. The other day, in conversation with a young lady, pupil of a school which enjoys the advantage of instruction from "Finishing Masters," I inquired what History she had lately been reading? She mentioned a well-known work on Modern Europe. I asked if she had read any of Macaulay's history. She had not, and took the opportunity of asking of me in return, "Who was Macaulay?" Pursuing my inquiries further for curiosity's sake, I ventured to inquire if she could tell me anything respecting Pope? "Pope," said I, "an author of great repute in English literature." Almost imploringly she looked at me, as if to beg that I would stop here, and replied, "Something to do with Rome, wasn't he?" Then, to wind up my short examination, thinking she might possibly have at command a fact or two concerning the author of a Dictionary of her own language, I asked if she knew "anything of the great Dr. Johnson?" She knew nothing of the great Dr. Johnson! I am not at liberty to mention the age of this young friend; but without betraying any confidence, I may say that it exceeded by a few months the age "Juniorum, qui ante diem primum mensis Julii immediate praecedentis decimum quintum aetatis annum non compleverint."* I may further remark that she had been attending "Establishments for Young Ladies" since the age of eight. It would be proper to add, however, that the mistresses of those institutions cannot with fairness be held altogether responsible for the present deficiencies in my young friend's education. The "Piano" should share the blame, along with "French" and the other "accomplishments," imperfectly taught her for the purpose, be it said, of enabling her, by and by, to earn her own living. Can anything be more deplorable than this? May I be allowed now to ask, in face of the above facts, whether it is a "Higher" culture or a "Proper" culture of women at which we should most especially aim, in attempting to improve and raise the present condition of Middle-class female education? The subjects dealt with at the Oxford and Cambridge Local Examinations are, as we have seen, the great fundamental ones of general knowledge; yet, forsooth, at some schools our daughters are taught them, as if an acquaintance with those subjects marked the culminating point of woman's education. Do let us, for these daughters' sake, strike for the Proper education of Englishwomen first, and discuss the motives to their Higher culture afterwards.

It seems to me—and I hope the reader may feel able to share this opinion—that in the interests of parents, no less than of schoolmistresses themselves, some system of inde-

* Extract from the Statute of Oxford University providing for the examination of candidates "qui non sunt de corpore Universitatis."

pendent examination of schools for Middle-class girls is in the highest degree necessary. It is desirable, on the one hand, that evidence should be forthcoming to the parent that his child is being properly and progressively educated; it is essential, on the other, that the mistress should have at command proof that her teaching is sound, and according to the approved methods of the day. The testimony of an impartial examiner is calculated to meet both these requirements. I would, however, keep the examination of Girls' Schools within reasonable limits; and in my humble judgment those limits could scarcely be more satisfactorily or precisely defined than in the qualifications set forth for candidates desiring to secure the certificates of the "Local" examiners of the Universities of Oxford and Cambridge. It is because I entertain this opinion, and know of no better way than independent inspection for setting the stamp of thoroughness, foundation, and system on a school's teaching, that I have considered the granting of such certificate to the pupils of a school a sufficient passport to its place in the chapters which follow. In the lists which have been therein given, no school has been inserted whose address is not likewise to be found in the last issued "Local Examinations" class lists of the English, Scotch, and Irish Universities.

CHAPTER IV.

SECONDARY EDUCATION — *continued*. PROPRIETARY COLLEGES, AND HIGH AND ENDOWED SCHOOLS.

It was a subject of frequent remark in the Report of the Schools Inquiry Commission of 1864, that Girls' Schools are more numerous in England, and very much smaller, than those for boys. At the period of that commission it was ascertained that the average number of pupils in Ladies Schools was about twenty-five, and, as an obvious consequence of their smallness, that they were generally more expensive than boy's schools. "They ought," remarked Mr. Fitch, in his report to the commissioners, "to be less so, seeing that women who do a given amount of work are satisfied with a smaller remuneration than men; and that the expenses of a household consisting entirely of female inmates need not be so great. But relatively to the advantages purchased, and to the teaching power employed, much more is always charged for girls than for boys. If a lady is to obtain even a humble livelihood out of the profits on twenty or twenty-five pupils, she must make a large demand on each. Accordingly all the means whereby the bill can be increased, the extra charges to which I have referred before, as swelling the total account in boarding establishments for the other sex, are to be found in still larger proportion in 'ladies' schools.' . . . Nothing can well be more extravagant than the waste of money and of educational resources in these small schools. There is little life, no collective instruction, and nothing to call forth the best powers of either teacher or learner in a school where each class consists of two or three pupils only. Even if a teacher were highly qualified, she would in time grow dispirited and mechanical under the sense that she was frittering away her strength in small efforts, and producing results so insignificant in proportion to them." So wrote Mr. Fitch in the year 1868–9, and there is unfortunately little reason for doubting that what he wrote then concerning the smaller ladies' schools, applies with any less force to schools of the same class now. As compared with boys' schools, the generality of girls' schools can scarcely be said to be organized at all. There is a certain number of classes, or of girls learning particular things; but there is neither any definite course of studies mapped out, nor any grouping of classes so as to work into one another. In the smaller and cheaper schools one mistress alone, or a mistress aided by a pupil not unfrequently very indifferently instructed herself, teaches every subject to every class in one or at most two rooms. The fifteen or twenty scholars are of all ages, from eight to sixteen; hence half or two-thirds are left to their own devices while the rest are saying their lessons, and thus contract dawdling and listless habits, which would destroy the effect even of far better teaching than they receive. There is no system in these little schools; things go as chance or the momentary convenience of the mistress directs; the pupil's progress is not marked and registered, for she is never examined, and there is no higher class for her to enter; the total number is too small to excite, not merely emulation, but any spirit or sense of movement. These, for the most part, are the words of Mr. Bryce, a colleague of Mr. Fitch on the same commission. They so completely describe the state of things in many Girls' Schools now—be it borne in mind ten years after the opinions expressed first appeared in print—that I have taken the liberty of reprinting them here as embodying my own present impressions after a careful perusal of a number of school documents in my possession.

It has been remarked that the education of boys in England has only been saved from the abyss of triviality and vulgarity by the application, however clumsy, of endowments.* In other countries the same purpose has been served, perhaps better (notably in the United States), by appropriations from the revenues of the State. For girls the same salvation can only be obtained in the same way, or by private enterprise: by the creation of Proprietary Schools or Colleges on the plan of some of the greater Public Schools for boys. A model of a school formed upon these lines presents itself in the existing Ladies' College at Cheltenham. I select this institution as worthy of attention, because it includes within its system the best example of a Girls' Boarding-school with the best example of a Girls' Day-school. The number of its pupils at present is 440. I have before me its Twenty-third Annual Report, containing the reports of the College Examiners; and comparing their statements with those of Examiners of other girls' schools at hand, I am little short of astonished at the degree of excellence to which the teaching at Cheltenham Ladies' College has attained.† In French, for instance, out of 155 pupils examined,

	63	pupils gained more than	70	per cent. of the marks allowed.
	71	" " " "	50	" " "
and	21	only failed to obtain	50	" " "
	155			

The Rev. P. H. Ernest Brette, B.D. (Head Master of the French School, Christ's Hospital; Examiner in the University of London; at Harrow School, &c., &c.), the Examiner, reports that the standard in French at the Ladies'

* Report of Mr. Hammond. † See *Note* following title-page.

College "is much higher than in any other school I have examined during the last twenty years." In German, out of ninety-three papers examined, twenty-seven rose above 75 per cent., and of these, seven above 90 per cent. In Latin, the Examiner (Rev. C. E. Graves, M.A., Classical Lecturer at St. John's College, Cambridge), reports that the "translations from Horace were in general most satisfactory." In History, Mr. Samuel R. Gardiner (Lecturer on English History at King's College, London), states that "the result of the examination, as far as the knowledge of facts is concerned, is eminently satisfactory." In Geography, of the total examined, by far the majority obtained 75 per cent. marks. Here is Mr. A. G. Fitch's (one of Her Majesty's Inspectors of Schools) report of his examination in English Literature :—"In regard both to accuracy and to the fulness and quality of the knowledge displayed, it appears to me that a higher level of merit has been attained this year than last. All the selected plays of Shakespeare have been studied with care and minuteness; the historical and other allusions have been investigated; and more attention seems to have been given than heretofore to the history of archaic and obsolete words. Some of the replies on the moral purpose and significance of the several dramas, seemed to me to possess great merit, and to amount to much more than a mere reproduction of criticism which had been learned from a book or a lecturer."

In Arithmetic, Algebra, Geometry, and Natural Philosophy, the Examiner (Mr. Philip Magnus, B.Sc. Univ. Lond.) states that the average answers have been highly satisfactory. Last, not least, in Religious Knowledge, the general results of the examination were "of a highly satisfactory character throughout." Each of the appointed Examiners is of recognized eminence in his own particular line of work, and was therefore not likely to slur over, or pass lightly upon the faults of the students.

It would have been impossible for these results to have been obtained in any school that had not good classification, organization, and teaching power. Few small schools, framed on the ordinary lines of ladies' schools, could furnish such testimony of their efficiency, for the chief reason, that in most of them a comprehensive and consistent course of study can very seldom be carried out. Pupils are received into such schools, without any regard to uniform age of admission, pass no examination as to their capabilities on entrance, and are drafted into classes, mostly at the whim of parents, according as each parent's views in regard to "accomplishments" are more or less pronounced. At Cheltenham Ladies' College a child may enter the junior class at seven years of age, and may go through an eight years' gradual but definite course of instruction, which, in respect to its fulness, and the method by which it is governed, far excels the best course that the best "finishing school for young ladies" could possibly supply. The reason for this is, that the College can afford to engage, and as a matter of fact does engage, a large permanent staff of teachers of first-rate ability. Its tutorial staff at present comprises a Lady Principal, assisted by about thirty English and four foreign Governesses and various Lecturers. Its course of instruction includes:—"Holy Scripture, History, Literature, English Language, Geography, Arithmetic, Geometry, Algebra, Natural Science, Natural Philosophy, Chemistry, French, German, Latin, Greek, Calisthenics." Its school terms are three, and following are the inclusive charges for each term:—

	Day Pupils.			Boarders.		
	£	*s.*	*d.*	£	*s.*	*d.*
For Pupils of 15 years and upwards	8	8	0	27	6	0
" under 15 but above 10	6	6	0	25	4	0
" under 10	4	4	0	23	2	0
" under 7	3	3	0			

The only extra charges are for Music and Drawing (both taught by first-rate masters), the ordinary fee being *2l. 2s.* "for the course." I am not prepared to say that an average of 75*l.* per year for board and tuition may not be a little in excess of the means of some parents of the Middle class. This I am, however, disposed to maintain, namely, that in no boarding-school for girls in the kingdom can a better education be had for the same amount of money than is offered, as above set forth, by the Ladies' College at Cheltenham. It should be pointed out that boarders at this institution are lodged in "Boarding-houses" on the same excellent plan that obtains at the great Public Schools for boys. The government of Cheltenham Ladies' College is vested in a Council elected by the proprietors. No teachers or officers of the institution are eligible for election—a guarantee that the interests of the pupils will be preferred to those of the teachers.

For purposes of comparison, let me now lay before the reader one or two facts gleaned from the prospectus of another "Ladies' College," under private management, in a town not a hundred miles from Cheltenham. "The course of instruction provided in this College" (I quote from the prospectus), "includes every study and accomplishment necessary to a finished education." That course, as set forth in the school's circular, is as follows:—"English, generally; French, German, Singing, Harmony, Pianoforte music, Drawing, and Water-colours." The school year is divided into three terms, and the school charges are as follows:— "Pupils under twelve years of age, 100 guineas per annum; pupils above twelve, 120 guineas." Fourteen weeks' holidays are allowed in each year, so that at this school the board and education of a girl over twelve years of age, costs her parents at the rate of 3 guineas per week. Allowing, for sake of argument, 30 shillings per week to be a fair charge for a young lady's board and lodging, it follows that at the "Ladies' College" under review an additional 33 shillings per week must be forthcoming for the purposes of her education. With, perhaps, one exception, there is not a Public School (for Boys) in the kingdom that would venture to make such a charge. When I say this, I am not alluding to the tuition fees of Foundationers, or boys educated from endowment funds; but to those which are charged to the ordinary students. Take Harrow School, for instance; I find that the educational expenses of a Boarder in the Head-master's House are as follows:—Public Tuition and School charges per annum, 28*l.* 10*s.*; Private Tuition per annum, 15*l.*: total for tuition per annum, 43*l.* 10*s.* There are thirty-eight weeks in the Harrow School year, so that the cost of a boy's instruction there, public and private, is about 23 shillings per week. At Winchester College, the expenses of a "commoner" are as follows:—For School fees an annual sum of 26*l.* 10*s.*; for board and private instruction by the House Master an annual sum of 78*l.* 10*s.*: Total for board and education, both, 105*l.* At Charterhouse the school expenses of a boarder are:—Tuition, 30*l.* per annum; Board, 70*l.* per annum: Total for board and education, both, 100*l.* per annum. Thus, at our best Public Schools, a boy may obtain board and education (with the possibilities of earning preferment to the University) for 20*l.* a year less than is charged for a young lady's board and instruction—granted that the latter, in this instance, includes "every study and accomplishment necessary to a *finished* education"—at a comparatively small private school which cannot possibly possess a tithe of the facilities for teaching. It would be charitable to suppose that the particular "Ladies' College," whose prospectus we have glanced at, is one of those institutions typified in the following little anecdote related by a lady at a meeting of the Social Science Association. In conversation with the mistress of a school, the relater of the story pointed out that the certificate of the Local Examiners of the Universities would enable any one of her pupils readily to obtain employment as a teacher, should occasion arise. "Madam," replied the mistress, "the young ladies attending my seminary will never require to put their education to any practical use." Fortunately, this handbook has not been undertaken in the interests of those who believe that the selectness and exclusiveness of a girls' school constitute the best tests of its merits. I have written my little book, principally, as an aid to those who desire, like myself, some more substantial guarantee that the education of a child shall be directed towards higher aims than the possibility that, in after-years, she may not have to turn that education to practical account.

In passing, I would ask the reader to call to mind for a moment what I incidentally mentioned in the first chapter of this book, namely, that I hoped myself to profit by the information it contains, in planning my own children's education. My position, therefore, is almost precisely that of the reader's, if, as I take it, he follows my statements solely with the view of seeing what he can glean from them likely to prove useful to himself. I shall but follow his example, when the book is before me bearing the imprint of the publisher. From the list of schools hereinafter given, it will be my care to make selection of the one most calculated to meet my requirements and means; and, in like manner, doubtless will the needs of the reader be the principal consideration in directing him to a choice. I can give no better assurance of the efficiency of the schools appearing in the following directory, than the fact, that pupils trained in them have secured (some with "Honours," some without) the "Local Examinations" certificate of the Universities and College of Preceptors.

PROPRIETARY COLLEGES AND HIGH SCHOOLS.

PLACE.	*SCHOOLS.*	*PRINCIPALS.*
BATH	Royal School *	Miss Kingdon.
,, ...	High School, Portland Place	Miss S. Wood.
BIRMINGHAM ..	Handsworth Ladies' College	Mrs. Kirkpatrick.
BISHOP'S STORTFORD.	East of England Nonconformist Girls' School.	Miss Lewin.
BRIGHTON ..	High School, Milton Hall, Montpelier Road.	Miss Creak.
,, ..	Proprietary Ladies' School, Marlborough Place.	Miss Allen.
,, ..	St. Mary's Hall, Kemp Town.†	Miss Newport.
CASTERTON ..	The Clergy Daughters' School.†	Miss Vincent.
CHELTENHAM ..	The Ladies' College ‡ ..	Miss Beale.
CLIFTON	The Ladies' College	Miss Baxter.
,, ...	Clifton Girls' School	Miss Arnold.
DEVONPORT ..	Devonport, Stoke, and Stonehouse High School.	Miss McCallum.
EDGBASTON ..	High School, 284, Hagley Road.	Miss A. J. Cooper.
FROME	Chantry School for Girls ..	Miss Senior.
GATESHEAD-ON-TYNE.	The High School, Prospect Cottage.	Miss Rowdon.
GRAVESEND ..	Milton Mount College ..	Miss Hadland.
,, ..	"The Laurels," Overcliffe	Miss Allcock.
GUERNSEY ..	The Ladies' College	Miss Eaton.
HALIFAX	The High School	Miss L. A. Robinson.
HEREFORD ..	The Ladies' College	Mrs. Jacob.
HUDDERSFIELD	The Girls' College	Miss Cheveley.
ISLEWORTH ..	Royal Naval Female School §	Miss Quinan.
LEEDS	The High School, Woodhouse Lane.	Miss Kennedy.

* For daughters of officers of the Army only.
† For daughters of Clergymen only.
‡ See also Chapter X.
§ For daughters of Naval and Marine officers only.

PLACE.	SCHOOLS.	PRINCIPALS.
LEEDS	Mechanics' Institution School, Cookridge Street.	Miss Ash.
"	Middle-Class School	Miss Sothern.
LIVERPOOL ..	Collegiate School for Girls, Bedford Street North ..	Miss Milward.
" ..	Blackburne House (Liverpool Institute School).	Miss Nicholson.
LONDON, AND ITS SUBURBS	Bedford College*	Miss Alice von Cotta.
" ..	Camden School for Girls, Camden Street, N.W.†	Miss Elford.
" ..	Chelsea High School, Durham House, Smith Street, Chelsea.	Miss Bishop.
" ..	City of London College School, 8, City Road, Finsbury Square, E.C.	Miss M. Murton, L.A.
" ..	Clapham Middle School, Clarence House, Clapham Common, S.W.	Miss O'Connor.
" ..	Croydon High School ..	Miss Neligan.
" ..	Dulwich High School, Thurlow Park Road, S.E.	Miss Alger.
" ..	Hackney High School, 275, Mare Street, Hackney, E.	Miss Pearse.
" ..	Hammersmith High School‡	Miss Page.
" ..	Highbury and Islington High School, 6, Canonbury Place, N.	Miss Whyte.
" ..	Maida Vale High School, Warrington Crescent, Warwick Road, Maida Vale, W.	Miss Andrews.
" ..	North London Collegiate School, 202, Camden Road, N.W.†	Miss Buss, F.C.P.
" ..	Notting Hill and Bayswater High School, Norland Square.	Miss H. M. Jones.

* See also Chapter X.

† These are Endowed Schools.

‡ This school is not under the control of "The Girls' Public Day-school Company (Limited)," for a list of whose schools see the Appendix.

PLACE.	*SCHOOLS.*	*PRINCIPALS.*
LONDON, ETC.—*continued.*	Queen's College School,* Harley Street, W.	Miss Hay.
,, ..	St. John's Wood High School, Winchester Road, N.W.	Miss Allen-Olney.
,, ..	Tooting High School † ..	Miss Hawes.
,, ..	Wandsworth High School, East Hill, Wandsworth. ‡	Miss Withiel.
,, ..	West Central London Collegiate School, 97, Southampton Row, Russell Square, W.C.	Miss Dimock.
,, ..	West Ham High School §	Miss Mortimer-Rowdon.
MANCHESTER ..	High School for Girls, 369, Oxford Road.	Miss Day.
,, ..	Ladies' High School, Lower Broughton.	Mrs. Fenis.
MIDDLESBRO' ..	The High School	Mrs. Plant.
NORWICH	The High School for Girls, Theatre Street.	Miss Wills.
NOTTINGHAM ..	The High School for Girls, 1, Oxford Street.	Miss Hastings.
OXFORD	The High School for Girls, 16, St. Giles's.	Miss Benson.
PLYMOUTH ..	The High School for Girls, North Hill.	Miss Kendall.
SHEFFIELD ..	The High School, Surrey Street.	Mrs. Woodhouse.
SHIPLEY	Salt Schools	Miss M. Griffiths.
SOUTHAMPTON	The Ladies' College	Miss Daniels.
,, ..	Girls' College, Sussex Place	(*Vacant*).
SOUTHPORT ..	Trinity Hall ‖	Miss C. Hay.
TORQUAY	The High School for Girls	Miss Trevor.
YORK	The Mount School	

* See also Chapter X. and Appendix.

† This school is not under the control of "The Girls' Public Day-school Company (Limited)," for a list of whose schools see the Appendix.

‡ This is a Private School, with no committee of supervision.

§ Not one of the Girls' High School Company's Schools.

‖ For daughters of Wesleyan Ministers only.

SCOTLAND.

PLACE.	SCHOOLS.	PRINCIPALS.
EDINBURGH ..	The Edinburgh Ladies' College (Edinburgh Merchant Company's Schools), Queen Street.	David Pryde, M.A., LL.D. (*Head Master*); Miss Key (*Lady Superintendent*).
,, ..	George Watson's College for Ladies, George Square.	Alex. Thomson (*Head Master*); Miss Wilson (*Lady Superintendent*).
ST. ANDREWS ..	St. Andrew's School for Girls	Miss Innes-Lumsden.

IRELAND.

PLACE.	SCHOOLS.	PRINCIPALS.
DUBLIN	Alexandra College for Ladies.*	Mrs. Jellicoe (*Lady Superintendent*); Rev. R. B. Carson, M.A. (*Secretary and Bursar*).
,, ...	Alexandra School, St. Stephen's Green.	Mrs. Jellicoe (*Lady Superintendent*); Miss Wright (*Head Mistress*).
,, ...	Queen's Institute Schools, Molesworth Street.	Miss Corlett (*Registrar*).

MIDDLE-CLASS ENDOWED SCHOOLS FOR GIRLS.†

The following is not a complete list of Endowed Schools for Girls, nor is it intended to be. Only such schools have been included in it as seem to come within the category of schools of the "Higher Grade" for Middle-class girls. I have experienced some difficulty in satisfactorily defining the term "Higher Grade," and have used it here in the sense of schools that are attended more or less by children of the poorer class of professional men and others of the same rank of life.

* See Appendix and Chapter X.

† I am indebted for the information given under this head, to Miss Brough, Secretary of the "Women's Education Union."

PLACE.	SCHOOLS.	SECRETARIES.
BRADFORD ..	The Girls' Grammar School. For Day Scholars. Fees per term, 4*l.* 4*s.* and 5*l.* 5*s.* Several Exhibitions are tenable in the school.	Miss Smiddy (*Secretary*); Miss Porter (*Head Mistress*).
BURTON-ON-TRENT.	Alsop's Girls' School. Fees per term, 1*l.* 13*s.* 4*d.* Registration, 1*s.*	Miss Brown (*Head Mistress*).
EXETER	Episcopal Schools, 83 and 84, Queen Street. Fees per annum, 3*l.*; admission fee, 5*s.*	Mr. W. Miller, St. David's, Exeter (*Clerk to the Governors*).
GRAYS THURROCK (Essex).	Palmer's Schools for Day Scholars and Boarders. Fees per term: Day Scholars, 1*l.* 18*s.* 4*d.*; Boarders, 11*l.* 13*s.* 4*d.* Entrance Fee, 3*l.*	Miss Beck (*Head Mistress*).
HACKNEY ..	Drapers' Company's Schools, Elmslea.	Miss Wallder.
HATCHAM ..	Aske's School. For 200 girls, day pupils. Fees per annum, 6*l.*; Books and Stationery, 5*s.* per quarter. Admission fee, 2*s.* 6*d.* Entrance fee, 10*s.* Several Exhibitions are tenable in the school.	Mr. G. W. Griffiths, (*Clerk to the Managers*).
HERTFORD ..	Christ's Hospital. Age of admission 8 to 10. Fees, none. Pupils must be nominated by a Governor.	M. S. S. Dipnall, Esq., Christ's Hospital, London (*Clerk to the Governors*).
HOXTON	The Haberdashers' Girls' School. For the education of about 300 girls. Fees, 15*s.* per quarter. Entrance fee, 1*s.* 6*d.*	Miss Powell (*Head Mistress*).
KEIGHLEY (YORKS.).	Drake and Tonson's School. Fees per quarter, 1*l.* 2*s.* 6*d.*, 1*l.* 10*s.*, and 1*l.*	Mr. J. Whiteley (*Secretary*).

PLACE.	SCHOOLS.	SECRETARIES.
LONDON	North London Collegiate School, 202, Camden Road, N.W. Fees per annum, 13, 16, and 19 guineas. Entrance fee, 1*l.* Preparatory School, 3*l.* 3*s.* per term. There are several Scholarships and Exhibitions to be competed for in this school.	Rev. A. J. Buss, B.A. (*Clerk*).
,, ...	Camden School for Girls, Camden Street, N.W. Fees per term, 1*l.* 11*s.* 6*d.* and 2*l.* 5*s.* 6*d.* Entrance, 5*s.* Several Exhibitions and Scholarships to be competed for in this school.	Miss A. Elford (*Secretary*).
,, ...	St. Clements Danes' Middle-class Girls' School, Houghton Street, W.C. Fees per term for parishioners of St. Clements Danes, 1*l.* 10*s.*; non-parishioners, 2*l.* 5*s.*, including Books and Stationery.	W. Raimondi, Esq. (*Clerk to the Governors*).
,, ...	St. Martin-in-the-Fields, Middle-class School for Girls, Castle Street, Leicester Square, W.C. Fees per term, 1*l.* 10*s.* and 1*l.* 5*s.*	Miss Derrick (*Head Mistress*).
,, ...	Datchelor's Middle-class Day School, Camberwell Grove, S.E. Fees per term, 3*l.*	Miss Appleford (*Secretary*).
,, ...	Burlington School for Girls, St. James's. Fees per term, 1*l.* 10*s.* and 1*l.* 5*s.*	Mr. J. Redman, St. James's Church Vestry, Piccadilly (*Secretary*).
,, ...	Westminster: The Greycoat Hospital (near Victoria Street). Tuition Fees, 2*l.* to 4*l.* a year.	C. Spencer Smith, Esq. (*Secretary*).

PLACE.	*SCHOOLS.*	*SECRETARIES.*
LOUGHBOROUGH	Upper Girls' School (Burton's Foundation). Fees, Day Pupils, per quarter, 1*l.*; Entrance, 2*s.*; Boarders, per annum, 31*l.* and 33*l.*	Miss Ruddle (*Head Mistress*).
NEWCASTLE-UNDER-LYME.	Orme Girls' School. Fees per annum, 4*l.* 4*s.* and 5*l.* 5*s.*	Miss Martin (*Head Mistress*).
READING (BERKS)	Kendrick School for Girls. Fees per term, 1*l.* 11*s.* 6*d.*; Registration fee, 1*s.*; Entrance fee, 5*s.*	Mr. W. F. Blandy, Friar Street, Reading (*Clerk*).
TAUNTON ..	Huish's School for Girls, The Crescent. Fees per term, from 1*l.* to 2*l.*, according to age; Entrance fee, 2*s.* 6*d.*; Registration fee, 1*s.* Two Exhibitions are competed for annually.	Mr. J. H. B. Pinchard, 37, Paul Street, Taunton (*Clerk to the Governors*).

It may be remarked, in connection with the foregoing list of Endowed Schools, that no steps have yet been taken to found "A High or High Schools to be called Dean Colet's School or Schools, for not less than 400 girls in all," sanctioned by the Queen in Council on the 24th March, 1876, as part of the new scheme for St. Paul's School, London; and there appears to be no immediate prospect of a school for girls (part of Alleyn's College scheme) being established in connection with that charity at Dulwich. A more complete list of Endowed Schools is given in Chapter XIII.

CHAPTER V.

SECONDARY EDUCATION—*continued*. PRIVATE SCHOOLS.

FOLLOWING is a list, in alphabetical order, of Private Schools whose pupils have been successful at the Senior and Junior Local Examinations of the Universities of Oxford, Cambridge, Durham, Edinburgh, and Glasgow, and in the Schools' examination of the College of Preceptors. It is to be noted that the University of Dublin issues no class lists in respect of its "Examinations for Women."

PLACE.	*SCHOOLS.*	*PRINCIPALS.*
ABERYSTWITH	Caerleon House..	Miss Trubshaw.
ABBOTS' BROMLEY	"St. Anne's"	Miss Rose Lacon.
AMBLESIDE ..	Fairfield House*	Mrs. Fleming.
APPLEBY	White House School ..	Miss Wright.
ASHFORD	The Collegiate School ..	Mrs. F. Badham.
ASHTON - UPON - MERSEY.	Ladies' College	Miss Bradshaw.
AYLESBURY ..	Havelock Collegiate School	Miss Terry Page.
,, ..	White House, Parson's Fee	Mrs. Dumas.
BANBURY	"The Mount"*	The Misses Tysoe Smith.
,, ...	Oxford Lodge	The Misses Brailey.
,, ...	Whately House	Mrs. Drury.
BATH	Abbey Churchyard, 5 ..	Mrs. Davies.
,, ...	Daniel Street, 2..	Miss Buckpitt.
,, ...	Duke Street, 2	Miss Long.
BECCLES	Waveney House..	Miss Garrard.
BEDFORD	French Protestant College*	Madame de Marchot.
,, ...	The Manse	Mrs. John Brown.

* See Appendix.

PLACE.	*SCHOOLS.*	*PRINCIPALS.*
BEDFORD—*contd.*	Moravian Ladies' School ..	Miss England.
,, ...	Windsor Villa	Mrs. Durley.
BIRMINGHAM ..	Clifton Terrace, Chapel Ash	Mrs. Sherwin and Miss Perkins.
,, ..	Erdington Ladies' College	Mdlle. Lefébvre and Miss Marsland.
,, ..	Spring Hill Ladies' College	Miss S. L. Brown.
BISHOP'S AUCKLAND.	Wear Terrace	Mrs. Cleminson.
BISHOP'S STORTFORD.	Ladies' College	Mrs. Clark and Miss Kelsey.
BOGNOR	Bucksbridge Hall	Miss Gurney Atkins.
BOSTON	South Square	The Misses Adams.
BOURNEMOUTH	"St. Margaret's"	Miss Williams.
BOWDON	Culcheth New Hall	Mrs. Williamson.
BRAINTREE ..	Grove House	Miss Ashley.
BRIGHTON ..	Brunswick Road, 31	Miss Scott.
,, ..	Lewes Crescent, 17	Miss Prangley.
,, ..	Marine Parade, 111	Miss Leakey.
,, ..	Montpellier Place, 20 ..	Mrs. H. H. Brown.
,, ..	Old Hove House School ..	Miss Meredith.
,, ..	Powis Square, 17	Miss Miller.
,, ..	Rokesley House	The Misses Maclaren.
,, ..	Somerset House, Hove ..	The Misses Pringle.
,, ..	Sussex Square, 10	Mrs. W. Harris.
,, ..	Waterloo Place, 10	Mdlle. Thiébaut.
BRISTOL (*see*, also, CLIFTON).	All Saints' Ladies' School ..	Sister Superior.
,,	Duncan House School ..	The Misses Cort and Bulkeley.
,,	Ellenborough House, Redland.	The Misses Appleton.
,,	Fairfield School, Cotham Park.	The Misses Elliott.
,,	Marlborough House, Bristol	The Misses Gould and Barns.
,,	St. Anne's School, Baltonsborough.	The Misses Neville.
BROMSGROVE ..	Abberley House	The Misses Jones.

PLACE.	SCHOOLS.	PRINCIPALS.
BROMSGROVE — *continued.*	Highfield House	The Misses Taynton and Johnson.
CAMBRIDGE ..	Bateman House School ..	The Misses M. and J. Thornton.
,, ..	Cavendish House School	The Misses Thurlbourn.
,, ..	Dorset Terrace, 2	Miss Mainprice.
,, ..	Regent Street, 56	Miss Smart.
CARDIFF	Belgrave House	Miss Tullis.
,, ...	Harrow House	The Misses Marks.
,, ...	Ladies' Collegiate School	Mrs. R. White.
CARLISLE	Cavendish House	Miss Fairlie.
,, ...	Castle Street School	Miss Sycalmore.
,, ...	George Street, 7	Miss Dick.
,, ...	Victoria Place, 4	The Misses Thorpe.
CHELTENHAM ..	Alstone Court	Miss Robinson.
,, ..	East Hayes	Miss Scott.
,, ..	Eckington House	Miss Chambers.
,, ..	Ellenborough House	The Misses White.
,, ..	Ormond Terrace	The Misses Headley.
CHESTER	Ashfield House, Neston ..	Miss Young.
,, ...	St. James's School, Llanddulas.	Mrs. Hick.
,, ...	Thorncliffe House	Mrs. R. L. Dew.
,, ...	Upper Northgate Street, 24	Miss Birch.
CLAUGHTON ..	Buckingham House	Miss Gibson.
,, ..	Grosvenor House	The Misses Harrison.
CLEVEDON ..	Woodbury	Miss Kelly.
CLIFTON (*see*, also, BRISTOL).	Avondale House	The Misses Harris.
,, ...	Badminton House	Mrs. M. Badcock.
,, ...	Cornwallis House	Madame d'Orsey.
,, ...	Duncan House	The Misses Cort and Bulkeley.
,, ...	Down End	Miss Crook.
,, ...	Essendene School	Mrs. White.
,, ...	King's Parade School ..	Mrs. Maynard.
,, ...	Northumberland House ..	Miss M. F. Mullock.
,, ...	Rodney Place, 1	Miss Brice.

PLACE.	*SCHOOLS.*	*PRINCIPALS.*
CLIFTON — *continued.*	Royal Crescent, 1	Miss Robe.
"	"St. Helens"	Mrs. Gaskin.
"	White Ladies' College ..	Dr. and Mrs. Tomkins.
COLCHESTER ..	Cambridge House	Miss Whitby.
" ..	Mindon House	Mrs. Grove.
COVENTRY ..	College House	The Misses Cave.
DARLINGTON ..	Ladies' College	Mrs. Fearnley.
" ..	Thornbeck House	Miss Wilkinson.
" ..	West Grove School	Miss Bamber.
DEAL	Ladies' Collegiate School	Miss A. Taylor.
DERBY	Normanton Villas	Mrs. Bookey.
"	Oldcroft House, Quarndon	The Misses Morgan and Newbold.
DEVONPORT ..	Ker Street, 31	Miss Moorshead.
" ..	Moorfield House, Stoke ..	Mrs. Rattenberry.
" ..	Private School, Stoke ..	Miss Barrett.
DORCHESTER ..	Icen Cottage	Miss Lock.
DORKING	Spreydon House	Miss Cunningham.
DOVER	Effingham Crescent	The Misses Haddon.
EASTBOURNE ..	Benhall House	Miss Simmonds.
" ..	Ladies' Collegiate School ..	The Misses Breeze.
" ..	Wellington House	Miss M. Collbran.
EDGBASTON ..	Brighton House	Miss York.
" ..	Derwent House	Miss Goode.
" ..	Wilton House	Mrs. Lance.
EXETER	Fairfield	Mrs. James.
"	Southernhay, 1	The Misses Lea.
GATESHEAD-ON-TYNE.	Mrs. Southgate and Miss Every's School.	
GLOUCESTER ..	Montpellier House	Miss Jitt.
GOSFORTH ..	Roxburgh House	The Misses Kell and Kirsopp.
GRANTHAM ..	The Ladies' College	Miss A. M. Wilson.
GREAT YARMOUTH.	Sunderland House	Mrs. Tomkins.
HALIFAX	Milton Place, 14	Miss Tyndall.

PLACE.	*SCHOOLS.*	*PRINCIPALS.*
HALIFAX—*contd.*	Savile Park: Ladies' College	Miss Cusworth.
,, ...	Willow Hall, Sowerby Bridge.	Miss Wilson.
HARBORNE ..	Walton House	Miss F. Johnson.
HARROGATE ..	Marlboro' House	Miss E. M. Kay.
HASTINGS ..	Beaufort House, St. Leonards.	Mrs. Halley Stewart.
,, ..	Hastings and St. Leonards College School.	Miss Hall.
,, ..	Kenilworth House, Hastings	Miss Price.
,, ..	Linfield House, St. Leonards	Miss Hill.
,, ..	Prospect House, Ore ..	Miss Ades.
HAVERFORDWEST	Hill House College	Miss Philpott.
HEATON NORRIS	"Hope Lea"	Mrs. Marcus.
HUDDERSFIELD	Imperial Road School ..	Mrs. Welsh.
HULL	Clareville House	Miss Pearce.
,, ...	Minerva Terrace, 4	Mrs. and the Misses Oake.
IPSWICH	Anglesea College *	Miss Butler.
,, ...	Dedham: Ivy Lodge ..	Miss Barber.
,, ...	East Hill, 71	Miss Viney.
,, ...	St. Nicholas Place School	Miss Bullock.
JERSEY	Angia House, St. Helier ..	The Misses Falle.
,, ...	Grosvenor House	Miss Simon.
,, ...	Pomeroy House..	Miss Holt.
,, ...	Warwick House	Miss A. E. Guiton.
KESWICK	Greta Hall	Miss Brindle.
LEAMINGTON ..	Leigh Bank	The Misses Ivens.
,, ..	Portland House	The Misses Browne.
LEEDS	Ashgrove: Masham House	Mrs. A. E. Wainwright.
,, ...	Fulneck	Rev. J. H. Willey.
,, ...	Moorland View, 5	Miss Lobley.
,, ...	Otley: Collegiate School	S. H. Kerr, Ph.D.
,, ...	Queen Square, 2	Miss E. P. Walters.
,, ...	Riversdale House	The Misses Newstead.

* See Appendix.

PLACE.	*SCHOOLS.*	*PRINCIPALS.*
LEEDS—*continued*	St. John's Terrace	The Misses Giles.
,, ...	Thorner Lodge	The Misses Howse and Ellis.
,, ...	Woodsley Road: St. Helens	Miss Tootal.
LEICESTER ..	Collegiate House	Mrs. Islip.
,, ..	De Mountfort House ..	Miss Plant.
LEWES	Linden House	Miss Dudeney.
LEYTON	Ascham House	Mrs. Hills.
LINCOLN	Chestnut House	The Misses Metcalf.
,, ...	Essendon House	Miss Barley.
,, ...	The Priory	Mrs. Walsh.
LITTLEHAMPTON	Marine Villa	Miss Dalton.
LIVERPOOL ..	Blundellsands: Rutland House.	The Misses Robinson.
,, ..	Cambridge House, Liverpool	Miss Dalling.
,, ..	Chatham Street, 132 ..	Miss C. Wells.
,, ..	Canning Street, 30	Miss Hughes.
,, ..	Creswell Street Ladies' School.	Mrs. Kent.
,, ..	Delahaye's (Mdlle.) School	Miss White.
,, ..	Fairfield: Eldon House ..	Miss Winchester.
,, ..	,, Ladies' College	Mrs. S. A. Grounds.
,, ..	Liscard: Withinfield House	Mrs. Millar.
,, ..	Litherland: Summerhill House.	Miss Jones.
,, ..	Sefton House, Liverpool ..	Miss M. Ackerley.
,, ..	Shaw Street School	Miss Watkinson.
,, ..	Stoneycroft: Derwent Road, 48.	Mrs. Parry.
,, ..	St. Domingo Grove, 14, Liverpool.	The Misses Thorneley.
,, ..	Waterloo: Sandholm ..	Mrs. Roscoe Jones.
LLANFAIRFECHAN (WALES).	Erifana	Mrs. Swan.

LONDON, AND ITS NEIGHBOURHOOD.

LONDON (CITY)	Artillery Court, Finsbury, 7	Mrs. J. Turner.
BATTERSEA ..	Vicarage House School ..	Miss Crofts.

PLACE.	*SCHOOLS.*	*PRINCIPALS.*
BAYSWATER ..	Doreck Ladies' College, Kensington Gardens Square.	The Misses Bailey and Neuhofer.
,, ..	Elgin College for Ladies ..	The Misses Gregson.
,, ..	Holland College, Notting Hill Square.	The Misses Stewart.
,, ..	Ladbroke Gardens, 34 ..	Miss Stokes.
,, ..	Lansdowne Road, 67; Notting Hill.	Mrs. Kingdon.
,, ..	Sunderland Terrace, 21; Westbourne Park.	Miss Macnier.
,, ..	Warrington Crescent, W., 26	Miss Clarke.
BECKENHAM ..	Broad Lea	Miss Bradley.
,, ..	Minshull House	The Misses Worthington.
BLACKHEATH (and vicinity).	Beth Combe School	Miss Cranch.
,, ..	Blackheath and Greenwich Ladies' College, Dartmouth House, Blackheath.*	Miss Burton.
,, ..	Blessington Road (Camden Lodge), Lee, S.E.	Miss Maclean.
,, ..	Ellerslie College, Lewisham High Road, S.E.*	Mrs. C. Russell Roberts.
,, ..	Gatefield House	Mrs. Catterns.
,, ..	Goldburn House, Lee, S.E.	Mrs. Bennett.
,, ..	Vanburgh Castle	Miss Nicholson.
BRIXTON	Arundel House, Acre Lane	Miss Dickson.
,, ...	Dorrington House, Brixton Hill.	Mrs. J. Geere.
,, ...	Saxon House, Brixton Hill	Mrs. and Miss Palmer.
CAMBERWELL ..	Camberwell Park, The Terrace, 6.	Miss Dale.
	Camberwell Green, S.E., 32	Miss Killingley.
CANONBURY ..	Marquess Grove, 3	Miss Lonsdale.
CLAPHAM ..	"Ashurst," Clapham Common, S.W.	Mrs. and Miss Turner.

* See Appendix.

PLACE.	*SCHOOLS.*	*PRINCIPALS.*
CLAPHAM—*continued.*	Mornington House, Clapham Road.	The Misses Morris.
,, ..	"The Woodlands," Clapham.	The Misses Smith and Parker.
CLAPTON	"Beechholme," Upper Clapton	Miss Rabett.
,, ...	Champion Place, 16; Upper Clapton.	The Misses Penn.
,, ...	"The Five Elms," Lower Clapton.	Miss Henley.
,, ...	Haddington Villa, Lower Clapton.	The Misses Inglis.
,, ...	Percy House, Stamford Hill	The Misses Crookshank.
CROYDON	Hereford House, Croydon	Mrs. Shrewsbury.
,, ...	London Road, 48; West Croydon.	The Misses Pearse and Power.
,, ...	Merton College, Croydon	Mrs. Dix.
EALING	"The Ferns," Warwick Road	Mrs. Satterthwaite.
,, ...	Grosvenor House, Windsor Road.	Mrs. Wristbridge.
HACKNEY	East London Collegiate School.	Miss Chaffer.
,, ...	Mile End Road, 141	Miss Youngman.
,, ...	North East District College	Miss Dodworth.
,, ...	Orford Road, Walthamstow	Miss Joscelyne.
,, ...	Stepney Green; Montgomery House.	Miss E. Gold.
HAVERSTOCK HILL.	Handel House	Mrs. Wm. Corke.
HENDON	"Highfield"	The Misses Metcalfe.
HIGHGATE ..	Grove, The	Mrs. Gallatly.
,, ..	Stratford House	The Misses Grimley.
HOLLOWAY ..	Seven Sisters Road, 216 ..	Mrs. Butcher.
HORNSEY	"Birklands," Hornsey Lane	Miss Leighton.
,, ...	Colebrooke Cottage, Green Lanes, N.	The Misses Salmon and Tucker.
HYDE PARK ..	Gloucester Terrace, 115 (Hyde Park College for Ladies).	The Misses Harrison and Edis.

PLACE.	SCHOOLS.	PRINCIPALS.
ISLINGTON (and vicinity).	Arundel Square; Westbourne College.	Mrs. Huxtable.
" ..	Finsbury Park; Alexandra Villas, 13 (Queen's College).	Miss Willoughby.
" ..	Finsbury Park, West Coombe House.	Miss Fletcher.
" ..	Hilldrop Road, 36	The Misses Hewitt.
" ..	Mildmay Park College, Stoke Newington.	Mrs. E. Coles.
" ..	North-east London Collegiate School.	Miss Whyte.
" ..	North London College, Canonbury Place.	The Misses Blissett.
" ..	St. Augustine's College ..	The Misses Seller.
KENSINGTON ..	Anglo-French College ..	Miss Clare and Mme. Quesnée.
" ..	Bullingham House, Kensington.	Miss Leighton.
" ..	Cedar House, West Kensington.	Miss Scoles.
" ..	Linden Gardens, 99	Miss Sibley.
" ..	St. Philip's College	Miss Wright.
KILBURN	Clyde Villa, Kilburn ..	The Misses Dymond and Bowman.
"	Priory Road, 26..	Mrs. McBean.
NORWOOD ..	Caerleon College, Lower Norwood.	Miss Grain.
" ..	Dagnall Park School, South Norwood.	Miss Beale.
" ..	Duffield House, Lower Norwood.	Miss Richardson.
" ..	Leighton College, Lower Norwood.	Miss Jermyn.
PIMLICO	Belgrave Collegiate School	Miss Brake.
	Lexham Gardens, S.W., 73	Miss Forster.
RICHMOND ..	The Church School	The Mother Superior
" ..	The Hermitage	Miss Cuff.
" ..	Montague House	Madame Philippart.
" ..	Private High School.. ..	Miss Smith.

PLACE.	*SCHOOLS.*	*PRINCIPALS.*
SHEPHERD'S BUSH	Adelaide Cottage	Mrs. Bonwick.
,, ,,	Askew College	Mrs. Laurance.
ST. JOHN'S WOOD (and vicinity).	Belsize College for Ladies	Miss Haswell.
,, ,,	Belsize Park Gardens, 14	Miss Bird.
,, ,,	Belsize Park Gardens, 23	The Misses Barker.
,, ,,	Carlton Hill, 82, St. John's Wood.	Miss Visick.
,, ,,	Claremont College, St. John's Wood Park.	Miss Cavan.
,, ,,	Finchley Road, "The Elms"	Miss Sutton.
,, ,,	King Henry's Road; Twyford House.	The Misses Locket.
,, ,,	Maida Vale, 83..	Miss Lounds.
,, ,,	Parkhurst Road, 29	Miss Smith.
,, ,,	Portsdown College	Miss Rachel D. Myers.
,, ,,	St. Alban's College, Greville Road, N.W.	Miss Stone.
,, ,,	St. John's Wood School ..	Miss Mardon.
,, ,,	Warwick Hall, Maida Hill, W.	Mrs. Rowe.
STRATFORD ..	London College..	Mrs. James Stocker.
SURBITON ..	"St. Stephens"..	Miss Carey.
SUTTON	Malvern House	Mrs. Bawtree.
SYDENHAM ..	Sydenham College for Ladies.	The Misses Jebb and Hooker.
,, ..	Forest Hill, Ladies' Collegiate School.	The Misses Cocks and Shillito.
,, ..	Forest Hill, Parkfield College.	Miss Strickland.
,, ..	Gipsy Hill, Dorpat House	Miss Haddon.
,, ..	Percy House School, Sydenham.	Miss Pierson.
TOTTENHAM ..	Fernhouse	Mrs. Fisher.
TUFNELL PARK	Queen's College Institution, Camden Road.*	Mrs. Morel.
TWICKENHAM..	Amyand Park	Miss Walker.
WEST CENTRAL LONDON.	Brunswick Square, 1, Grenville Street.	Mrs. Ainger.

* See Appendix.

PLACE.	SCHOOLS.	PRINCIPALS.
WEST CENTRAL LONDON—*cont.*	Gower Street School	Miss Harrison.
WIMBLEDON ..	Binfield House	Mrs. Maude Roxby.
,, ..	Codrington House	Miss Harral.
LYMINGTON ..	Arnewood House	Mrs. H. J. Banks.
LYTHAM	Ribble House	The Misses Sharp and Hall.
MAIDSTONE ..	Rock House	The Misses Dobie.
MALTON	Prospect House	The Misses Hall.
MALVERN	Elmsdale : The Ladies' College.	Mrs. R. Gilbert.
,, ...	Hazel Bank, Malvern Link	Miss Somerville.
,, ...	The Birches, Malvern Link	Mrs. and Miss Piper.
MANCHESTER ..	Acomb House, Ladies' College.	Miss Broadhead.
,, ..	Albert Terrace, Old Trafford.	Miss M. Woodcock.
,, ..	Buckingham Crescent School, Victoria Park.	Miss C. Anthony.
,, ..	Enville Place School, Ashton-under-Lyne.	Rev. J. Bleasdell, B.A.
,, ..	"Glenbrooke," Fulshaw ..	The Misses Gratrix.
,, ..	Horwich Bank, Whaley Bridge.	Mrs. Harris.
,, ..	Mechanics' Inst. Ladies' School, Manchester.	Mrs. K. R. Smith.
,, ..	Oakleigh Ladies' School, Higher Broughton.	Mad. Delhavé and C. Delhavé, B.ès-L.
,, ..	Park Terrace, 3, Higher Broughton.	Miss Miall.
,, ..	St. John's Place School, Manchester.	Mrs. and Misses Butcher.
,, ..	St. Matthew's Middle School, Manchester.	Miss Hannen.
MARGATE	Burleigh House	Mrs. Jolly.
,, ...	Charlesville House	The Misses Valder.
,, ...	Cliftonville House	Mrs. Killick.
,, ...	Hawley House	Miss Ray.

PLACE.	*SCHOOLS.*	*PRINCIPALS.*
MARGATE—*cont.*	Hawley Square, 35	Miss Brooke.
MIDDLESBRO' ..	Bonchester House, Coatham	The Misses Turner.
,, ..	Ormesby College, Middlesbro'.	Madame Gouget de Fenouillet.
NEWCASTLE ..	Miss Glass' School.	
NORTHAMPTON	Castle Hall School, Northampton.	Mrs. Martin.
,,	College Street School ..	Miss Gulland.
,,	Waterloo, 38	Miss Hinton.
NORWICH.. ..	Mornington House	Mrs. C. Hall.
,, ...	Surrey Street School ..	Miss Clark.
,, ...	Unthanks Road, 17	Miss Steel.
NOTTINGHAM ..	"Brincliffe," The Park ..	Mdlle. Courtial.
,, ..	The Park	Miss Adcock.
,, ..	Regent Street, 4	Miss Barnett.
,, ..	Western House, Nottingham	Miss Clark.
OXFORD	Oxford House	Miss Crapper.
,, ...	St. Giles's, 4	Miss Newbury.
,, ...	St. Giles's, 60	The Misses Howe and Beaufoy.
,, ...	Walton Street, 149	Miss Taylor.
PENMAENMAUR, N. WALES.	Ladies' School	The Misses Ridgway.
PLYMOUTH ..	"Educational Home," Torrington Place. ..	The Misses Grose.
,, ..	Leigham House	Mdlle. Issanchon.
,, ..	Moorfield House	Mrs. Rattenberry.
,, ..	Mulgrave House	The Misses Highmore.
,, ...	Mutley, 4, Ford Park ..	The Misses Peake.
,, ..	Portland College	Miss Ellen Stevens.
PRESTEIGNE ..	Ladies' Educational Home	Miss Newark.
RAMSGATE ..	Augusta Villa	Mrs. Winmill.
READING	Albion Place	The Misses Butler.
,, ...	Blenheim House School ..	The Misses Buckland
,, ...	Downshire House	Mrs. Legg.
,, ...	Summerbrook	Miss Hamley.
,, ...	Wilton House	Miss White.
ROCHESTER ..	Lindon House	Mrs. Topple.

PLACE.	SCHOOLS.	PRINCIPALS.
ROCHESTER—*cont.*	Nile Terrace	The Misses Pike.
,, ...	St. Margaret's Bank	Miss Spreck.
ROCKFERRY ..	"Briarfield"	Miss Hobson.
,, ..	"Elmhurst"	Miss Spence.
RUGBY	South Corner School ..	Miss C. Woods.
RUSHOLME ..	Buckingham Crescent, 6 ..	Miss Anthony.
SAFFRON WALDEN	Cambridge House	Miss Barrett.
SALISBURY ..	The Ladies' Collegiate School.	The Misses Edmunds.
,,	Montague Villas	Miss Jarman.
ST. AUSTELL ..	Bellevue House..	Miss Gummoe.
SCARBOROUGH	Haddo House School ..	Miss Theedam.
,, ..	Haddo Terrace, 6	Miss Mitchell.
,, ..	Ravensworth Lodge	Miss Woodhead.
,, ..	Westwood Collegiate School	The Misses Pickering and Barrett.
SEAFORTH ..	Claremont House	Miss Mamage.
SHEFFIELD ..	Eton House, Wilkinson Street, Sheffield.	Mrs. Bottom.
,, ..	Fern Bank, Victoria Road	Mrs. Gover.
,, ..	Holmesfield House School	Miss J. Brown.
,, ..	Shrewsbury House School, Sheffield.	Miss Witheford.
,, ..	Stand Field, Sheffield ..	Miss Biram.
,, ..	Western Bank, 267	Miss Graysmark.
SHREWSBURY ..	St. John's Hill School ..	The Misses Harrison.
SLOUGH	Halidon House	Miss Goddard.
,, ...	Upton Park	Mrs. H. K. Cornish.
SOUTHAMPTON	Alexandra College	Miss Sherrat.
,, ..	Bevois Mount House ..	Mrs. Barns.
,, ..	Blenheim House	Mrs. Jones.
,, ..	Cumberland Place, 15 ..	Mrs. Roberts.
,, ..	Emsworth School	Mrs. Jewell.
,, ..	Rockstone House	Miss Barratt.
SOUTHPORT ..	Bath Street, 53, Southport	Miss Rothwell.
,, ..	Brighthelmston, Birkdale Park.*	Mrs. Wallis.

* See Appendix.

PLACE.	*SCHOOLS.*	*PRINCIPALS.*
SOUTHPORT—*cont.*	Cleveland House, Westlands	Mrs. Cheetham.
,, ..	Lansdowne House, Southport.	The Misses Sumner.
,, ..	Leighton College, Southport	The Misses Batham.
,, ..	Malvern House, Birkdale Park.	Miss M. S. Hobbs.
,, ..	Temple House, ,,	Miss Hunter.
SOUTHSEA ..	Byculla House	Miss Charlesworth.
,, ..	St. Bernard's Collegiate School.	Mrs. Hollier.
STAFFORD ..	"The Green"	Miss E. Stanley.
STONE	St. Dominic's Convent ..	Mrs. Drake.
STOURBRIDGE ..	Greenhill House	Miss Moorhouse.
STRATFORD-ON-AVON.	Cambridge House College	Mrs. J. O. Stewart.
STROUD	Roxburgh House	Miss Betts.
,, ...	Stratford Abbey College ..	Miss Isackë.
SUNDERLAND ..	Salem House School.	
SWANSEA	Oakley House	Miss Phillips.
TAMWORTH ..	Lady Bank House	The Misses Gilman and Fairclough.
TAUNTON	"Corfe"	The Misses Leigh.
,, ...	Hope House	Mrs. Sibley.
TENBY	St. Mary's Hill School ..	Mrs. Goward.
TIVERTON ..	Middle School	Miss Elphick.
TORQUAY	Leigh Court	Miss Trevor.
WALSALL	Lime House School	Mrs. N. E. Best.
WANTAGE ..	St. Mary's School	Sister Ellen.
WELLINGBOROUGH.	Hill-Side	Miss Brown.
WELLINGTON ..	The Ladies' College	Mrs. Elizabeth Hiatt.
,, ..	Swan House	Mrs. Duley.
WESTON-SUPER-MARE.	"Dunmarklyn"	The Misses Latham and Dyke.
,, ,,	"King's Holme"	Miss Ballin.
,, ,,	Southside House	Miss Ferris and Mrs. Smith.
,, ,,	Stanmore House	Mrs. A. A. White.
,, ,,	Sydney House	Miss Needham.

PLACE.	SCHOOLS.	PRINCIPALS.
WEYMOUTH ..	Lansdowne Villas, 7	Miss Parker.
WIMBORNE ..	Private School	Miss Twinch.
WINCHESTER ..	Kingsgate Street, 9	The Misses White.
WINDSOR	St. Stephen's College ..	Miss Hutchinson.
WITNEY	Church Green	The Misses Tarrant.
WOLVERHAMPTON	Clifton Terrace School ..	Mrs. Sherwin and Miss Perkins.
,,	Oakfield	Mdlle. Geney.
WORCESTER ..	Cripplegate House	Miss Bullock.
,, ..	The Ladies' College* ..	Mrs. Reader.
,, ..	Raby House	The Misses Osborn.
WORTHING (EAST)	Giddinap House	Miss Butler.
WREXHAM ..	Wynnstay House	Mrs. Simmes.
YORK	Blossom Street House, York	The Misses Sumner.
,, ...	Gillygate, York	The Misses Tiplady.
,, ...	Lendal House, York ..	Miss Mosey.
,, ...	Park Villa School	Miss M. Dale.
,, ...	Springfield School, Easingwold.	The Misses Blyth and Koch.

SCOTLAND.

ABERDEEN	Miss Andrew's School.
,, ...	Miss Warrack's School.
ALLOA	Alloa Academy.
AYR	Ayr Academy.
BANFF	St. Leonard's School.
BROUGHTY-FERRY ..	Home Park School.
CUPAR	Baxter House.
DUMBARTON	Burgh Academy.
DUNSE	Newtown House.
EDINBURGH	Miss Brown's School.
,, ...	Miss Elwert's School.
,, ...	Mr. Gibbs' School.
,, ...	Mr. Hood's School.
,, ...	Mr. Oliphant's School.
,, ...	Mr. Sampson's School.

* See Appendix.

FORRES .. .. Tulloch Park.
GALASHIELS .. .. .. Miss Buist's School.
GLASGOW .. .. .. Albion Crescent School.
" .. .. .. Alfred Terrace School.
" .. .. .. Mrs. Allan, 2, Woodside Crescent.
" .. .. .. Misses Allan, Hill Street.
" .. .. .. Misses Barlas' School.
" .. .. .. Messrs. Chalmers and Dick's School.
" .. .. .. Craigpark House, Dennistoun.
" .. .. .. Miss Gray's School.
" .. .. .. Hamilton Crescent School.
" .. .. .. Miss Langland's, Hamilton Park Terrace.
" .. .. .. The Middle-Class School.
" .. .. .. Miss Morison, 15, Rosslyn Terrace.
" .. .. .. Miss Nicolson, 14, Newton Place.
" .. .. .. Pollokshields Young Ladies' Institute.
" .. .. .. Rosemount School.
" .. .. .. Mrs. Smith, 12, Sandyford Place.
" .. .. .. Misses Watson, Pollokshields.
" .. .. .. Western Academy.
GREENOCK .. .. .. Greenock Academy.
" .. .. .. Kilblain Academy.
HAMILTON .. .. .. Miss Nelson's School.
" .. .. .. St. John's Grammar School.
HELENSBURGH .. .. Glenfruin House.
IRVINE .. .. Mrs. Wilson's School.
KILMARNOCK .. .. Kilmarnock Academy.
LENZIE .. .. Glen Bank College.
LOCKERBIE .. .. .. Public School, Lockerbie.
MELROSE .. .. .. Glenview House.
PAISLEY .. .. The Grammar School.
PERTH .. .. Mrs. Weiss' School.
ROTHESAY .. .. .. Rothesay Academy.

CHAPTER VI.

SECONDARY EDUCATION—*continued.* SCHOOL EXPENSES.

I PROPOSE to discuss in this chapter the expenses of secondary education for girls of the Middle Class. The subject is one of considerable importance, that, sooner or later, engages the attention of parents of moderate means having children to educate, and therefore it deserves consideration. In the last chapter but one I touched upon the topic in comparing the educational expenses of boys and girls generally; in the present I shall enter into the matter more fully, with special reference to those schools which have been selected as deserving notice of the reader. From the list of PROPRIETARY and HIGH SCHOOLS, given in the previous pages, I have chosen ten, as being fairly representative of the whole class. These, in alphabetical order, are as follows:—

(1) Brighton Proprietary Ladies' School.
(2) Clapham Middle School.
(3) Devonport, Stoke, and Stonehouse High School.
(4) East of England Nonconformist Girls' School.
(5) Edgbaston High School for Girls.
(6) Frome, Chantry School for Girls.
(7) Gravesend, Overcliffe High School.
(8) Handsworth Ladies' College, Birmingham;

and in Scotland and Ireland:—

(9) The Ladies' College, Edinburgh.
(10) Alexandra School, Dublin.

Stated briefly, and in general terms, the aim of these institutions is to educate girls of all classes above those provided for by the Elementary Education Acts, and to supply on moderate terms, general instruction of the highest class, together with moral and religious training. The system of instruction which each school follows may be said to be adapted to meet and correct the defects pointed out in the Report of the Schools Inquiry Commission, viz. "Want of thoroughness and foundation; want of system; slovenliness and superficiality; inattention to rudiments; undue time given to accomplishments, and these not taught intelligently or in any scientific manner; want of organization." The following subjects are specified in the curriculum of all, viz. Religious Knowledge; Reading and Writing; Arithmetic and the Elementary parts of Mathematics; English Grammar, Composition, and Literature; History and Geography; French; Elementary Drawing; the Elements of Natural Science; Class Singing and Harmony; Needlework and Calisthenics. In a few of the selected schools, Latin and German are included in the general course. Each of the ten selected schools was started by private enterprise, and is governed by a council or association of gentlemen elected from among, and by, the general body of proprietors. This statement does not altogether apply to the Chantry School of Frome, or Edinburgh Ladies' College; but, inasmuch as each is under independent government of a committee, to all intents and purposes these rank as public schools. The fees charged by each school are as follows:—

BRIGHTON PROPRIETARY SCHOOL. A Day School. The school year is divided into three terms.

Elementary Class,	21*s*. per Term,	with Fee at	Entrance	of	10*s*. 6*d*.
Third Class	55*s*.	,,	,,	,,	21*s*. 0*d*.
Second Class	70*s*.	,,	,,	,,	42*s*. 0*d*.
First Class	88*s*.	,,	,,	,,	63*s*. 0*d*.

A considerable reduction in the foregoing fees is made to Shareholders. No extras.

School Books (Music and Atlases excepted) are provided.

CLAPHAM MIDDLE SCHOOL. A Day School. The school year is divided into three terms. Entrance Fee 10*s*.

For pupils under 12 years of age	.. ..	50*s*. per term.
,, above ,, ,,	.. ..	60*s*. ,,

The following subjects are extras:—German, Latin, the higher branches of English Literature and Drawing, Instrumental Music, Mathematics, and Natural Science. The fee for each extra subject is 21*s*. per term, excepting for Instrumental Music, which is 42*s*. per term. School Books are not provided by the School.

DEVONPORT, STOKE, AND STONEHOUSE HIGH SCHOOL. A Day School. The school year is divided into three terms. Entrance Fee 21*s*.

For pupils under 10 years of age	.. .. ..	63*s*. per term.
For the above Pupils remaining after 13, and for Pupils entering between 10 and 13	..	84*s*. ,,
For Pupils entering above 13	.. .. ..	105*s*. ,,

These fees are inclusive; the only extras being for Solo Singing and Instrumental Music. A reduction in the above fees is made to Shareholders,

EAST OF ENGLAND NONCONFORMIST GIRLS' SCHOOL. A Day and Boarding School. The school year is of three terms. Entrance Fee 21*s*.

Boarders.—Under 14 years of age	.. ..	£16	16	0	per term.
,, Over 14 years of age (if already two years in the school)	..	18	18	c	,,
,, Over 14 years of age (if entering as new pupils)	.. ..	23	2	0	,,
Day Boarders.—Under 14 years of age	..	6	6	0	,,
,, Over 14 ,,	..	8	8	0	,,

The extras for Boarders are for Solo Singing, Printed Music and Examination Fees; for Day Boarders as follows:—Instrumental Music (with Professor), 3*l*. 13*s*. 6*d*. per term; Piano and Harmony, 2*l*. 12*s*. 6*d*. per term; Solo Singing, 3*l*. 3*s*. per term.

EDGBASTON HIGH SCHOOL. A Day School. The school year is of three terms. No Entrance Fee.

For Girls nominated by Shareholders, under 14 years of age	£6	6	0	per term.
Ditto, ditto, over 14 years of age	7	7	0	,,
Ditto, not so nominated, under 14 years of age ..	7	7	0	,,
Ditto, ditto, over 14 years of age	8	8	0	,,
Extras.—Advanced Drawing	2	2	0	,,
Instrumental Music	3	13	6	,,
Solo Singing	3	13	6	,,
Dancing	2	2	0	,,
Religious Instruction for those pupils whose parents desire that they should receive it	1	1	0	,,

These fees are exclusive of books and stationery.

FROME: CHANTRY SCHOOL FOR GIRLS. A Boarding School. Terms for Board and General Instruction, 42*l.* per annum.

Extras are as follows: Piano and Harmony, 6*l.* 6*s.* a year, or, by a Junior Mistress, 4*l.* 4*s.* a year.

GRAVESEND: OVERCLIFFE HIGH SCHOOL. A Day School. The school year is of three terms. Entrance Fee 20*s.*

For pupils under 10 years of age	42*s.*	per term.
,, entering from the Preparatory School	63*s.*	,,
,, under 16 years of age	84*s.*	,,
,, above that age	105*s.*	,,

The fees are inclusive of all subjects except Music and Harmony, Solo Singing, and Advanced Drawing, which are charged as follows per term:—

Instrumental Music	£3	13	6
Pianoforte and Harmony (Elementary) ..	2	2	0
Pianoforte and Harmony (Advanced)	2	12	6
Harmony without Piano..	1	11	6
Solo Singing	2	2	0
Advanced Drawing	1	11	6

HANDSWORTH LADIES' COLLEGE. A Day School. The school year is of three terms. Entrance Fee 10*s.* 6*d.*

For Pupils in the Elementary Class	63*s.*	per term.
,, under the age of 14 years	84*s.*	,,
,, above ,, ,, ...	105*s.*	,,

Extras are as follows:—German and Mathematics, 28*s.* per term; Harmony, 21*s.* per term; the Pianoforte (under a master), 52*s.* 6*d.*, and (under a lady) 42*s.* per term.

SCOTLAND.

THE LADIES' COLLEGE,* EDINBURGH. A Day School. Boarders received by the Lady Superintendent. No Entrance Fee.

Elementary Department	12s 6d.	per quarter.
Junior Department—*Lower Division*	27s. 6d.	,,
,, *Upper Division*	40s. od.	,,
Senior Department	50s.	,,
,, *Advanced*	60s.	,,

IRELAND.

ALEXANDRA SCHOOL,† St. Stephen's Green, Dublin. A Preparatory Day and Boarding School for Alexandra College. Boarders received at Residence House under sanction of the Council. No Entrance Fee.

For Pupils in the Senior School	70s.	per term.
,, ,, Junior School	60s.	,,

Stationery, in addition to the foregoing, 7s. 6d. per term. These Fees include the use of books. The charge for Boarders is 45*l.* per school year. Total for education and board, 55*l.*

It will be seen from a comparison of the foregoing particulars that the cost of educating a girl, under the age of fourteen years, in all essential subjects in a good Middle-class Day-school, ranges at present from 15*l.* 15*s.* to 22*l.* per annum. The difference in charge is explained by the fact that some schools include in the general school course subjects which other schools rank as "extras." In general, however, the only "extras" of importance in the schools of the class under notice are Instrumental Music, Solo Singing, and Advanced Drawing. Above the age of fourteen the cost of a girl's education becomes more expensive; but I have been unable to ascertain that it anywhere exceeds—in the case, at least of the Proprietary and High Schools mentioned in this book—a total sum of 30*l.* per annum. In some of those schools the cost is materially less. At Liver-

* See page 72 and Appendix. † See Appendix.

pool Collegiate School for Girls, for instance, 11*l.* per annum will cover the charges for the general course in the senior department; while the fees at the North London Collegiate School for Girls (one of the very best Middle-class Day-schools in England) amount to 16*l.* 16*s.* for instruction in all subjects but Pianoforte and Harmony. At the City of London College for Ladies (another excellent school), with a very liberal curriculum, the annual charges amount to 15*l.* 15*s.* per annum for the Upper School. Here, again, the only important extras are Pianoforte, Singing, Drawing, and German.

Practically, then, it amounts to this, that parents ought to be able to obtain the highest kind of education that the Girls' Schools of England—and I do not except any, whether fashionable, expensive, or "finishing"—at present afford for 30*l.* per annum. Of course, I am referring now only to Day-schools, and to those of them which employ the highest trained teachers. I arrive at the sum stated in the following way. The general course of a good school should include all of the following subjects, viz.:—

(*a*) English: i. e. Scripture; History, Ancient and Modern; Geography, Physical and Political; Literature.

(*b*) Language: i. e. French, German, and Latin.

(*c*) Science: i. e. Arithmetic; Algebra; Geometry; Natural Philosophy; Natural Science.

(*d*) Calisthenics and Needlework.

For this curriculum not more than 17*l.* per annum should be charged—and, in point of fact, this sum seldom is exceeded in a High School—leaving 13*l.* to be expended for instruction in Art, i. e. Music, Singing, and Drawing. Music and Singing would probably rank as one subject, Drawing as another. Most pupils would desire to become proficient in one, rather than to be mere smatterers in both subjects; so that the sum left over seems to be amply sufficient to secure competent teaching in either of the two that may be selected.

At present there are but few large Proprietary Schools for girls which receive Boarders. From such as do, I have been able to collect the following particulars respecting terms for ***board, including tuition:***—

SCHOOL A charges as follows:—						
For Pupils under 15 years of age	..	£94	0	0	per annum.
" over 15 "	..	112	5	0	"
SCHOOL B:—					
For Pupils under 15 "	..	99	15	0	"
" over 15 "	..	105	0	0	"
SCHOOL C:—					
For Pupils under 15 "	..	81	18	0	"
" over 15 "	..	88	4	0	"
SCHOOL D:—					
For Pupils under 15 "	..	73	10	0	"
" over 15 "	..	84	0	0	"
SCHOOL E:—					
For Pupils under 15 "	..	75	12	0	"
" over 15 "	..	81	18	0	"
SCHOOL F:—					
For Pupils under 15 "	..	75	12	0	"
" over 15 "	..	81	18	0	"

In one of the larger Scotch Schools (Edinburgh Ladies' College) the Lady Superintendent receives pupils to board in her house for 42*l.* per school year. This sum includes private superintendence of studies, but not college fees, which amount in the aggregate to about 10*l.* per annum.

Turning to the PRIVATE SCHOOLS given in the previous chapter, I have selected the following ten as fairly representing the whole number. Four of the ten are well-known schools in the suburbs of London; two are located in the neighbourhood of Liverpool; one is an old-established school at Plymouth; another at Leamington; a third at Dover; a fourth at a town near Oxford. All are schools supported by persons in the Middle class of society. Following are the charges made by each:—

SCHOOL NO. 1 (LONDON). A Boarding School. School Year of three terms. Fees for tuition and board:—Elementary School, Thirty Guineas per annum; Junior School, Forty Guineas per annum; Finishing School, Fifty Guineas per annum. Extras:—Elementary Music, 1*l.* 1*s.* per term; Pianoforte, from 1*l.* 11*s.* 6*d.* to 4*l.* 14*s.* 6*d.* per term; Vocal Music, from 1*l.* 11*s.* 6*d.* to 3*l.* 13*s.* 6*d.* per term; German, 10*s.* 6*d.* per term; Drawing, 1*l.* 11*s.* 6*d.* per term.

SCHOOL NO. 2 (LONDON). A Boarding School. School Year of three terms. Fees for tuition and board:—For children under 12 years of age, Eighty Guineas per annum; above 12 and under 15, One Hundred Guineas per annum; above 16, One Hundred and Twenty Guineas per annum. No extras but for books and stationery.

SCHOOL NO. 3 (LONDON). A Boarding School. School Year of three terms. Fees for tuition and board:—For children under 12 years of age, Fifty-four Guineas per annum; above 12, Sixty-four Guineas per annum. Extras:—Pianoforte, from 1*l.* 8*s.* to 3*l.* 10*s.* per term; Vocal Music, 3*l.* 3*s.* per term; German, 1*l.* 8*s.* per term; Drawing, 4*l.* 4*s.* per term; Calisthenics, 2*l.* 2*s.* per term.

SCHOOL NO. 4 (LONDON). A Boarding School. School Year of three terms. Fees for tuition and board:—Pupils under 14 years of age, Seventy-five Guineas per annum; over 14, Ninety Guineas per annum. The only extras are Music, Solo Singing, Drawing: fees for these not stated.

SCHOOL NO. 5 (LIVERPOOL). A Boarding School. School Year of three terms. Fees for tuition and board, Fifty Guineas per annum. Extras:—Latin and Mathematics, Four Guineas per annum, each.

SCHOOL NO. 6 (LIVERPOOL). A Boarding School. School Year of three terms. Fees for tuition and board, Sixty Guineas per annum. Extras:—Pianoforte, from 1*l.* 11*s.* 6*d.* to 2*l.* 12*s.* 6*d.* per quarter; Harmony, 1*l.* 1*s.* per quarter; German, 1*l.* 1*s.* per quarter.

SCHOOL NO. 7 (PLYMOUTH). A Boarding School. School Year of three terms. Fees for tuition and board:—Pupils under 12 years of age, Thirty Guineas per annum; over 12, Thirty-five Guineas per annum. Extras:—Music, from 4*l.* 4*s.* to 6*l.* 6*s.* per annum; Drawing, 4*l.* 4*s* per. annum; German, 6*l.* 6*s.* per annum; Latin, 3*l.* 3*s.* per annum; Calisthenics, 1*l.* 1*s.* per annum; use of Books and Piano, 2*l.* 2*s.* per annum.

SCHOOL NO. 8 (LEAMINGTON). A Boarding School. School Year of three terms. Fees for tuition and board:—Pupils under 12 years of age, Thirty-two Guineas per annum; above that age, Thirty-six Guineas per annum; Extras:—Music, 4*l.* 4*s.* per annum; singing, 4*l.* 4*s.* per annum; Drawing, 4*l.* 4*s.* per annum; French, 4*l.* 4*s.* per annum; German, 4*l.* 4*s.* per annum; Latin, 4*l.* 4*s.* per annum; Calisthenics, 2*l.* 2*s.* per annum.

SCHOOL NO. 9 (DOVER). A Boarding School. School Year of three terms. Fees for tuition and board:—Pupils under 11 years of age, Sixty Guineas per annum; under 15, Seventy Guineas per annum, Extras:—Music and Singing: fees for these not stated.

SCHOOL NO. 10 (OXON). A Boarding School. School Year of three terms. Fees for tuition and board:—Pupils under 13 years of age, Thirty-six Guineas per annum; over 13, Forty-five Guineas per annum. Extras:—Accomplishments, by visiting professors, from 8*l.* 8*s.* per annum; by resident foreign and English governesses, 4*l.* 14*s.* 6*d.* per annum.

As it is quite clear that it is impossible for all girls of the Middle class between the ages of ten and fifteen, now requiring education, to secure admission to the few Proprietary Colleges in existence, the above figures must have some interest for parents. The average charge for board and tuition (in which I have included Music, a Modern Language, and Calisthenics) will be found to amount to about Sixty Guineas per annum.

CHAPTER VII.

SECONDARY EDUCATION—*continued.* ITS GENERAL AIMS IN SCHOOLS FOR GIRLS OF THE MIDDLE CLASS.

Of Girls' Schools in general it may be said, that they are lacking in stimulus and inducement to work. It will not be difficult to find a reason for this. Apathy and the want of co-operation, sometimes active opposition, on the part of parents, are primarily responsible; associated with these evils is the prevalent notion that education is only something which the recipient is to turn into money. Those who hold to this notion can see why a boy should learn Latin or Mathematics. These acquirements fit him out for a remunerative employment, or may even obtain for him University preferment, the capital value of which can be expressed in pounds sterling. But when told that a girl is studying such subjects, parents ask where is the necessity—what is the use of them? reading the Latin poets will not make her more attractive. Those who argue in this manner have no adequate conception of the objects of education. Literature, science, classics, and mathematics are not taught to boys chiefly that they may make money by them; but because those subjects enter into the approved scheme of English education, and are considered best adapted to develop the intelligence, to increase the mental capacity, and to add to the interest of life. It is as general, not as special education, that the subjects above enumerated are most valuable.

Let us, by way of explanation, take the case of a boy admitted into one of our Public Schools, divided, after the fashion of the day, into two departments, "Classical" and "Modern." Seldom does the lad enter the Modern school direct from without, unless, indeed, he has reached the maximum limit of age for admission. In the ordinary way he takes his place on the Classical side, where the education is not limited to any special or professional purpose, but is classical and general upon the public school system, comprising English, Greek, Latin, at least one Modern language, Mathematics, and Natural Science. All these subjects form regular portions of the school work, i. e. (1) they are all taught within the proper limits of school hours; (2) they are encouraged in the same way, and proficiency in each of them advances a boy's place in the school; (3) none are extras in the school accounts. When the pupil has reached a certain age or place in the school, and the father has determined on the profession in life his son is to follow, the lad retains his place in the Classical, or enters the Modern school, according as the father decides in consultation with the head-master. Supposing that the boy is to enter the Army, the education which he has received in the Classical department fits him to join in the Modern, a class corresponding in seniority to that which he is leaving, and he may be said to enter the new class without break in the continuity of his studies. The education on the Modern side of the school differs from that on the Classical mainly in the following points:—(1) The amount of time given to mathematics is largely increased, and that subject has the preponderating weight in deciding promotions; (2) Both French and German are taught simultaneously, and the time given to them is considerably increased; (3) Greek is entirely dropped, and Latin diminished. I think I shall be correct if I say, that few boys of any decided capacity enter the Modern classes of a public school until the age of fourteen or fifteen has been reached. I have carefully looked through the prescribed subjects for the entrance examinations of our principal Public Schools for boys, and in no single instance do I find Latin and French absent from the list; in general, Greek is included, and where it is omitted, one subject, either of History or Science is substituted. This, be it borne in mind, applies to the admission examinations for all boys, whether desirous of entering the Classical or Modern department of the school; conclusive evidence, one would say, that no difference of opinion exists among the best authorities, as to whether the intellectual training of a boy should be limited to a special purpose, or be so directed as to develop his general intelligence.

"Nothing is more common," wrote Mr. Fitch in his report to the Schools Commissioners, "than to hear the difference in the future destiny of boys and girls assigned as a reason for a difference in the character and extent of their education. A girl is fated to be a wife and a mother, and must therefore be educated for a domestic life. But (significantly adds Mr. Fitch) I cannot find that any part of the training given in Ladies' Schools educates them for domestic life, or prepares them for duties which are supposed to be especially womanly. I am repeatedly told that cooking, the government of servants, the superintendence of their work, the right management of the purse, and the power to economize all the resources of the household are of more importance to a girl than learning. All this is confessedly true. But these things are not taught in schools. Nor are the laws of health, the elements of chemistry, the physiology which would be helpful in the care of children, the political economy which would preserve ladies from mistakes in dealing with the poor; nor any, in short, of those studies which seem to stand in a close relation to the work a woman has to do in the world.* Everywhere the fact that the pupil is to become a woman and not a man operates upon her course of study negatively, not positively. It deprives her of the kind of teaching which boys have, but it gives her little or nothing in exchange. It certainly does not give to her any exceptional teaching adapted to her career as a woman.

"And it may well be doubted," continues Mr. Fitch, "whether such exceptional instruction could be given with advantage. Considering how the teaching staff of a Girls' School is generally constituted, I think it very unlikely that a course of lessons on wifely and household duties, or on the best mode of dealing with sick and young, or the poor, would serve any useful purpose. Such efforts, if made, would probably share the fate of the many futile attempts in Boys' Schools to adapt the teaching to the mercantile or the professional life of the pupil. The best teachers are abandoning such attempts. They attend less to a pupil's special calling and more and more to his general capacity. It is not by thinking of the pupil as a future manufacturer or master, or even as a husband and father, that the best systems of instruction have been devised for boys; but by seeking to develop to their full extent the highest powers the pupil possesses. It is the human, not necessarily the masculine, character which the best teachers try to improve in youth—the love of knowledge, the power of acquiring it, and the art of retaining and wisely employing it. And if it were once admitted, that relatively to the duties of a woman's life, intellectual culture would be as useful and appropriate as to a man, the same principle would probably be adopted by teachers in Girls' Schools."

At present, governesses are more to be pitied than

* Two of the subjects mentioned are now taught in Proprietary and High Schools.

blamed for the failures made in educating girls of the Middle class as compared with boys of the same rank of life. A well-educated and skilled schoolmistress is the equal, in point of attainments and social position, of a well-educated and skilled schoolmaster. It is in the power of either to command the respect and support of parents who move in, what are known as, the better classes of society. Let us suppose that master and mistress open a private school. At the outset the master has the advantage. Setting aside the possibility of his being a man of spirit, imbued with the Public School system, tenacious of its principles, and resentful of any interference in the method of his teaching; he has before him a fixed, I might almost add authorized, standard by which he may measure the requirements and progress of each individual pupil. I am presupposing that his school consists of boys drawn from the better ranks of life, and that their aim is to enter one or other of the professions. Let us note what those Professions are. There is the Navy, the Army, the Home and Indian Civil Service, the Church, the Bar, the profession of Solicitor, the Medical profession. For the entrance examination to each one of these professions certain common subjects of learning are essential, e. g. English, Arithmetic, Elementary Algebra, Elementary Geometry, Latin, French. I am beginning at the very beginning; I am here considering the educational qualifications for a Naval cadetship adapted to boys of twelve and thirteen years of age. The subjects which carry a youth through this examination are useful, nay, essential, as I have already said, for admission to the other professions. The schoolmaster, therefore, from the very day his school is opened, has a prescribed elementary course, we may almost term it, which it will be necessary for all his pupils to follow. Advancing a little higher, we find that the following subjects are common to the prescribed examinations for admission to some of the senior branches of the Navy,* and to all the other professions above enumerated: viz. Classics (Latin or Greek); Mathematics (generally); Languages (French or German); English (Language, Literature, and History); and in most Natural Science is held to be important. Of course, I am only laying before the reader the qualifications for entry to the several professions in outline. The schoolmaster, therefore, has a wide general scheme of education open before him, which he is bound to follow, if his pupils are to enter the professions. Parents cannot meddle with, or alter that scheme. It bears the stamp of the highest authority, and the master is at once exempt from all possibilities of parental interference by the mere fact of his following the course which the scheme prescribes.

Now let us take the case of the schoolmistress. Her school likewise consists of pupils drawn from the better ranks of society. She is, we will suppose, a woman of mind and culture, valuing learning for learning's sake, and honestly intent on doing her utmost to teach thoroughly, and in a broad and liberal spirit. At the outset of her career she is opposed by, what may be called, the drawing-room theory of education. She finds that if she is to make any headway as a teacher, if she is to retain her school, and, along with it, her means of livelihood, she must listen to the clamorous demand of mothers for "ladylike accomplish ments." Probably out of the whole number of the schoolmistress's supporters, not one will be found brave enough to uphold her endeavours to establish in her school a solid system of education. All will clamour for the "accomplishments," and without these, so far as the direct interest of parents in her labours is concerned, the schoolmistress

* In making this statement, I have in mind the course of study prescribed for officers joining the Royal Naval College, Greenwich.

may be left to teach herself into the workhouse. To satisfy the general demand, then, her school must be cut up into minute classes of twos and threes, one reading a little German, another a little Italian, a third venturing upon the elements of Geometry, a fourth, possibly, studying Botany, and so on. The only subjects at which the whole school works in common, are instrumental and vocal music, and, in endeavouring to master these accomplishments, very persistent and very laborious efforts are made. Presently the mistress will be pestered with the suggestions and requests of parents. Miss A.'s mamma will present her compliments, and request that, as Miss A. "has no head for mathematics," she may be allowed to devote the time saved in omitting to read this branch of knowledge to the cultivation of vocal music, which Miss A.'s mamma holds to be of infinitely higher value. Miss B.'s parents will follow suit, and demand, that, as that young lady "will probably go to Paris with her papa in the autumn," she may be allowed to "brush up her French a little in place of giving so much time to arithmetic." Miss C. will hand in a note written on pink paper, begging that a little more attention may be paid to her deportment, as Miss C.'s mamma is of opinion that "ladylike manners and deportment are far more important than learning." Mrs. D. who has a daughter at the school, and who, with motherly concern, has remarked that her child reads more than she has been in the habit of doing, at once protests. The harassed schoolmistress is begged on no account to allow Miss D. to overwork herself—to strain her mental powers, which Mrs. D. points out are none of the strongest, but which the mistress, on the contrary, knows are beyond the average, and only need proper cultivation to be made to produce abundant results. And so the lady who rules the private school is interfered with, and annoyed. Being conscientious, and desirous of doing the best for the mind and character of her pupils, she comes to the conclusion that school-keeping is at the best a thankless and troublesome task. She must either throw it up, or submit to bear the whims of, and be thwarted by, the very people for whose children she is trying to do her best. She must sacrifice her only means of living, a living for which she has been striving vigorously and earnestly from girlhood, or be content to float with the stream and to advertise her school as "a select college for young ladies attended by eminent visiting professors." As an act of charity to herself, on the whole, perhaps, it might be desirable for her to do so. Let her sit in the drawing-room and receive the visits and solicitations of parents, leaving the teaching to ill-paid governesses and to "eminent professors." Until fathers and mothers can be stirred-up to oppose the showy and attractive in the teaching of their daughters, and to demand what is solid and enduring, school-keeping can offer few inducements to an earnest-minded and cultivated woman.

What is now needed, and most urgently needed in Girls' Schools, is some aim, some after purpose that provides a motive to work. If marriage be insisted on as the most encouraging goal for which a young girl should strive, by all means let her strive for it. But for her future husband's sake, if for no other, let her education be of such a kind, that, when she takes her place as a wife and mother, she may add to his happiness by her ability to appreciate and share his highest intellectual pursuits, and lessen his cares by her power to aid in the education of his children.

The Bishop of Manchester, the other day,* quoting an

* At the meeting at Manchester for distributing the honours and prizes awarded at the annual Oxford and Cambridge examinations in the Manchester centre, 1878.—*Reported in the 'Daily News.'*

opinion of the late Bishop of Orleans, on the education of women in France, spoke of their sisters in England as follows:—"The hope of England was in her homes, and a home was very much what a mother made it. He went along with Pericles and St. Paul, when the first gave the palm to the women least talked of among men, and the second to those who were stayers or workers at home. The harder and ruder toil of life should certainly be done by men; but while he wished women to be educated as highly as they could, he hoped that when they were educated they would choose those departments of life, for which men at least thought them best suited." And so, indeed, do all who have the common sense to appreciate the meaning of the Bishop. But "stayers or workers at home" may promote its attractiveness, strengthen its ties, add to its enjoyment and repose, in more ways than in exhibiting habits of order and thrift; displaying judiciousness in the control of servants, cunningness with the needle, skill in the matter of cookery, or right-hearted tenderness in dealing with the little-ones in the nursery. There comes a time when the husband may be considered apart from the exigencies of his household. In the long, dreary winter evenings (for a homely illustration), when the qualities of the cookery have been recognized and discussed, and the present necessities of the children provided for in the security and comfort of bed, then is the season when the culture of a wife should prove an inestimable boon to her husband. She may share with him his literary pursuits, or engage with him in endeavouring to investigate this new mystery of science, or to master the arguments advanced by the more prominent writers of the day; in short she may interest herself in those very topics and matters of popular inquiry which men for the most part are driven to discuss only with men, for the reason, that they find the majority of women unable to enter into discussion upon them. "It would not be difficult to point to thousands of instances of men," writes Mr. Fitch, "who have started in life with a love of knowledge, and with a determination to master at least some department of honourable thought or inquiry; yet, who have gradually sunk into habits of mental indolence, have allowed all their great aims to fade out of view, and have become content with the reading supplied by Mudie and the newspapers, simply from a dread of isolation, and because these resources sufficed for the intellectual aliment of the rest of the household. There is no hope for the middle classes (insists Mr. Fitch) until the range of topics which they care about, includes something more than money-making, religious controversies, and ephemeral politics; nor until they consider that mental cultivation, apart from its bearing on any of the business of life, is a high and religious duty.* When they come to consider this, they will set as great a value on intellectual power or literary taste when they are put forth by a girl as by a boy; and they will feel that the true measure of a woman's right to knowledge is her capacity for receiving it, and not any theories of ours, as to what she is fit for, or what use she is likely to make of it."

What is needed in most schools for Girls is an induce-

* "It was said that by this high-class education women would be taken out of their proper sphere; but he (Lord Granville) would ask, was it probable that a first-class religious, moral, and intellectual education would prevent a woman from doing her duty as daughter, wife, and mother, or as a single woman? He utterly disbelieved anything of the kind. He believed that the times were past when, as was said by a great literary character (who, he was happy to say, did not belong to this country), it was easier for a coquette to marry than a highly educated woman. He believed that the time would come, if it had not already,

ment to work, higher and more honourable than that put forward by too many persons, to wit, that it is the first duty of a girl to glean knowledge solely with a view of becoming attractive, and making conquests among men. The co-operation of parents is the first thing essential in the way of providing such inducement. Let them join hand in hand with those thoughtful high-minded women who are now bent upon lifting the education of girls from the slough of decay into which it has fallen, by reason of years of apathy, and indifference on the part of fathers and mothers, and we shall have a standard of learning forthcoming for girls, at once as ample and satisfactory as that for boys. To accomplish this most desirable end we must first get rid of that singular theory of girls' education by which parents are at present governed; we must make them believe that it is not to refinement and modesty that a cultivated intelligence is opposed, but to vapidity and langour, and vulgarity of mind, to the love of gossip, and the love of dress.*

At the risk of being thought tedious, and of incurring the charge of too great prolixity in one branch of my subject, I must ask the reader once more to consider with me the advantages of the Universities' examinations as furnishing

when men would know how to appreciate those of the other sex who had fitted themselves, by industry and by study, to become really useful members of the community to which they belonged. There was another thing which should not be laid aside in considering this question, that after all, women constituted half of mankind, and to a remarkable degree they exercised a most important influence on the moral and intellectual teaching of the other half, and therefore it was of the utmost importance that the best possible education should be given to women."—*Speech of Lord Granville at St. James's Hall in distributing Prizes to Students of the North London Collegiate School for Girls, Midsummer*, 1878.

* Mr. Bryce's Report to the Schools Inquiry Commission.

an educational standard for Girls' Schools. In my previous remarks on this subject, I discussed the *Junior* local examinations for girls as providing a fit test of their progress *at* school; in what I have to lay before the reader in the next chapter, I propose to deal with the *Senior* local examinations for girls as affording a sufficient test of their general education at the time of *leaving* school.

CHAPTER VIII.

SECONDARY EDUCATION—*continued*. THE SENIOR "LOCAL EXAMINATIONS" OF THE UNIVERSITIES, AND OTHER EDUCATIONAL BODIES, CONSIDERED AS A TEST FOR GIRLS AT THE TIME OF LEAVING SCHOOL.

I HAVE no statistics at hand wherewith to support the opinion; but I believe that a girl's education is, generally, supposed to finish at, or about the age of eighteen. If this be conceded, we may take it for granted that she has been under instruction—I mean "secondary" as distinct from "primary" instruction—for not less than eight years. Of this period, six years may have been spent continuously at one school. I am given to understand, however, that, at present, this rarely is the case, even with girls attending the larger proprietary schools. Let us hope that it is, and that the results of an uninterrupted educational course of six years, are as satisfactory and advantageous to them, as in the case of boys attending our Public Schools. Abundant fruit ought to accrue from a six years' continuous course of instruction under a competent schoolmistress. At the end of that time a girl should be sufficiently advanced in her studies to pass with comparative ease an examination equivalent to that prescribed for matriculation at the University. And no doubt if it were once to be the recognized rule, that all Girls' Schools, whether Proprietary, High, Private or Endowed, should be examined and inspected by appointed authority, girls would be found only too willing to submit their educational attainments to a test such as I have indicated. Personally, I may say that I have no faith in the competitive examination system (and I have had some opportunity of judging of its working from practical experience) of our public services; although I am not competent to show, how it would be possible to make appointment to those services, but by means of an examination test, unless, indeed, by the infinitely more objectionable method of governmental patronage. I do very strenuously advocate, however, the introduction into schools, generally, of independent examination, as affording the only satisfactory guarantee to parents that their children are being properly educated. At present, as I have already pointed out in the preceding pages of this book, we have no sufficient assurance of the kind. It is true that now-a-days parents are presented with what are known as "terminal reports," setting forth the progress of their children at school; but these statements are altogether too partial, too much in the language of the schoolmistress, and altogether unsatisfactory in the way of providing a safe index to a child's capacity and merits.

Periodical examinations, strictly non-competitive, conducted by independent examiners, are in my opinion desirable as tests of a girl's advancement while at school; and an examination answering to the "leaving examination" of Germany might very well be made general in England, as furnishing an educational standard for girls at the period of their leaving school. This examination is held at the close of the school course by examiners appointed by Government in conjunction with the school teachers. On the result of such examination a certificate is given, which takes the place of a preliminary or matriculation examination at the University. Such a certificate from a school of high standing is in some respects more useful than one obtained after examination by a University, inasmuch as it certifies not merely that the holder possesses a specified amount of knowledge, but that the knowledge has been acquired in a certain way, and under certain conditions.* "Its object undoubtedly is," Mr. Arnold pointed out in his report on Prussian Schools, "not the illusory one of an examination test as in our public service it is employed; but the sound one of insuring, as far as possible, that a youth should pass a certain number of years under the best school-teaching of his country. This tries him, which the mere application of an examination test does not; but an examination test is wisely held in conjunction with this training to take care that a youth has really profited by it." The establishment of the Oxford and Cambridge Schools Examination Board was due to a movement among the head-masters of our Public Schools for boys who wished for the introduction into England of an examination similar to this "leaving examination." They preferred, however, that it should be conducted by the Universities, rather than by Government, and the Oxford and Cambridge local examinations for senior candidates (i. e. for those under eighteen years of age), was the outcome of the negotiations. At first girls were not admitted to these examinations; now they may present themselves, not only for these, but for the matriculation examination of the University of London, and the local examinations held by the Universities of Edinburgh, Dublin, Durham, St. Andrews, Glasgow, the Queen's University of Ireland,† &c. I propose to lay before the reader extracts from the regulations of, and examples of the examination papers used by, each University, in order that he may judge for himself, how far the "senior candidates" examination of Oxford and Cambridge, and its equivalents

* Reports issued by the Schools Inquiry Commission on the Education of Girls, with extracts from the Evidence, and a Preface. By D. Beale, *Principal of the Ladies' College, Cheltenham.*

† See also Chapter XII.

of the other Universities, seem to meet the necessities of Middle-class female education at the present day. It will be more convenient, perhaps, if we take the "Regulations" first, reserving the examples of examination papers for notice in another chapter.

I. THE UNIVERSITY OF OXFORD.

Examination of Senior Candidates. Regulations for the year 1879.

The examinations will commence on Monday, May 26, 1879. Any person of either sex born on or after April 30, 1861, may be received as a Candidate. No one born before that day can be received.

I. Preliminary Subjects.

Every Candidate will be required to satisfy the Examiners in

1. A paper on Pope's 'Essay on Man,' Epistles I., II. Candidates will be expected to write passages of the poem from memory, and questions will be set testing power of interpretation, and knowledge of English Grammar (including Analysis of sentences not necessarily taken from the poem).
2. A Short English Composition.
3. Arithmetic.

N.B.—The quality of the handwriting and the spelling will be taken into account.

Every Candidate will be required to satisfy the Examiners either in the "Rudiments of Faith and Religion" and one of the Sections marked B, C, D, *or in two of the Sections marked* A, B, C, D.

II. The Rudiments of Faith and Religion.

Questions will be set in

1. The First Book of Samuel, the Gospel according to St. Matthew, and the Acts of the Apostles.
2. The Catechism, the Morning and Evening Services, and the Litany; and the outlines of the History of the Book of Common Prayer.

   Some of the questions will relate to the Greek text of the Gospel according to St. Matthew.

No Candidate will pass in the "Rudiments of Faith and Religion" who does not satisfy the Examiners in each of the two portions of the Section.

All Candidates must be examined in the "Rudiments of Faith and

Religion," unless their Parents or Guardians object on conscientious grounds (*conscientiae causa*) : and must show at least *some* knowledge of each portion, even if they fail to show so much as will *satisfy* the Examiners ; otherwise they cannot obtain certificates, whatever may be the value of their work in other subjects.

Candidates on whose behalf the Section is declined may pass in Holy Scripture only, by showing a satisfactory knowledge of the *first* portion of the Section, and may count it as one of their two required subjects. But in that case they must also show sufficient knowledge of the Book of Genesis and Exodus i.–xx.

III. Optional Subjects.

Section A.—English.

This will include questions in

1. English History from the Accession of Henry VII. to the Death of Elizabeth, and the outlines of the History of English Literature during the same period, together with the general outlines of English History.
2. Shakspeare's 'Julius Cæsar,' and Johnson's 'Lives of Dryden and Pope.'
3. The elements of Political Economy; and the outlines of English Law, so far as regards the Law affecting persons.
4. Physical, Political, and Commercial Geography, with the filling up of an Outline Map of England and Wales, Scotland, India, United States of America, France, Italy, and Sicily, Spain and Portugal, or the Austrian Empire.

No Candidate will pass in this Section who does not show a fair knowledge of two of these four classes of subjects.

Section B.—Languages.

1. Latin. 2. Greek. 3. French. 4. German. 5. Italian.

No Candidate will pass in this Section who does not show a fair knowledge of one of these languages. Opportunity will be given for showing advanced scholarship in each of them.

Candidates who offer Latin will be examined in Cicero (De Amicitia) and in Virgil (Aen. I.), and those who offer Greek in Herodotus (Book V.) and in Æschylus (Prometheus Vinctus); but no one will obtain a place among the first twenty in either language unless she satisfies the Examiners in unprepared work as well as in the books here specified.

SECTION C.—MATHEMATICS.

Pure Mathematics to Algebraical Geometry inclusive, Mechanics (including Mechanism), and Hydrostatics.

No Candidate will pass in this Section who does not show a fair knowledge of Four Books of Euclid, and of Algebra to the end of Quadratic Equations.

The answers should be illustrated by diagrams, where these can be introduced.

SECTION D.—PHYSICS.

1. Electricity, Magnetism, Light, and Heat.
2. Chemistry. Questions will be set on the facts and general principles of Chemical Science. There will be a practical examination in the elements of Analysis. Candidates will not be able to pass in this Subject on the Questions alone.
3. Vegetable and Animal Physiology to the extent represented by Bentley's 'Manual of Botany,' Book I. and Book II., chapters i. and ii.; Huxley's 'Lessons in Elementary Physiology,' and Huxley's 'Introduction to the Classification of Animals.'

Candidates will be expected to show a special knowledge of the leading characters of the following Natural Orders:— Ranunculaceæ, Cruciferæ, Caryophyllaceæ, Leguminosæ, Rosaceæ, Umbelliferæ, Compositæ, Labiatæ, Primulaceæ, Polygonaceæ, Euphorbiaceæ, Salicaceæ, Orchidaceæ, Liliaceæ, Graminaceæ, Coniferæ, Filicales, Muscales, Fungi, Algæ.

4. Geology and Mineralogy.

No Candidate will pass in this Section who does not show a fair knowledge of one of these four classes of subjects. In all cases a practical acquaintance with the subject-matter will be indispensable.

The answers should be illustrated by diagrams and drawings, where these can be introduced.

Candidates may also offer themselves for examination in Drawing and in Music.

SECTION E.—DRAWING.

1. Drawing from the solid with light and shade.
2. Drawing in perspective.
3. Drawing in colour from a natural object.
4. Drawing from memory.

No Candidate will pass in this Section who does not satisfy the Examiners in Drawing from the Cast.

SECTION F.—MUSIC.

In addition to a thorough knowledge of the subjects prescribed for Junior Candidates, the Seniors must show an acquaintance with the chords of the Added Ninth and Minor Ninth and their inversions, and must be able to harmonize a figured bass introducing these chords. They may be called upon to add three parts to a given melody. A few questions may be set in Musical History.

Every Senior Candidate is required to pay a fee of 30*s*. before proceeding to examination.

The title of *Associate in Arts* is conferred upon successful Candidates.

II. THE UNIVERSITY OF CAMBRIDGE.

Examination of Senior Students.

Regulations for the year ending December 31, 1878.* No Candidates born before January 1, 1861, were admitted to this Examination.

I. PRELIMINARY SUBJECTS.

Every Student was required to satisfy the Examiners in (*a*) English Grammar, including Parsing and the Analysis of Sentences; (*b*) the principles and practice of Arithmetic.

The Examination comprised the subjects mentioned in the following NINE Sections; and every Student was required to satisfy the Examiners in THREE at least of the Sections marked A, B, C, D, E, F, G, or in TWO of them, and in one of the Sections marked H, I; but no one was permitted to be examined in more than five of the Sections A, B, C, D, E, F, G. Section A was compulsory; unless a Candidate's Parents or Guardians objected to his or her examination in that Section.

SECTION A.—RELIGIOUS KNOWLEDGE.

The Examination consisted of questions in (*a*) Ezra, Nehemiah, and the historical parts of Jeremiah, and on St. Matthew, credit being given for a knowledge of the original Greek of the Gospel. (*b*) The Order for Morning Prayer, the Litany, and the Order for Confirmation, in the Book of Common Prayer. Especial attention was paid to the Apostles'

---

* The Regulations for 1879 were not issued when this was in type. I thought it desirable to print those for 1878 in order to allow the reader to judge of any differences that may exist in the prescribed subjects of each University.

Creed. (*c*) Paley's 'Horæ Paúlinæ,' to the end of the Epistle to the Galatians.

Every Student examined in this Section was required to satisfy the Examiners in (*a*), and in either (*b*) or (*c*). No Student was examined in both (*b*) and (*c*).

SECTION B.—(*a*) HISTORY OF ENGLAND, from the accession of William III. to the accession of George III., with questions on the literature of the period.

Some general questions were also set on the history of England from the Norman Conquest to the battle of Waterloo.

(*b*) GEOGRAPHY, Physical, Political, and Commercial (Medal).
(*c*) Shakspeare's 'Julius Cæsar,' with philological and other questions arising out of the subject.
(*d*) The outlines of POLITICAL ECONOMY.

Every Student examined in this Section was required to write a short English Composition, and to satisfy the Examiners in two at least of the above four divisions.

SECTION C.—LATIN (see the note on following page relating to Latin, French, and German).

Passages were given from Cicero, Pro Archiâ and Pro Balbo (Pitt Press Texts), and Ovid, Fasti VI. (Pitt Press Texts), for translation into English, with questions on the historical and geographical allusions and on grammar. Without a fair knowledge of Accidence a Candidate could not pass.

GREEK:

Passages were given from Isocrates, Panegyricus, and Æschylus, Prometheus Vinctus, for translation into English, with questions on the language and subject-matter. Also one or more passages for translation from other Greek authors, in which Candidates were required to satisfy the Examiners; a vocabulary of the less familiar words was given. Without a fair knowledge of Accidence a Candidate could not pass.

A fair knowledge of either of these languages enabled a Student to pass in this Section.

SECTION D.—FRENCH (see the note on following page relating to Latin, French, and German).

Passages were given from X. de Maistre, 'La Jeune Sibérienne,' and 'Le Lépreux de la cité d'Aoste' (Pitt Press Texts), and from Corneille,

'La Suite du Menteur' (Pitt Press Texts), for translation into English, with questions on the historical allusions and on grammar. Without a fair knowledge of Accidence a Candidate could not pass.

GERMAN (see the note relating to Latin, French, and German):

Passages were given from 'Der erste Kreuzzug (1095—1099) nach Friedrich von Raumer' (Pitt Press Texts), and from a Book of German Dactylic Poetry (Pitt Press Texts), for translation into English, with questions on the historical allusions and on grammar. Without a fair knowledge of Accidence a Candidate could not pass.

A fair knowledge of either of these languages enabled a Student to pass in this Section.

The following note relates to the examination in Latin, French, and German:—

(1) "One or more easy passages not contained in the books named will be set for translation from the language into English, a vocabulary of the less familiar words being given. A Student cannot pass in the language without satisfying the Examiners in this part of the paper. (2) One or more passages will be set for translation from English into the language. A Student cannot obtain the mark of distinction in the language without satisfying the Examiners in this part of the paper."

SECTION E.—Every Student examined in this Section was required to satisfy the Examiners in EUCLID, Books i., ii., iii., iv., vi., and xi., to Prop. 21 inclusive, and in Algebra.

Questions were also set on the following subjects:—

1. PURE MATHEMATICS:

Plane Trigonometry, including Land-surveying, and the simpler properties of the Conic Sections treated geometrically.

2. APPLIED MATHEMATICS:

The elementary parts of Statics, including the equilibrium of forces acting in one plane, the laws of friction, the conditions of stable and unstable equilibrium, and the principle of virtual velocities. The elements of Mechanism. The elementary parts of Hydrostatics, namely, the pressure of elastic and inelastic fluids, specific gravities, floating bodies, and the construction and use of the more simple instruments and machines. The elementary parts of Astronomy, so far as they are necessary for the explanation of the more simple phenomena.

SECTION F.—NATURAL PHILOSOPHY:

(*a*) The facts and general principles of Chemical Science.
(*b*) Practical Chemical Analysis.

Credit was given for well-chosen experiments, good observations precisely recorded, and for well-drawn inferences from them.

(*c*) Statics, Dynamics, and Hydrostatics experimentally treated.
(*d*) Experimental laws and elementary principles of Heat.
(*e*) Experimental laws and elementary principles of Electricity and Magnetism.

Every Student examined in this Section had to satisfy the Examiners in (*a*), and in one of the three (*c*), (*d*), and (*e*). No one was examined in more than one of the divisions (*c*), (*d*), (*e*). Division (*b*) was taken or not at the option of the Student. A fair knowledge of Inorganic Chemistry enabled a Student to pass in (*a*).

SECTION G.—(*a*) ZOOLOGY, and the elements of Animal Physiology.

(*b*) BOTANY, and the elements of Vegetable Physiology.
(*c*) PHYSICAL GEOGRAPHY with GEOLOGY (Medal).

Candidates for the Medal were not obliged to enter for Geology; but all Students who desired to pass in this Section had to satisfy the Examiners in Geology as well as in Physical Geography.

Questions were set on the present physical condition of the earth, and the physical agencies modifying it or affecting the conditions of life upon it; on the principal minerals and rocks, their characters, mode of formation, and classification; on the outlines of stratigraphical geology, and the most common and characteristic genera of fossils.

Specimens of minerals, rocks, and fossils were given for identification or description.

No Student was examined in more than one of the three divisions (*a*), (*b*), (*c*). A practical acquaintance with specimens was expected.

SECTION H.—(*a*) DRAWING from the FLAT, (*b*) from MODELS, (*c*) in PERSPECTIVE, and (*d*) IMITATIVE COLOURING.

Every Student examined in this Section was required to satisfy the Examiners in drawing from the flat, and in one at least of the other divisions.

SECTION I.—MUSIC. A knowledge of the elements of Harmony and Musical Composition was required. Questions were also set upon the history and principles of the art.

Every Senior Student presenting herself for the Cambridge Examination pays a fee of 20*s*. Students who pass with credit or satisfy the Examiners receive certificates to that effect. These Certificates, under certain conditions, are accepted in lieu of the previous Examination, the preliminary Examination for Candidates of the degree of Bachelor of Music, and the entrance Examinations for the Legal and Medical professions.

III. UNIVERSITY OF LONDON.

The "General Examination for Women" at this University is superseded by the Ordinary "Matriculation Examination," which is now open to Candidates of both sexes.* Following are the Regulations at present in force for such examination.

Two Examinations for Matriculation are held in each year; one commencing on the Second Monday in January, and the other on the Last Monday in June.†

Candidates will not be approved by the Examiners unless they have shown a competent knowledge in each of the following subjects, according to the details specified under the several heads :—

1. Latin;
2. Any two of the following Languages :—Greek, French, German, and either Sanskrit or Arabic;
3. The English Language, English History, and Modern Geography;
4. Mathematics;
5. Natural Philosophy;
6. Chemistry.

The following are the particulars of the foregoing subjects of Examination :—

---

* Eleven ladies presented themselves for examination at the January Matriculation Examination of the University of London: of these nine passed; out of the nine, six were in the Honours division, four being marked as deserving prizes, and one standing second among the whole number of candidates examined.

† These Examinations may be held not only at the University of London; but also, under special arrangement, in other parts of the United Kingdom or in the Colonies.

A.—LANGUAGES.

1. LATIN.

One Latin subject to be selected by the Senate one year and a half previously from the works of the undermentioned authors: *—

Virgil, One Book of the Georgics, and One Book of the Æneid.
Horace, Two Books of the Odes.
Sallust, The Conspiracy of Catiline, or the War with Jugurtha.
Cæsar, Two Books of the Gallic War.
Livy, One Book.
Cicero, De Senectute or De Amicitiâ, with One of the following Orations:—Pro Lege Maniliâ, one of the four Catilinarian Orations, Pro Archiâ, Pro M. Marcello.
Ovid, One Book of the Metamorphoses, and One Book of the Epistles or Heroides.

The Paper in Latin will contain passages to be translated into English, with questions in History and Geography arising out of the subjects of the book selected. Short and easy passages will also be set for translation from other books not so selected. A separate Paper will be set containing questions in Latin Grammar, with simple and easy sentences of English to be translated into Latin.†

2. GREEK.‡

One Greek subject, to be selected by the Senate one year and a half previously from the works of the undermentioned authors: §—

Homer, One Book.
Xenophon, One Book.

The Paper in Greek will contain passages to be translated into

---

* The Latin Subjects for 1879 and 1880 are—
For June 1879:—*Cicero*, De Senectute, and the First Speech against Catiline.
For January 1880:—*Cicero*, De Amicitiâ, and the Speech pro Lege Maniliâ.
For June 1880:—*Sallust*, De Bello Jugurthino.

† Special stress is laid on accuracy in the answers to the Grammar questions, and on the correct rendering of English into Latin.

‡ Candidates may substitute German for Greek.

§ The Greek Subjects for 1879 and 1880 are—
For June 1879:—*Xenophon*, Anabasis, Book iii.
For January 1880:—*Xenophon*, Agesilaus.
For June 1880:—*Homer*, Odyssey, Book xi.

English, with questions in Grammar,* and with questions in History and Geography arising out of the subjects of the book selected. Short and easy passages will also be set for translation from other books not so selected.

3. FRENCH.

The Paper in French will contain passages for translation into English, and questions in Grammar limited to the Accidence.

4. GERMAN.

The Paper in German will contain passages for translation into English, and questions in Grammar, limited (except when German is taken as an alternative for Greek) to the Accidence.

5. SANSKRIT; ARABIC.

The Paper in Sanskrit and the Paper in Arabic will contain passages for translation into English, and questions into Grammar.

6. THE ENGLISH LANGUAGE, ENGLISH HISTORY, AND MODERN GEOGRAPHY.

Orthography; Writing from Dictation; The Grammatical Structure of the Language.

History of England to the end of the Seventeenth Century, with questions in Modern Geography.

B.—MATHEMATICS.

1. ARITHMETIC.

The ordinary Rules of Arithmetic.
Vulgar and Decimal Fractions.
Extraction of the Square Root.

2. ALGEBRA.

Addition, Subtraction, Multiplication, and Division of Algebraical Quantities.
Proportion.
Arithmetical and Geometrical Progression.
Simple Equations.

3. GEOMETRY.

The First Four Books of Euclid, or the subjects thereof.

C.—NATURAL PHILOSOPHY.†

1. MECHANICS.

Composition and Resolution of Statical Forces.

---

* Special stress is laid on accuracy in the answers to questions in Greek Grammar.

† The questions in Natural Philosophy will be of a strictly elementary character.

Simple Machines (*Mechanical Powers*): Ratio of the Power to the Weight in each.

Centre of Gravity.

General Laws of Motion, with the chief experiments by which they may be illustrated.

Law of the Motion of Falling Bodies.

2. Hydrostatics, Hydraulics, and Pneumatics.

Pressure of Liquids and Gases, its equal diffusion, and variation with the depth.

Specific Gravity, and modes of determining it.

The Barometer, the Syphon, the Common Pump and Forcing-Pump, and the Air-Pump.

3. Optics.

Laws of Reflexion and Refraction.

Formation of Images by Mirrors and Simple Lenses.

4. Heat.

Its sources. Expansion. Thermometers — relations between different Scales in common use. Difference between Temperature and Quantity of heat. Specific and Latent Heat. Calorimeters. Liquefaction. Ebullition. Evaporation. Conduction. Convection. Radiation.

D.—Chemistry.

Chemistry of the Non-Metallic elements; including their compounds as enumerated below—their chief physical and chemical characters—their preparation—and their characteristic tests.

Oxygen, Hydrogen, Carbon, Nitrogen, Chlorine, Bromine, Iodine, Fluorine. Sulphur, Phosphorus, Silicon.

Combining Proportions by weight and by volume. General nature of Acids, Bases, and Salts. Symbols and Nomenclature.

The Atmosphere—its constitution; effects of Animal and Vegetable life upon its composition.

Combustion. Structure and properties of Flame. Nature and composition of ordinary Fuel.

Water. Chemical peculiarities of Natural Waters, such as rain-water, river-water, spring-water, sea-water.

Carbonic Acid. Carbonic Oxide. Oxides and Acids of Nitrogen. Ammonia. Olefiant Gas, Marsh Gas, Sulphurous and Sulphuric Acids, Sulphuretted Hydrogen.

Hydrochloric Acid. Phosphoric Acid and Phosphuretted Hydrogen. Silica.

A fee of 40*s.* must be paid by every Candidate before examination. A Pass Certificate signed by the Registrar will be delivered to each Candidate who passes, after the report of the Examiners has been approved by the Senate.

IV. UNIVERSITY OF EDINBURGH.

The Local Examinations of this University have been instituted to supply a common test of attainment both for pupils of public schools and for those privately educated. The Board of Management grant Local Examination Certificates of two grades—Ordinary and Honour Certificates. These certificates are signed by the Vice-Chancellor of the University and specify the subjects in which Candidates have passed. The subjects of examination are divided into three classes,—Preliminary Subjects to be taken by all Candidates; Special Subjects, from which all Candidates must make a selection, according to the grade of Certificate desired; and Extra Subjects in which any Candidate may volunteer. The Examination for the Honour Certificate seems to correspond very nearly to the Examinations of Oxford and Cambridge for Candidates under 18 years of age. We have therefore here only to consider that Examination. Following are the Regulations for the examination in 1879, commencing June 17.

I. PRELIMINARY SUBJECTS,

In which all Candidates must undergo examination.

1. ENGLISH. — Reading aloud, with proper accent and emphasis. Writing from Dictation. The elements of English Grammar and analysis. English Composition; the structure of sentences.

2. HISTORY AND GEOGRAPHY.—(*a*) History of Scotland from 1513 to 1603. (*b*) The Geography of Europe. Only the principal mountains, rivers, and towns required, except in the geography of Great Britain and Ireland, of which more detailed knowledge will be expected. The Candidate will also be required to fill in an outline map of either Scotland, England, or Ireland.

3. LATIN.*—Grammar; with an easy passage for translation into English, and parsing.

4. ARITHMETIC, INCLUDING FRACTIONS.

---

* This subject will be optional for Female Candidates, except when Latin is taken as a Special Subject.

5. Scripture History.—The First Book of Samuel, and the Gospel according to St. Matthew.

No. 5 will not be required when parents or guardians request that it be omitted.

II. Honour Certificate.

At least *two*, and not more than *four* of the following subjects are to be selected by the Candidate. The selection must be made from at least two of the Departments A, B, C, and D.

Department A.

1. Latin.—A paper consisting of, 1st, a passage of plain English to be translated into Latin; 2nd, four short and plain passages, such as the Candidate might, without previous preparation in them, be expected to translate, two of these, at the choice of the Candidate, to be translated into English; and 3rd, a few grammatical questions, either arising out of the passages, or general.

2. Greek.—A paper including grammatical and general questions; the translation of an easy passage; and the translation of a few English sentences into Greek.

3. French.—*Ad aperturam* translation and retranslation, with questions on the accidence and the syntax of French grammar, and the history of French literature.

4. German.—*Ad aperturam* translation and retranslation, with questions on the accidence and syntax of German Grammar, and the history of German literature.

Department B.

1. English.—Composition; Higher Grammatical Questions, including Derivation of Words and Prosody; History of English Literature in the seventeenth century; Shakspeare's 'Merchant of Venice'; Chaucer's 'Prologue to the Canterbury Tales.'

2. History and Geography.—(*a*) General History of Europe from A.D. 1517 to 1648. (*b*) Geography of Asia.

3. Logic.—Jevons's 'Elementary Lessons in Logic' (Macmillan and Co.).

4. Bible Knowledge.—Coneybeare and Howson's 'Life and Epistles of St. Paul,' 2 vols., popular edition, vol. i., chapters i.–xiii.

Department C.

1. Mathematics.—Arithmetic. Euclid, Books i.–iv. and vi. Algebra to Quadratic Equations. Plane Trigonometry.

2. Natural Philosophy.—Elements of Mechanics and of Experimental Physics. (Balfour Stewart's 'Lessons in Elementary Physics'; and Blaikie's 'Elements of Dynamics,' or Thomson and Tait's 'Elements of Natural Philosophy.')

Department D.

1. Chemistry.—The relations to one another of Acids, Bases, Salts, and Metals—Oxidation and Reduction. The physical characters, methods of preparation, and chemical characters of the following non-metallic elements and their chief compounds:—Oxygen, Hydrogen, Nitrogen, Carbon, Sulphur, Phosphorus, Chlorine, Bromine, Iodine, Silicon. The oxides and salts of the following metals:—Potassium, Sodium, Barium, Calcium, Magnesium, Iron, Zinc, Manganese, Chromium, Aluminium, Cobalt, Nickel, Copper, Mercury, Lead, Silver, Gold, Platinum, Tin, Arsenic, Antimony, Bismuth.

The following text-books are referred to as indicating the amount and kind of knowledge expected:—Roscoe's 'Lessons in Elementary Chemistry,' Lessons I.-XXVI.; Williamson's 'Chemistry for Students,' Chaps. I.-XXXIII.; Wilson's 'Inorganic Chemistry' (Chambers's Educational Course); Brown's 'Chemistry' (Chambers's Elementary Science Manuals).

2. Zoology.—The general principle of Zoological Classification. The characters of the Classes of the Vertebrata, founded upon Anatomical and Physiological characters. The general characters of the Vertebrate Orders. The Morphological, Anatomical, and Physiological characters of the sub-kingdoms of the Invertebrata, and the general characters of the Invertebrate Orders. Dr. Stirling's Zoology, in Chambers's 'Information for the People,' and Dr. Alleyne Nicholson's 'Manual of Zoology.'

3. Botany.—Botanical organography. Functions of leaves and flowers. Process of fertilization in flowering and in flowerless plants. Demonstration of orders Ranunculaceæ, Cruciferæ, Caryophyllaceæ, Leguminosæ, Rosaceæ, Umbelliferæ, Compositæ, Labiatæ, Liliaceæ, and Grasses, in conspicuous specimens. General distribution of Plants in Britain. (Balfour's 'Elements of Botany.')

4. Physiology.—The structure and functions of the tissues of the body,—namely, epithelium, fibrous tissues, cartilage, bone, muscle, nerve-fibres, and nerve-cells. The structure and functions of the heart and blood-vessels. The circulation of the blood. The functions of the blood-corpuscles. The composition of the blood and its changes in the capillaries of the lungs, and in those of the system generally. The structure of the lungs, the mechanism by which the air is moved into

and out of the lungs during ordinary respiration. The changes of the air during respiration. Food, mastication, secretion and functions of saliva, deglutition. Secretion and functions of the gastric juice, bile, pancreatic and intestinal juices. Matters absorbed from stomach and intestine by radicles of portal vein and lacteals. The glucogenic function of the liver. The functions of the lymphatic system. The functions of skin and kidneys. The nature of reflex action. The functions of the two roots of a spinal nerve. The functions of the spinal cord, medulla oblongata, and convolutions of the cerebrum. A general knowledge of the structure and functions of the parts concerned in sight, hearing, smell, taste, and touch. Works recommended:—Huxley's 'Lessons in Physiology'; Newton's 'Animal Physiology.'

5. GEOLOGY.—Operations of the chief geological agents in effecting changes upon the earth's surface at present—air, rain, springs, rivers, frost, glaciers, the sea, earthquakes and volcanoes. Geological history of the earth, origin of mountains, table-lands, and valleys; leading features of plant and animal life during the primary, secondary, and tertiary periods. (Geikie's 'Elementary Lessons in Physical Geography'; Juke's 'School Class-Book of Geology.')

EXTRA SUBJECTS,

In which Candidates may volunteer for Examination, values obtained in either being acknowledged in the Certificate granted, but not added to the Candidate's aggregate marks.

A.—DEPARTMENT OF DRAWING.

(*a*) Drawing or Painting from a Model, with Light and Shade, or in Colour.

(*b*) Drawing in Perspective.

Candidates may undertake either of these Sections.

B.—DEPARTMENT OF MUSIC.

The Grammar of Music and the Principles of Musical Composition.

Every Candidate for an Honour Certificate is required to pay a fee of 30*s*. Ladies who obtain the Honour Certificate are exempted from the Entrance Examination for Girton College, Cambridge.

V. UNIVERSITY OF DUBLIN.

The "Examinations for Women" in 1879 commence on the Tuesday of the second week before Easter. There are three Examinations held by this University open to female students, which may be attended in succession at intervals of one or more years.

1. The First, or Junior Examination;
2. The Second, or Intermediate Examination;
3. The Third, or Senior Examination.

The Second, or "Intermediate Examination" seems to rank with the "Senior Candidates" Examination of Oxford and Cambridge, and we will therefore consider more particularly the regulations relating to it.

A.—INTERMEDIATE EXAMINATION.

In order to obtain a Certificate at this Examination, a Candidate is required to answer in the following subjects:—

1. ENGLISH COMPOSITION.

2. ENGLISH LANGUAGE AND LITERATURE. — English Grammar. Trench's 'English Past and Present' (last Edition). 'Student's Manual of English Literature,' in Dr. W. Smith's Series (last Edition), from Chap. xiv. (inclusive) to the end, with the Chapters on Shakspeare and Milton. Palgrave's 'Golden Treasury.' Shakspeare, 'Hamlet' (Clarendon Press Series); 'Merchant of Venice' (ditto). Milton, 'Paradise Lost,' Books i., ii.; 'Comus.'

3. ARITHMETIC, including Vulgar and Decimal Fractions; Rule of Three; Practice; Simple Interest; Decimal Currency; Extraction of Square Root.

4. GEOGRAPHY.—Clyde's 'School Geography.' The Geography of Europe and that of North America to be studied with special care. Questions of a more general kind will be set on the rest of the Geography.

5. HISTORY OF ENGLAND.—Green's 'History of the English People,' to end of Chap. vii. The period from A.D. 1509 to A.D. 1603 to be studied with special care.

6. HISTORY OF ROME.—'The Student's Manual of the History of Rome,' in Dr. W. Smith's Series, to end of Book iv. The period from B.C. 263 to B.C. 202 to be studied with special care.

7. HISTORY OF GREECE.—'The Student's Manual of the History of Greece' to end of Book iv. The period from B.C. 500 to B.C. 404 to be studied with special care.

[At least one-half of the questions in each Examination Paper in History and Geography will be from the specified portions of the Text-Books. Candidates will be expected to possess such a knowledge of Ancient Geography as is necessary for the intelligent study of the Histories of Greece and Rome.]

8. One Language from the following list, viz.:—

FRENCH.—Racine, 'Athalie'; Molière, 'Misanthrope'; Souvestre, 'Au coin du feu.' Grammatical questions will be set.

A passage from some modern French author will be set for translation into English; also a passage of English for translation into French.

Or, ITALIAN.—Tasso, 'Gerusalemme Liberata,' Canti i.–vi. (inclusive); Manzoni, 'I promessi Sposi,' Cap. i.–iv. Grammatical questions will be set. A passage from some modern Italian author will be set for translation into English; also a passage of English for translation into Italian.

Or, SPANISH.—Calderon, 'La Vida es sueño'; Caballero, 'La Gaviota,' Cap. i.–iv. (inclusive). Grammatical questions will be set. A passage from some modern Spanish author will be set for translation into English; also a passage of English for translation into Spanish.

Or, GERMAN.—Goethe, 'Hermann und Dorothea'; Freytag, 'Soll und Haben,' Chaps. i.–v. (inclusive). Grammatical questions will be set. A passage from some modern German author will be set for translation into English; also a passage of English for translation into German.

Or, LATIN.—Virgil, Æneid, Book vi.; Cicero, Pro Archiâ. Grammatical questions will be set. A passage from some Latin author will be set for translation into English; also a passage of English for translation into Latin.

Or, GREEK.—Plato, 'Apology of Socrates.' Grammatical questions will be set. Also Greek sentences for translation into English, and English sentences for translation into Greek.

B.—OPTIONAL SUBJECTS.

Candidates may offer themselves in the following subjects in addition to those above named; but a Candidate cannot present the same subject for both Examinations.

1. PURE MATHEMATICS.—Euclid, Books i., ii., iii., and vi. (omitting Props. 27, 28, and 29 of Book vi.); Algebra, to the end of Quadratic Equations; Trigonometry, to the end of the Solution of Plane Triangles.

2. MECHANICS.—Todhunter's 'Mechanics for Beginners'; 'Statics,' sections i.–xvi. (inclusive); 'Dynamics,' sections i.–iv. (inclusive), and vii. and viii. Galbraith and Haughton's 'Manual of Hydrostatics.'

3. ASTRONOMY.—Herschel's 'Outlines of Astronomy,' the first eleven Chapters.

4. PHYSICS.—Ganot's 'Natural Philosophy for General Readers and

Young Persons' (translated by Atkinson); Book v., or Book vi., or Books vii. and viii.

5. CHEMISTRY.—Roscoe's 'Lessons in Elementary Chemistry,' first twenty-six lessons; Fownes' 'Manual of Elementary Chemistry' (tenth Edition), Part ii.

6. BOTANY.—Oliver's 'Lessons in Elementary Botany'; Henfrey's 'Elementary Course of Botany,' Part i.

7. ZOOLOGY.—Huxley's 'Lessons in Elementary Physiology'; T. Rymer Jones's 'Animal Creation.'

8. GEOLOGY AND PHYSICAL GEOGRAPHY.—Page's 'Introductory Text-Book of Geology'; Juke's 'School Manual of Geology'; Hughes' Outlines of Physical Geography.'

9. LOGIC. — Thompson's 'Outline of the Laws of Thought'; Whateley's 'Logic,' Analytical Outline and Chapter on Fallacies.

10. THEORY OF MUSIC.—Dr. Stainer's 'Theory of Harmony.'

Or a Candidate may select, as an additional subject, a second Language, from the list given for the Examination of her Division.

Every Candidate presenting herself for Examination is required to pay a University fee of 20*s*., together with a Local fee of 5*s*.

VI. UNIVERSITY OF DURHAM.

The "Local Examinations" of this University are open to women, and will, in 1879, commence at Durham on Monday, June 2. The "Senior Candidates" Examination, for those under the age of 18, consists of four divisions, namely:—

Examination A, which will be directed (1) to the Elements of Christianity, as contained in the Bible and the Book of Common Prayer; (2) to English Grammar, Composition and Literature; (3) to Arithmetic; (4) to Geography and History.

Examination B, which will be directed to the Latin, Greek, French, German, and Italian languages.

Examination C, which will be directed to pure Mathematics.

Examination D, which will be directed to Physical Science and Art.

Every Candidate is required to pass Examination A, and no one who fails in it will be allowed to proceed to any of the other Examinations. But if any Candidate with the consent of her Parent or Guardian makes application to be exempted from Branch (1) of Examination A, the Warden and Senate have authority to grant such exemption. Following are the prescribed subjects of examination.

EXAMINATION A.

1. The Books of Ezra, Nehemiah, and the historical parts of Jeremiah. The Gospel according to St. Matthew. The Catechism.
2. Reading aloud. Writing from Dictation. Analysis and Parsing of English sentences. Questions in English Grammar.
   English Composition, to be tested by the narrative of some event, description of some place, or the like exercise.

   N.B.—Orthography and handwriting will be taken into account.
3. Arithmetic.
4. To draw from memory an outline Map of some country in Europe, showing the boundary lines, the names and position of the adjacent countries, the chief rivers, mountain ranges and towns, and the degrees of latitude and longitude.

   Questions will also be set on the Geography of Europe and Asia.
5. The outlines of the History of England, from the Invasion by the Romans to the end of the reign of George III.

All the Candidates except those who are exempted from branch (1) will be required to pass in the above-named subjects.

Candidates who are exempted from branch (1) will be examined in—

(1) Macaulay's 'Essay on Lord Bacon.'

(2) Milton's 'Paradise Lost.' Books x., xi., xii. (Passages will be given, and the Candidates will be required to explain their meaning and grammatical construction.)

The examination in these subjects will be accepted in lieu of that appointed in the Old and New Testament.

(3) Trench 'On the Study of Words,' Lectures iv., v., vi., vii.

Candidates will not be required to show a knowledge of the quotations in foreign languages.

The examination in this subject will be accepted in lieu of that appointed in the Church Catechism.

There will be an Examination also in the following additional subjects :—

1. The Acts of the Apostles, and the Morning Prayer. (Procter and Maclear's 'Elementary Introduction to the Book of Common Prayer.' Macmillan.)
2. Shakspeare's 'Julius Cæsar' (Clarendon Press Series), and Goldsmith's 'Vicar of Wakefield' (Rivington : edit. by C. Sankey).
3. Higher Questions in Arithmetic, Book-keeping, and Mensuration.

4. To draw from memory an outline Map, showing the coast-lines, chief ranges of mountains, the chief rivers and towns of France.
   Questions will be set on the geography of France.
5. History of England during the reigns of George I., II., and III., and notices of the chief English writers of the same period.

Examination B.

Latin.

1. Grammar.
2. Translations with questions—(1) Cicero, Pro Archiâ. (2) Cicero, Pro Balbo. (3) Ovid, Fasti vi. (Pitt Press Texts.)
   Candidates will be required to pass in two at least of these three subjects, of which (3) must be one.
   A passage for translation from some other Latin work.
3. A passage of English to be translated into Latin.

Greek.

1. Grammar.
2. Translations with questions—(1) Æschylus, Prometheus Vinctus. (2) Xenophon, Anabasis v. and vi.
   A passage for translation from some other Greek work.

French.

1. Grammar.
2. Translations, with grammatical, geographical, and historical questions from X. de Maistre, 'La Jeune Sibérienne' and 'Le Lépreux de la cité d'Aoste,' and Corneille's 'La Suite du Menteur.' (Pitt Press Texts.) Passages from some other French writers.
3. Translation of a passage from English into French.
   Each Candidate will be required to read a passage aloud.

German.

1. Grammar.
2. Translations, with grammatical, geographical, and historical questions from 'Der erste Kreuzzug (1095 - 1099) nach Friedrich von Raumer' (Pitt Press), and 'A Book of German Dactylic Poetry' (Pitt Press Texts). Passages from some other German writers.
3. Translation of a passage from English into German.
   Each Candidate will be required to read a passage aloud.

Italian.

1. Grammar.
2. Translations, with grammatical questions, from Silvio Pellico's 'Le Mie Prigioni,' chap. xxi.–xxx. ; Dante's 'La Divina Commedia,' Cantos i., ii.

3. Translation of a passage from English into Italian.

Each Candidate will be required to read a passage aloud.

A knowledge of one only of these languages will be required.

EXAMINATION C.

1. EUCLID, Books, i., ii., iii. and iv. First Twelve definitions of Book v. and Book vi.

2. GEOMETRICAL CONIC SECTIONS.

The questions on this subject will be confined to the properties of the Parabola.

3. ALGEBRA.

The questions will be chiefly elementary. Considerable weight will be attached to the solution of Equations. Questions will not be given on the Multinomial Theorem, Exponential Series, Converging and Diverging Series, Continued and Partial Fractions, Indeterminate Equations, Theory of Numbers or Probability.

4. PLANE TRIGONOMETRY AND LOGARITHMS.

Great importance will be paid to a thorough knowledge of the elementary principles. The questions will not include De Moivre's Theorem nor the propositions on Logarithms depending upon the Exponential Theorem.

In order to pass this examination a Candidate must show a knowledge of at least three books of Euclid, and Algebra as far as Quadratic Equations.

EXAMINATION D.

1. CHEMISTRY.

Questions will be set on the following elementary subjects :—(1) Definition of elements and compounds. (2) Character of Chemical Force. (3) Numerical laws of combination by weight and volume, and their application. (4) Nomenclature of compounds and Symbolic notation. (5) Character of Acids, Bases, and Salts. (6) Classification of Elements. (7) The non-metallic Elements, their occurrence, preparation, properties, and principal compounds.

It will be assumed that the experiments described in Miller's 'Inorganic Chemistry' (Longman's Text-Books of Science), *or parallel experiments*, have been exhibited and explained to the Candidates.

Practical Examination in the Elements of Chemical Analysis.

It is essential that Candidates should be able to explain the reasons for each step in their analysis.

2. Mechanics, Hydrostatics, and Pneumatics.

The examination will include the elementary portions of Statics and Dynamics treated in the ordinary text-books. The chapter on "Motion on a Curve" may be omitted.

A general knowledge will also be required of the construction and action of Pumps, Balances, the Barometer and Thermometer, Bramah's Press, the Steam-Engine, and methods of determining specific gravity.

3. Botany and Vegetable Physiology.

Questions will be set upon the structure, classification, and geographical distribution of plants, and also upon their several uses to man.

4. Zoology and Animal Physiology.

Questions will be set upon the classification and geographical distribution of animals, as well as upon their structure, aliment, and functions; also upon the laws which regulate the preservation of health.

5. Geology and Mineralogy.

Questions will be set upon the classification, structure, and relative ages of rocks, upon the distribution of organic remains in them, upon the chemical and physical characteristics of minerals, and upon the application of geological and mineralogical knowledge to agricultural and mining operations.

6. Drawing.

(1) Freehand. Outline drawing from the flat without shading. (2) Model. Freehand drawing from the solid with shading. (3) Practical Geometry, with the use of drawing instruments. (4) Linear Perspective. (5) Mechanical and Architectural. (6) Painting in Water Colours.

A Candidate will be required to pass in two branches at least, of which Freehand Drawing must be one.

Each Candidate in branch (6) will be required to bring to the examination a painting executed by himself, of such a kind as may best show his proficiency. Two hours will be allowed for a copy of the whole or a portion of the work, and this exercise will be judged with the finished work.

7. MUSIC.

In order to pass this examination, Candidates must be able to harmonize a given melody correctly in four-part score, employing the usual clefs—soprano, alto, tenor, and bass; and to show a fair general knowledge of the grammar of music, and the principles of musical composition.

A Certificate will be granted to any Candidate who passes a satisfactory examination in any of these subjects.

Every Candidate will be required to pay a fee of 20*s*. when she sends in her name for examination. Every one who at the examination for "Senior Candidates" passes Examination A, and any one of the other examinations also, will, in addition to the Certificate, receive the title of Literate.

VII. UNIVERSITY OF ST. ANDREWS.

The Senatus of the University of St. Andrews holds, at convenient centres, Examinations, which are conducted by Professors, of such Pupils (girls and boys) as may be presented to them. The University grants two sets of certificates, Junior and Senior. These Local examinations for 1879 will be held on June 17, and the prescribed subjects for the Senior Certificate are as follows:—

A.—PRELIMINARY SUBJECTS.

Every Candidate will be required to satisfy the Examiners in

1. ENGLISH.—Reading aloud a passage from an English author, Writing from Dictation, Grammar, and Structure of Sentences.
2. HISTORY.—History of England from the Conquest to the end of the reign of Elizabeth; or of Scotland, from the beginning of the reign of Alexander III. to the end of that of Queen Mary, as given in any of the School Histories.
3. MODERN GEOGRAPHY.—The Geography of England, Scotland, and Ireland; with a knowledge of the usual geographical terms.
4. ARITHMETIC.—Notation, Simple and Compound Rules, Practice, Proportion, and Vulgar Fractions.
5. SCRIPTURE HISTORY.—The Book of Genesis, and St. Matthew's Gospel.

In addition to the foregoing, each Candidate for the Senior Certificate will be examined in at least *two*, and not more than *four* of the following subjects:—

1. ENGLISH: Chaucer's 'Prologue,' and Shakspeare's 'Tempest'; ENGLISH LITERATURE: Stopford Brook's Primer, second half (from 1660 to present time); English Essay.

2. HISTORY AND GEOGRAPHY: Freeman's 'General Sketch of European History,' chaps. iv. to xii. inclusive; Geography of Asia, with a special study of British India.

3. MODERN LANGUAGES: FRENCH—Passages from Standard French writers to be translated into English; translations from English into French; Brachet's 'Historical Grammar of the French Language,' book ii. (Inflexion) "to conjugation of irregular verbs (so called)," exclusively; correspondence in French.

4. GERMAN: Passages from standard German writers to be translated into English; translations from English into German; correspondence in German.

5. ITALIAN: Passages from standard Italian writers to be translated into English; translations from English into Italian.

N.B.—Special value will be attached to ability to converse in any of the above languages.

6. ANCIENT LANGUAGES: LATIN—Books I., II., III., of the Odes of Horace, and Livy, Book XXI., with grammatical and general questions; a passage of English for translation into Latin.

7. GREEK: Homer's Iliad, Book III. and Xenophon's Anabasis, Book IV., with grammatical and general questions; narrative sentences for translation into Greek.

8. MATHEMATICS AND PHYSICAL SCIENCE: MATHEMATICS—Euclid, Books I., II., III., IV., and VI.; Elements of Plane Trigonometry — (Todhunter's 'Trigonometry for Beginners,' chaps. i.–xx.); Algebra as far as Quadratics, including Surds.

9. LOGIC: Jevons's Elementary Lessons in Logic—(Macmillan and Co.).

Any one, but only one, of the following subjects to be professed:—

10. NATURAL PHILOSOPHY.—Newth's First Book (last edition).

11. BOTANY.—Hooker's Primer of Botany.

12. ZOOLOGY.—Nicholson's Introductory Text-Book.

13. PHYSIOLOGY.—Huxley's Physiology for Schools.

14. CHEMISTRY.—Wilson's Inorganic Chemistry, or Roscoe's Lessons in Elementary Chemistry.

15. PHYSICAL GEOGRAPHY.—Page's Introductory Physical Geography.

16. GEOLOGY.—Page's Elementary Geology.

Every Candidate for the Senior Certificate will be required to pay an Examination fee of 20*s*.

VIII. UNIVERSITY OF GLASGOW.

The Local Examinations' Board of the University of Glasgow grants two certificates to students, (1) the Ordinary or Junior, and (2) the Honour or Senior. For these Certificates, Candidates must pass in the Common Subjects and also in a certain number of the Special Subjects as hereunder specified. It is not necessary that Candidates should take the Common and Special Subjects at the same time; if successful in the former, they will be registered as having passed, but no Certificate will be issued till the Special Subjects are taken at the next or a subsequent Examination. The Board will hold an examination in 1879, commencing on May 21.

COMMON SUBJECTS.

The quality of the handwriting and the spelling will be taken into account in judging the following exercises:—

1. ENGLISH.—Writing to Dictation. English Composition: an essay on a theme to be prescribed. Grammar: Syntax, and Parsing.

2. HISTORY.—The leading events in the History of England and Scotland from 1603 to 1660. (Books suggested: Gardiner's Two Stuarts; the relative portion of Green's Short History of the English People.)

3. GEOGRAPHY.—Geography of Asia. Outline Maps will be supplied on which Candidates will be required to indicate the position of rivers, mountains, towns, &c.

4. ARITHMETIC.—Elementary Arithmetic, including Simple Proportion and Vulgar Fractions.

5. SCRIPTURE HISTORY.—A knowledge of the contents of St. Matthew's Gospel (Cambridge Bible for Schools: Matthew).

6. LATIN.—Grammar. Translation of easy sentences into English, and Parsing.

Girls are not required to take Latin.

SPECIAL SUBJECTS FOR SENIOR CERTIFICATE.

Candidates must profess not less than *two*, nor more than *six* subjects. The selection requires to be made from at least two of the following Departments.

DEPARTMENT A.

1. ENGLISH LITERATURE.—English Literature of 17th century. Shakspeare's 'Tempest' and Milton's 'Comus'; Dowden's 'Shakspeare Primer.'

2. HISTORY.—French Revolution from 1789 to 1803.

3. POLITICAL ECONOMY.—Mrs. Fawcett's 'Political Economy for Beginners.'

4. LOGIC.—Jevons's 'Lessons in Logic—(Terms, Judgments, Reasonings, Fallacies).'

DEPARTMENT B.

1. LATIN.—Translation into English of passages from Virgil, Æneid I., and Cicero, Orations against Catiline. Translation of an easy passage from a book not prescribed. Translation into Latin of an easy English passage.

2. GREEK.—Translation into English of passages from Homer, Iliad, Book I., and Herodotus, Book V., Chap. i.–xxx. Translation into Greek of simple English sentences.

3. FRENCH.—Translations into English of French passage selected by the Examiner. Questions in Grammar. Translation of English passage into French.

4. GERMAN.—Translation into English of German passage selected by the Examiner. Questions in Grammar. Translation of English passage into German.

DEPARTMENT C.

1. MATHEMATICS.—Arithmetic. Euclid, Books I.–IV. and VI. Algebra—(Elementary Algebra, Equations with one or two unknown quantities, Fractions, Surds, Quadratic Equations, Arithmetical and Geometrical Progression, and Combinations). Plane Trigonometry—(Mensuration of the Circle, the Trigonometrical Ratios, the solution of Triangles by Logarithms).

2. NATURAL PHILOSOPHY.—Elements of Mechanics and of Experimental Physics. (Balfour Stewart's 'Lessons in Elementary Physics,' and Goodwin's 'Mechanics,' or Thomson and Tait's 'Elements of Natural Philosophy.')

3. ASTRONOMY.—The subjects treated in Dunkin's edition of Lardner's 'Astronomy,' or in equivalent books.

DEPARTMENT D.

1. CHEMISTRY.—General principles of Chemistry, including calculations with combining weights. Chemistry of the more important metals, including testing. (The relative portions of Roscoe's 'Elementary

Chemistry,' Williamson's 'Chemistry for Students,' or Wilson's 'Inorganic Chemistry.)

2. BOTANY. — Vegetable Organography. Elementary Physiology. Flowering and flowerless plants. Demonstration of Orders—Ranunculaceæ, Cruciferæ, Caryophyllaceæ, Leguminosæ, Rosaceæ, Umbelliferæ, Compositæ, Labiatæ, Liliaceæ, and Gramineæ. (Oliver's 'Lessons in Botany'; Balfour's 'Elements of Botany.')

3. ZOOLOGY —The characters of Molluscs, Insects, and Birds. The common plan of the Vertebrates compared with that of Nonvertebrated animals. (Nicholson's 'Manual of Zoology.')

4. HUMAN PHYSIOLOGY.—The mechanical arrangements of bones, joints, and muscles. A general knowledge of the cells, fibres, and tubes in the body, as revealed by the microscope. Food. Digestion. Absorption. Circulation of the blood. Respiration. Secretion and Excretion. The structure and functions of nerves. A general knowledge of the functions of the brain and spinal cord. Reflex actions. The general mechanism of the organs of sense. Special knowledge of the functions of various parts of the eye. (Cleland's 'Physiology,' Collins' series; Huxley's 'Physiology.')

5. GEOLOGY.—Stratification and its disturbances. Volcanoes and their products. The division and characters of the Palæozoic Strata.

VOLUNTARY SUBJECTS (SENIOR CERTIFICATE).

DEPARTMENT A.

1. DRAWING.—Drawing from a Model with Light and Shade, or in Sepia.

2. Drawing in Perspective.

The Candidate may take either or both.

DEPARTMENT B.

MUSIC.—Knowledge of Common Chords, major and minor. Resolution of the discord of the seventh. Writing a harmony to a given bass.

Candidates for the Senior Certificate holding a Junior Certificate of Glasgow University, or of any University whose Certificates may be recognized by the Board, are required to pay a fee of 20*s*. Candidates who do not hold such a Certificate are required to pay 30*s*.

IX. THE QUEEN'S UNIVERSITY IN IRELAND.

This University holds annually two Examinations open to girls—one for Junior, the other for Senior Candidates. Following are the prescribed subjects of examination for Senior Candidates :—

I.—Obligatory Group.

All Candidates are required to satisfy the Examiners in

1. Writing a continuous passage, and a list of difficult words from Dictation.
2. Analysis of English sentences, and parsing, and correction of faulty sentences.
3. A short English composition.
4. Arithmetic.
5. Geography.

Every Candidate will be required to fill up an outline Map of some country in Europe, or in North America, to be named by the Examiners, by inserting the great physical features of the country, the chief towns and remarkable places.

Questions will also be set in Geography. Clyde's 'School Geography' is recommended.

6. Outlines of English History, including the succession of sovereigns, the chief events, and the characters of the leading men in each reign.

N.B.—The quality of the handwriting and the spelling in the several exercises will be taken into account.

II.—Optional Subjects.

Every Candidate will also be required to satisfy the Examiners in two at least of the following Sections, of which one shall be either A, B, or C.

Section A.—English.

A fair knowledge of one of the following subjects will enable a Candidate to pass in this Section.

1. English History from 1589 to 1873, and the outlines of the History of English Literature during this period. Green's 'Short History of the English People' is recommended.
2. English Language and Literature.—English Grammar; Morley's First Sketch of English Literature, chapters iv., vii., sections 37–99, viii., x., xi.; *Chaucer, Prologue; *Shakspere, As You Like It; *Milton, Comus, Lycidas, Sonnets, and Samson Agonistes; *Pope, Satires and Epistles; Bacon, Essays xxx.–lviii.; *Addison, Arnold's Selections.

---

* Clarendon Press Series.

SECTION B.—LANGUAGES.

A fair knowledge of one of the following languages will enable a Candidate to pass in this Section.

1. LATIN.

Any two of the following, provided that one of the books selected be in prose and the other in verse.

Virgil, Æneid, Book III.
Horace, Odes, Book II.
Cæsar, Gallic War, Book IV.
Cicero, De Senectute.

2. GREEK.

Any two of the following, provided that one of the books selected be in prose and the other in verse.

Homer, Iliad, Book XVIII.
Sophocles, Ajax, omitting choral passages.
Plato, The Apology of Socrates.
Xenophon, Anabasis, Book IV.

3. FRENCH.

Corneille, Polyeucte.
Racine, Britannicus.
Molière, Les Fourberies de Scapin, and L'Avare.
Ségur, Histoire de la Grande Armée.

A passage from some other French author may be also selected for translation into English.

For translation into French an exercise of detached sentences will be set, testing the Candidate's knowledge of Syntax, especially the syntax of the pronouns, the use of the tenses, of the subjunctive mood and the participles.

A passage or some sentences selected from Ségur, Livre VIII., chaps. iv.–viii. inclusive, will be set for translation into French.

A passage from some easy English author.

4. GERMAN.

Freytag, Ingo und Ingraban.
Schiller, Jungfrau von Orleans.
Goethe, Hermann und Dorothea.

A passage for translation into English may also be selected from some other German author.

An exercise will be set testing the Candidate's knowledge of Syntax, especially of the arrangement of words in relative and dependent clauses, and the use of inversion.

A passage for translation into German will also be set from some modern English author.

5. ITALIAN.

Vasari, Vite de' più eccelenti Pittori, Scultori e Architetti, *scelte da Milanesi.* (Firenze, Barbèra.)

Dante, Inferno, i.–x. Fraticelli's edition is recommended.

A passage for translation into English may also be selected from some other modern Italian author.

An exercise, consisting of detached sentences, testing the Candidate's knowledge of Syntax, will be set for translation into Italian.

A passage, or some sentences, selected from Vasari's 'Life of Raffaelle' for re-translation.

A passage fıom some modern English author.

SECTION C.—MATHEMATICS.

GEOMETRY, the portions treated of in Euclid, Books I., II., III.

ALGEBRA to the end of Quadratic Equations.

This amount of knowledge will enable a Candidate to pass in this subject.

Questions will also be set in the Geometry treated of in Euclid, Books IV. and VI.

SECTION D.—LOGIC AND POLITICAL ECONOMY.

A fair knowledge of one of the following subjects will enable a Candidate to pass in this Section :—

LOGIC.—Fowler's Deductive Logic (Clarendon Press Series).

POLITICAL ECONOMY.—Fawcett's Manual of Political Economy.

(The following books will be found useful by Students in this group :—

LOGIC.—Jevons's Lessons in Logic ; Whateley's Logic, Books II., III. ; Mill's Logic, Book III., chapters i.–xiv. inclusive, xx., xxiii., Book V. ; Fowler's Inductive Logic.

POLITICAL ECONOMY.—Mill's Political Economy.

SECTION E.—NATURAL SCIENCES.

A fair knowledge of one of the following subjects will enable a Candidate to pass in this Section :—

ASTRONOMY.—The first eleven chapters of Herschel's Outlines of Astronomy.

CHEMISTRY.—Text-books — Roscoe's Lessons in Elementary Chemistry; Williamson's Chemistry for Students (Clarendon Press Series); Galloway's First Step in Chemistry. For consultation—Miller's Elements of Chemistry.

HEAT.—Ganot's Physique, Book VI.; or Everett's Translation of Deschanel's Traité Elémentaire de Physique, part ii.; or Balfour Stewart's Elementary Treatise on Heat.

SOUND.—Tyndall's Lectures on Sound.

BOTANY.—Text-book — Oliver's Lessons in Elementary Botany; Thomé's Structural and Physiological Botany. For consultation—Asa Gray's Structural and Systematic Botany.

ZOOLOGY.—Text-books — Nicholson's Text-book of Zoology for the Use of Schools; Huxley's Lessons in Elementary Physiology; Cleland's Physiology. For consultation—Milne Edwards's Cours Elémentaire de Zoologie (English Translation); Huxley's Introduction to Classification of Animals.

PHYSICAL GEOGRAPHY.—Text-books—Maury's Physical Geography for Schools and General Readers; Young's Physical Geography, in Collins' Advanced Science Series; Geikie's Elementary Lessons in Physical Geography; Johnston's School Atlas of Physical Geography. For consultation—Ansted's Physical Geography; Humboldt's Cosmos.

GEOLOGY.—Text-books—Juke's School Manual of Geology; Lyell's Student's Elements of Geology. For consultation—Juke's Manual of Geology, by Geikie; Ramsay's Physical Geography and Geology of Great Britain.

Each senior Candidate is required to pay before examination a fee of 10*s.* The Certificate given to each successful Candidate will specify the subjects in which she has answered with credit or satisfied the Examiners.

X. SCHOOLS' EXAMINATION OF COLLEGE OF PRECEPTORS.

This Corporation undertakes the examination of Girls' in common with Boys' Schools.

The First-Class Certificates of the College, it may be remarked, are recognized as guarantees of "*good general Education*" by several important corporate bodies connected with the learned professions. Following are the prescribed subjects for the "First-Class Certificate."

I.—OBLIGATORY SUBJECTS.

1. English Grammar with Analysis of Sentences, and Composition, and Outlines of the History of English Literature.

2. English History.
3. Geography, including Physical and Mathematical.
4. Arithmetic.
5. Algebra.
6. Euclid, Books I.–IV.*
7. Latin.
8. Foreign Languages,† (*a*) French, (*b*) German, (*c*) Spanish, (*d*) Italian, (*e*) Greek.

II.—OPTIONAL SUBJECTS.

Candidates may be examined in five, or any less number, of the following subjects :—

Scripture History; Trigonometry; Mechanics; Mensuration; Experimental Physics,‡ (*a*) Acoustics, (*b*) Light, (*c*) Heat, (*d*) Electricity and Magnetism; Chemistry; Natural History,‡ (*a*) Physiology, (*b*) Zoology, (*c*) Botany, (*d*) Geology; Political Economy; Book-keeping; Music (theoretical); Drawing,‡ (*a*) from the Flat, (*b*) from Models, (*c*) in Colours, (*d*) Geometrical.

Every Candidate must be prepared to pay an Examination fee of 10*s*.

XI. EXAMINATIONS OF THE SOCIETY OF ARTS.

These Examinations are specially intended for the benefit of Members of Institutions in union with the Society of Arts, and are, therefore, not ordinarily attended by girls from Schools of the higher grade. The Society grants certificates and prizes for proficiency in "Commercial Knowledge," "Domestic Economy," the "Fine Arts applied to Industries," the "Theory and Practice of Music," Technology of Arts and Manufactures. The subjects for examination in "Commercial Knowledge" are as follows :—1, Arithmetic; 2, English (Composition and Correspondence, and Précis Writing); 3, Book-keeping; 4, Commercial Geography and History; 5, Shorthand; 6, Political Economy; 7, French; 8, German; 9, Italian; 10, Spanish. The subjects for

---

* In the case of all Female Candidates, Algebra, Geometry, and Latin are optional; but such Candidates must be examined in as many subjects as are required of other Candidates.

† Only one of these is obligatory. See preceding note.

‡ Physics, Natural History, Drawing.—No Candidate will be examined in more than *two* branches of Physics, Natural History, or Drawing; and no Special Certificate will be awarded for less than 120 marks.

examination in "Domestic Economy"—an examination applying particularly to women—are as follows :—1, Clothing and its materials, 2, Health; 3, Housekeeping and Thrift; 4, Cookery.

XII. SCIENCE AND ART DEPARTMENT'S EXAMINATIONS.

These are of two kinds—the Class Examinations, of which there are two grades, the first or Elementary, and second or Advanced; and the Honours Examination. Prizes and certificates are given on the results of the Examination. The Examinations are conducted by a Committee approved by the Department. Following are the prescribed subjects of examination :—1, Practical, Plane, and Solid Geometry; 2, Machine Construction and Drawing; 3, Building Construction; 4, Naval Architecture and Drawing; 5, Pure Mathematics; 6, Theoretical Mathematics; 7, Applied Mechanics; 8, Acoustics, Light, and Heat; 9, Magnetism and Electricity; 10, Inorganic Chemistry; 11, Organic Chemistry; 12, Geology; 13, Mineralogy; 14, Animal Physiology; 15, Elementary Botany; 16–17, Biology (including Animal and Vegetable), Morphology and Physiology; 18, Principles of Mining; 19, Metallurgy; 20, Navigation; 21, Nautical Astronomy; 22, Steam; 23, Physiography; 24, Principles of Agriculture.

Art Subjects.—1st Grade: Freehand Drawing from Copies, Freehand Drawing from Models, and in Practical Geometry. 2nd Grade: Freehand (more advanced), Geometric, Perspective, and Model Drawing.

CHAPTER IX.

SECONDARY EDUCATION — *continued.* EXAMPLES OF THE PAPERS SET TO GIRLS, UNDER THE AGE OF 18 YEARS, IN THE SENIOR LOCAL EXAMINATIONS OF THE SEVERAL UNIVERSITIES.

THE following Papers have been selected from those which were set at the last Senior Local Examinations held by the following Universities, viz. Oxford, Cambridge, Dublin, Edinburgh, Durham, St. Andrews, Queen's University of Ireland, and at the last Midsummer examination of the College of Préceptors, and the last Annual examination of the Society of Arts. I have thought it desirable to print these papers, in order that persons interested in the subject of Female Education may judge, whether, or not, they seem to indicate a fair standard of general knowledge for Girls at the age of leaving school. I am given to understand that female candidates very rarely attempt Mathematics or Classics at these examinations, so that I have omitted from the list papers on those subjects.

DICTATION.

Time allowed: ¾ hour.

The Hellenic civilization, as it spread eastward into Asia, was adulterated by foreign elements, and in the west it was gradually crushed out by barbarism. A revolution took place in the principles which regulated social and political order. The small civic communities, in which the Hellenic civilization had sprung up and flourished, were absorbed by larger states. In the east there were formed the various monarchies of Syria and Asia Minor, where the Greek spirit of personal freedom received a strong admixture of

Oriental despotism. In the west was growing up the empire of the Roman republic, where fixed rules equally repressed personal greatness and personal government. What military and political organization was able to accomplish in a contest with the greatest personal qualities, has been shown in the course of the first collision between Romans and Greeks. The next three centuries completed the triumph of the Roman arms and of Roman policy, and at the same time the triumph of the Greek mind.

perquisite	brewery	suffrage
subtlety	disbursement	demagogue
adjournment	secular	heraldry
suspense	archæology	emergency
facilitate	mechanism	supremacy
inadequacy	crisis	pamphlet
inappreciable	irresistible	vengeance
commentary	prevalence	protocol

ENGLISH GRAMMAR.

Time allowed: 1½ hour.

1. Enumerate the Parts of Speech. How do grammarians differ in their enumeration?

2. Mention all the inflexions of which *nouns* admit.

Give the feminines of *sorcerer*, *actor*, *fox*, *lord*, *hero*, *margrave*, and the plurals of *brother*, *ox*, *child*, *sheep*, *cloth*, *index*, *formula*, *chief*, *thief*, *bandit*, *court-martial*. Mention the two forms of the plurals, where such exist.

3. What is the meaning of *tense?* What different forms of the present, past, and future tenses are in use?

How are verbs classified with reference to the formation of their past tense? Give the past tense and past participle of the following verbs, and classify them :—

To burst, to bring, to build, to cast, to dream, to dig, to freeze, to make, to melt, to ring, to tear, to weave.

4. What is an *Adverb?* Give two instances of adverbs of number, affirmation, degree, manner, place, time, cause and effect.

Give three examples of adjectives used as adverbs.

What is the meaning of an *adverb-sentence?* Give an example.

5. Give rules respecting the concords of verbs with their subjects, when subjects differing in number or person or both are connected by a conjunctive or disjunctive conjunctive.

On what grounds can you justify the following constructions from Milton and Shakspeare?

Bitter complaint and sad occasion dear
Compels me to disturb your season due.
No ceremony that to great ones 'longs,
Not the king's crown, nor the deputed sword,
The marshal's truncheon, nor the judge's robe
Become them with one half so good a grace
As mercy does.

6. Parse the words in Italics in the following lines :—

Forth rushed *in haste* the great Consulting Peers,
Raised from their dark Divan, *and* with like joy
Congratulant approached him, *who* with hand
Silence, and with these words *attention* won.

MILTON.

7. Analyse the following sentence :—

But this rough magic
I here abjure, *and*, when I have required
Some heavenly music, *which* even now I do,
To work mine end upon their senses, *that*
This airy charm *is for*, I'll break my staff,
Bury it certain fathoms in the earth,
And *deeper* than did ever plummet sound
I'll drown my book.

SHAKSPEARE.

Parse the words in Italics in this passage.

ENGLISH COMPOSITION.

Time allowed: 1½ *hour.*

N.B.—Every Candidate is required to satisfy the Examiners in this Paper. Attention should be paid to Spelling, Handwriting, Punctuation and Correctness of Expression.

The Composition is to be written on *one only* of the following subjects, and should not be less than two nor exceed four pages in length.

1. Give in outline the story of any tale of fiction you have read.

Or

2 Describe any place you have visited, pointing out its historical associations or physical features.

Or

3. Sketch the life and character of any illustrious person in ancient or modern history.

Or

4. Discuss the influence on mankind, politically, socially, morally, and religiously, of the invention of printing.

ENGLISH HISTORY.

Time allowed: 2 hours.

1. Trace the descent from James I., of William III., and Mary his wife, Prince Rupert, and George I.

2. Give the dates and results of the battles of Worcester, Sedgmoor, Naseby, and Killiecrankie.

3. Sketch the career of George Villiers, Duke of Buckingham.

4. What grievances were dealt with in the Petition of Right? Narrate the circumstances that attended the granting of it.

5. Give some account of the foreign policy of Oliver Cromwell.

6. What is the origin of the names "Whig" and "Tory"? Under what circumstances did they appear as party names during the reign of Charles II.?

7. Briefly indicate the nature of the events that are alluded to as the Self-denying Ordinance, the Hampton Court Conference, the Triple Alliance, the Petition and Advice, the Declaration of Breda, the Trial of the Seven Bishops.

8. What part did John Milton take in the politics of his time? Mention his principal works.

9. Describe in general terms the following works, naming the author of each: Leviathan, Hudibras, Absalom and Achitophel, Religio Medici.

10. Give some account of the contents of Magna Charta, with a brief outline of the events in the reign of John that led to his signing it.

11. Explain the causes of the separation of the English Church from Rome in the reign of Henry VIII.

12. At what times were representatives from Ireland, Scotland, and Wales, respectively, incorporated with the English Parliament?

ENGLISH LANGUAGE AND LITERATURE.

Time allowed: 2 hours.

1. (*a*) What is meant by "phonetic decay"?
   (*b*) What is the force of the English prefix *for*? What of the prefix *um*?

(*c*) By what marks may you discover that a word is not yet thoroughly naturalized in our language? Give examples.

(*d*) Write a note on the word "Its."

(*e*) What changes have taken place in the meaning of the following words?—Fairy, starve, polite, humourous, influence.

2. Name the author, and briefly state what is the nature, of each of the following works:—Thalaba, The White Doe of Rylstone, Adonais, The Dream, The Rivals, The Jolly Beggars, Sir Eustace Grey, The Castle of Indolence, Memoirs of a Cavalier, Fable of the Bees.

3. Give some account of

(*a*) The fourth period of Shakspeare's career as a dramatist.

(*b*) Addison's periodical Essays.

4 In what poem does each of the following passages occur?—

(*a*) But that two-handed engine at the door
Stands ready to smite once, and smite no more.

(*b*) Nothing's so dainty sweet as lovely melancholy.

(*c*) Such sights as youthful poets dream
On summer eves by haunted stream.

(*d*) Yet oft before his infant eyes would run
  Such forms as glitter in the Muse's ray
With orient hues, unborrowed from the sun.

(*e*) They would have thought who heard the strain
  They saw, in Tempe's vale, her native maids,
  Amidst the festal-sounding shades,
To some unwearied minstrel dancing.

(*f*) I set her on my pacing steed,
  And nothing else saw all day long,
For sidelong would she bend and sing
  A fairy's song.

(*g*) Thou dost preserve the stars from wrong.
And the most ancient Heavens through thee are fresh and strong.

(*h*) Now more than ever seems it rich to die,
  To cease upon the midnight with no pain.

(*i*) Wild Spirit, which art moving everywhere,
Destroyer and Preserver; Hear, O hear!

(*j*) Behold the Child among his new-born blisses—
A six-years' darling of a pigmy size.

5. Give as accurate an account as you can of 'Il Penseroso,' or 'The Passions,' or the two poems in which Wordsworth's 'Matthew' appears.

6. (*a*) Give some account of the scene in which Nerissa names her lady's wooers and Portia criticizes them.

(*b*) What is Ophelia's account of her silent interview with Hamlet?

(*c*) How do the speeches of the Player King and Player Queen illustrate the general theme of the play of 'Hamlet'?

7. Write notes on the following passages:—

(*a*) We have done but greenly
In *hugger-mugger* to inter him.

(*b*) In the dead *vast* and middle of the night.

(*c*) Unhousel'd, disappointed, unaneled.

(*d*) And thus do we of wisdom and of reach
With windlasses and with *assays of bias*,
By indirections find directions out.

(*e*) For look where my *abridgment* comes.

(*f*) His master and he . . . are scarce cater-cousins.

(*g*) And with affection wondrous sensible
He wrung Bassanio's hand.

(*h*) Some men there are love not a *gaping pig*.

(*i*) Look how the floor of heaven
Is thick enlaid with *patines* of bright gold.

(*j*) Nothing is good, I see, *without respect*.

8. (*a*) Give the substance of Belial's speech in the infernal consultation.

(*b*) Exhibit your acquaintance with some lyrical passage of 'Comus.'

GEOGRAPHY.

Time allowed: 2 hours.

1. Draw an outline Map of France, showing the boundary and the degrees of latitude and longitude.

2. State the different causes which produce the winds. What *general* classification of them may be made? Give a brief description of Cyclones and Typhoons.

3. Compare the Old and New World in the following points:— (*a*)

Direction of mountain systems. (*b*) Nature and extent of coast-line. (*c*) Climate and Vegetation.

4. What parts of the present Italian kingdom formerly belonged to Austria? State the circumstances of their transfer, and mention any Austrian possessions which formed part of the ancient kingdom of Italy.

5. Give the boundaries of British America. What countries does it comprise? Mention their chief towns, and say on what river, if any.

6. Draw a sketch map of America, inserting the names of its straits, gulfs, and mountains.

7. What and where are The Maelstrom, La Plata, The Pampas, Corfu, San Salvador, The Great Antilles, New Orleans, Wisconsin, Otranto, Coimbra, Ratisbon.

ADDITIONAL QUESTIONS.

1. An outline map of Turkey. Can you mention the changes proposed in the Treaty of San Stefano?

2. What different races are included in the Turkish Empire? Notice some leading characteristics of each.

3. State accurately the position of the following places:—Scutari, Bagdad, Rodosto, Erzeroum, Aleppo, Saida, Beirout, the Golden Horn, Saloniki.

SCRIPTURE HISTORY.

Time allowed: 2 hours.

1 AND 2 KINGS, AND THE GOSPELS OF MATTHEW, MARK, AND LUKE.

1. What caused the secession of the Ten Tribes under Jeroboam?

2. What means did Jeroboam take to make the severance of the kingdoms permanent?

3. What was the distinction between the idolatry of Jeroboam and that of Ahab?

4. Name the kings of Jeroboam's line.

5. What did Jezebel mean when she said, "Had Zimri peace who slew his Master?"

6. Athaliah, Jehoiada, Huldah, Ahijah,—state what you know of them.

7. What tribes were lead into captivity by Shalmanezer, Tiglath Pileser, and Nebuchadnezzar respectively?

8. What miracles did Elisha work?

9. What was the character of Hezekiah?

10. Wherein did the good work of Josiah, as king, differ from that of the good kings before him?

11. What incidents in the beginning of the Gospel History are recorded by Matthew alone? and what by Luke alone?

12. What parables are found in St. Luke's Gospel only?

13. What indications do we find in St. Matthew that he wrote for Jews?

14. What does our Lord teach by the illustration of a house founded on a rock?

15. Do you remember any cases in the Sermon on the Mount, in which our Lord draws lessons from the fact that God is our Father in Heaven?

16. Quote texts or refer to passages teaching that we should not set our hearts on money or other perishable things.

ARITHMETIC.

Time allowed: 2 hours.

1. Seven millions two hundred thousand penny stamps, and nine millions four hundred and six thousand halfpenny stamps were issued in a year; what is their value in pounds, shillings, and pence?

2. Find the value of 157 miles, 3 furlongs, 24 poles of telegraph wire at 11*l.* 10*s.* per mile.

3. Prove that if the numerator and denominator of a fraction be divided by the same number, the value of the fraction is not altered.

4. Reduce $\frac{595}{1071}$, $\frac{1547}{5712}$ to their lowest terms and express their difference as a decimal.

$$\frac{\frac{1}{4}+\frac{11}{13}}{\frac{2}{7}+\frac{9}{11}} \div \frac{\frac{1}{5}+\frac{3}{4}}{\frac{1}{3}+\frac{2}{7}}.$$

5. Give a general rule for the division of decimals.

The weight of a cubic inch of water is 253·17 grains, that of a cubic inch of air 31 grains; find, to three places of decimals, how many cubic inches of water are equal in weight to one cubic foot of air.

6. If $\frac{7}{15}$ of a guinea be taken from $\frac{3}{12}$ of $\frac{5}{9}$ of 5*l.*; what fraction of 3*l.* 9*s.* will remain?

7. Find the value of

$$\cdot 3\dot{8}\dot{7} \text{ of } 8l.\ 16s.\ 3d. + 6\tfrac{1}{2} \text{ of } \frac{16}{65} \text{ of } 7s.\ 8\tfrac{1}{2}d. + \frac{7}{11} \text{ of } 1d.$$

8. What is the length of the edge of a cubical cistern which contains as much as a rectangular one whose edges are

154 ft. 11 in., 70 ft. 7 in., and 53 ft. 1 in.?

9. In 1861 three towns had populations of 17,650, 19,600, and 18,760 respectively. In 1871 the population of the first had decreased 18 per cent., that of the second had increased 21 per cent., while the population of the three had increased by 4691; find the change per cent. in the population of the third town.

10. What sum will amount to 1591*l.* 13*s.* 2·16*d.* in 3 years at compound interest, the interest for the 1st, 2nd, and 3rd years being 3, 2, and 1 per cent. respectively?

11. A bankrupt has goods worth 975*l.*, and had they realized their full value, his creditors would have received 16*s.* 3*d.* in the pound; but $\frac{3}{8}$ths were sold at 17·5 per cent. and the remainder at 23·75 per cent. below their value. What sum did the goods fetch, and what dividend was paid?

12. A man has stock in the 3 per cents. which brings him 240*l.* a year. He sells out $\frac{1}{4}$th of the stock at $87\frac{1}{4}$ and invests the proceeds in railway stock, at $174\frac{1}{2}$*l.* What dividend per cent. per annum ought the railway stock to pay, so that he may increase his income 40*l.* per annum by the transaction?

FRENCH.

Time allowed: 3 *hours.*

[N.B.—Give simply the answers: do not copy the words of the different questions unless you are particularly requested to do so.]

1. Write the plural of: Héros, tuyau, filou, mal, maille, émail, joujou, bleu, impérial, naval, œil, ave-maria, basse-taille, porte-drapeau, contre-ordre, réveille-matin, coup-d'œil, essuie-mains, porte-voix, tête-à-tête.

2. Write the feminine singular of: Facile, actif, époux, net, inquiet, bas, aigu, pécheur, créateur, épais, mou, chasseur, cheval, girafe, pair, grognon, larron, diacre, perroquet, pastoureau.

3. Conjugate *s'asseoir* in the 3rd pers. sing. of the simple tenses *negatively*; in the 3rd pers. plur. of the compound tenses *interrogatively*; and in the 2nd pers. plur. of both simple and compound tenses *interrogatively negatively*. (*Names of tenses to be omitted.*)

4. Write the Participles Present and Past, and the 2nd pers. sing. of all the simple tenses of: Envoyer, tenir, voir, pouvoir, naître, vivre. (*Abbreviations allowed, and names of tenses to be omitted.*)

5. State the four elementary rules of agreement of the Past Participle, and illustrate them by six different examples.

6. Write out the following, and correct the mistakes: Un orange; un orage; un ouvrage; un sphère; un atmosphère; un hémisphère. Tête nu; nu-tête. Il possède une maisonnette et un jardin assez grands. Il est quatre heure et demi. Les cinq lettres ci-inclus. Ils sont tous-puissants. Des cerises aigre-doux. Une couleur grise-obscure. Il vaut mieux être un homme galant qu'un galant homme. L'an mille et un de l'ère chrétienne. J'espère que votre promenade a été agréable. Je ne doute pas que vous viendrez demain. Elle a donné le moi. N'avez-vous pas donné les leur? Donnez-le moi. Ne donnez pas le moi. Vous n'aviez pas envoyé les en. Enverront-ils la vous? Envoyez la y. Ne donnez-pas moi en. .Sa montre et cette de sa sœur. Le livre qui vous voyez n'est pas mien.

7. Translate into English:—

I. La nation la plus riche du monde devient bientôt incapable de fournir à un roi absolu tout l'argent dont il a besoin, parce que la nature humaine est insatiable. Si grandes que soient les ressources de la nation, les dépenses d'un prince que rien n'arrête sont toujours plus grandes. Et puis, dans son avidité imprudente, il tarit les économies de ses peuples, et, sans avances, les peuples ne peuvent pas refaire leur richesse. A la profusion s'ajoute le désordre, le gaspillage. Il se passe en grand dans cette nation ce qu'on voit dans la maison d'un prodigue insouciant. Nous avons eu bien peu de rois, je ne dis pas économes, mais raisonnables.

(*a*) What is meant by: *la taille* and *la gabelle?*

(*b*) What was the general situation of the French people between 1650 and 1750?

(*c*) Say what you know of Louis XIV.

II. L'un dit que vous faites imprimer des almanachs particuliers, où vous faites doubler les quatre temps et les vigiles, afin de profiter des jeûnes où vous obligez votre monde; l'autre, que vous avez toujours une querelle toute prête à faire à vos valets dans le temps des étrennes ou de leur sortie d'avec vous, pour vous trouver une raison de ne leur donner rien. Celui-là conte qu'une fois vous fîtes assigner le chat d'un de vos voisins, pour vous avoir mangé un reste de gigot de mouton; celui-ci, que l'on vous surprit, une nuit, en venant dérober vous-même l'avoine de vos chevaux; et que votre cocher, qui était celui d'avant moi, vous donna, dans l'obscurité, je ne sais combien de coups de bâton, dont vous ne voulûtes rien dire. Enfin, voulez-vous que je vous dise? on ne saurait aller nulle part où l'on ne vous entende accommoder de toutes pièces. Vous êtes la fable et la risée de tout le monde;

et jamais on ne parle de vous que sous les noms d'avare, de ladre, de vilain, et de fesse-mathieu.

(*a*) Who speaks these words?

(*b*) Who are Cléante, Valère, Mariane, Anselme, Elise, Frosine?

(*c*) Write a short life of Moliere.

III. Ménalque descend son escalier, ouvre sa porte pour sortir, il la referme: il s'aperçoit qu'il est en bonnet de nuit, et, venant à mieux s'examiner, il se trouve rasé à moitié, il voit que son épée est mise du côté droit, et que ses bas sont rabattus sur ses talons. S'il marche dans les places, il se sent tout d'un coup rudement frapper à l'estomac ou au visage; il ne soupçonne point ce que ce peut être, jusqu'à ce qu'ouvrant les yeux et se réveillant il se trouve ou devant un limon de charrette, ou derrière un long ais de menuiserie que porte un ouvrier sur ses épaules. On l'a vu une fois heurter du front contre celui d'un aveugle, s'embarrasser dans ses jambes, et tomber avec lui, chacun de son côté, à la renverse. Il lui est arrivé plusieurs fois de se trouver tête pour tête à la rencontre d'un prince et sur son passage, se reconnaître à peine, et n'avoir que le loisir de se coller à un mur pour lui faire place.

LA BRUYÈRE.

8. Translate into French:—

I should very imperfectly execute the task which I have undertaken, if I were merely to treat of battles and sieges, of the rise and fall of administrations, or intrigues in the palace, and of debates in the parliament. It will be my endeavour to relate the history of the people as well as the history of the government, to trace the progress of useful and ornamental arts, to describe the rise of religious sects and the changes of literary taste, to portray the manners of successive generations, and not to pass by with neglect even the revolutions which have taken place in dress, furniture, repasts, and public amusements. I shall cheerfully bear the reproach of having descended below the dignity of history, if I can succeed in placing before the English of the nineteenth century a true picture of the life of their ancestors.

MACAULAY.

GERMAN.

Time allowed: 2 hours.

1. Translate into English:—

Friedrich eilte seinem Bruder Heinrich zu Hülfe, der in Sachsen durch Marschall Daun hart bedrängt wurde. Bei dem Dorfe Hochkirch in der Nähe von Bautzen bezog er ein offenes Lager Seine Generäle machten ihn auf das Gefährliche seiner Lage aufmerksam.

"Wenn uns die Œstreicher hier nicht angreifen," sagte Seydlitz, "so verdienen sie gehängt zu werden" Aber Friedrich meinte: "Sie werden nicht, denn sie fürchten sich vor uns mehr als vor dem Galgen!" Aber in der Nacht auf den 14. October, als noch Alles im preussischen Lager schlief, näherten sich die Œstreicher dem Dorfe und begannen früh morgens um fünf Uhr den Ueberfall. Das Niederschiessen der Vorposten weckte die schlafenden Preussen, die sich zu sammeln suchten; aber eine die Hauptstrasse des Dorfes beherrschende Batterie streckte sie haufenweise nieder. Allein gerade jetzt zeigte sich die Ordnung im preussischen Heere und Friedrichs Geistesgegenwart im glänzendsten Lichte. Lager und Geschütz gingen zwar verloren, aber in bewundernswerther Haltung führte er sein geschlagenes Heer zurück, und wusste durch geschicktes Manövriren den Œstreichern die Früchte ihres Sieges zu rauben.

2. Translate into German:—

Three young men, Lewis, Peter, and Paul, were travelling together and came to an inn where there was nothing to eat except one egg. "This," said Lewis, "is too little for us all to eat; come, let us go to bed, and he who has the best dream shall have the egg." They lay down accordingly; but Paul got up in the middle of the night and ate the egg. The next morning each recounted (*erzählen*) the dream he had had. Peter said: "I dreamt *that* (*omit*) I was sitting (*subjunct.*) beside the king's throne." Lewis said: "I dreamt *that* I was the king himself and thou wert sitting beside me. My dream is better than thine; and the egg belongs to me." "And I," said Paul, "I dreamt *that* I was eating the egg." In vain they looked (*suchen*) for it (*danach*); for he had really swallowed (*verschlucken*) it.

3. (1) Write out the third person singular and the first person plural, present, imperfect, and perfect indicative active of *vertreiben, beginnen, sich besinnen, ausgehen, únterhalten, unterháltén, entweichen.*

(2) Give the German words in the singular and plural with the definite article for *window, song, street, pain, sea, lake, river, face, merit, damage, wealth, sex.*

(3) Form the respective abstract nouns of *hoch, schön, schlecht, frei, gut, sanft, tapfer, schnell, nah.*

(4) Illustrate by examples the government of *sich schämen, gehorchen, spotten, froh, warten, verdriessen.*

4. State what you know of *Lessing* and his writings, and the place he occupies in the history of German Literature.

[It is to be noted that none of the following subjects are *Obligatory* on female Candidates. The papers are printed simply with the purpose of allowing the reader to judge of the nature of the questions set.]

ZOOLOGY.

Time allowed: 2 hours.

(Not more than five questions should be attempted.)

1. In what respects do *Birds* differ in their organization from Mammals? What are the chief Orders and Families of Birds?
2. To what Order of animals does the *frog* belong? Define the characteristics of that Order, and mention its chief divisions.
3. Describe the structure of some *sponge;* and mention some of the animals that are allied to the Sponges.
4. In what particulars do *whales* differ from other mammals? Enumerate the chief members of the Cetacean group.
5. What are the *Polyzoa?* Give some account of their structure, habitats, and classification.
6. Make a classified table of the *Mollusca;* and describe an example of any one kind in particular.
7. Mention the different kinds of *Chelonia;* indicate their habits, and where they are met with.
8. Make orderly lists of the kinds of animals that are allied to the *cat* and the *dog* respectively.

BOTANY.

Time allowed: 2 hours.

(Not more than five questions should be attempted.)

1. Name the classes of Phanerogamous plants, state the characters on which they are founded, and mention any British plants which are exceptional in each of such characters, respectively.
2. Define the following organs:—(i) *tuber*, (ii.) *bulb*, (iii.) *tendril*, (iv.) *runner*, (v.) *cyme.*

   How does (i.) differ from a *tuberous root?* How does (ii.) differ from a *corm?* What organs are metamorphosed into (iii.)? How does (iv.) differ from a *stolon* and a *sucker?* What modifications are there of (v.)?
3. What are *stipules?* Mention as many different forms as you can and state their uses respectively.
4. From what plants, and from what part of them, are the following

substances obtained :—*sago, indigo, opium, cotton, linen, cloves, mace, vegetable ivory, flour, liquorice?*

5. Describe the processes of Respiration and Assimilation in plants with green leaves. What modifications occur in colourless parasites?

6. Describe the fructification of any sea-weed or other *alga.*

7. What part do Insects play in Vegetable Physiology? Describe in detail any instances known to you where they are at least important, if not absolutely necessary agents.

8. A British plant has opposite *entire* leaves, a *subgamosepalous* calyx of five sepals, a *hypogynous* polypetalous corolla, many *triadelphous* stamens, and a *superior syncarpous* pistil. Name the plant, and give the meaning of the terms printed in *italics.*

GEOLOGY AND PHYSICAL GEOGRAPHY.

Time allowed: 2½ hours.

1. State the true figure of the Earth, and give an account of some one method by which it has been determined.

2. Draw and describe a rough contour map of the bed of the North Atlantic Ocean, and a generalized section taken across it from Ireland to Newfoundland.

3. Describe and explain as far as you are able the circulation of the waters of the North Atlantic basin.

4. State the laws of rainfall.

In what way and from what causes do the North-east and South-west winds of our Islands differ from each other in regard to temperature and the quantity of aqueous vapour they contain?

5. Describe fully the phenomena of a volcanic eruption.

Discuss the arguments for and against that theory which you consider to afford the most probable explanation of a volcanic eruption.

6. Write a complete history of a glacier from its source to its termination.

Point out its effects as a denuding agent.

7. Define the terms isothermal, isochimonal, and isotheral lines.

Account for the general direction of the isothermal lines which cross the North Atlantic Ocean.

---

8. What is meant by the phrase "crust of the earth"? Give a concise outline of what is known of the general structure and composition of the earth's crust.

9. Describe, and state the mineral and chemical composition of each of the following rocks :—*granite, gabbro, felstone, basalt, limestone.*

Trace the changes by which limestone may be derived from basalt.

10. On what principles are strata grouped together into formations? Write out a list of the formations which occur in Britain in the order of their age, and mention a fossil peculiar to each.

11. Draw a rough sketch map to indicate the distribution of land and sea and of active volcanic vents over the site of the British Islands during the Carboniferous limestone period.

12. Identify the rocks A, B, and the fossils D, E.

NATURAL PHILOSOPHY.

Time allowed: 2 hours.

1. Enuntiate Newton's first two Laws of Motion; show how far they enable us to carry Dynamics; and thence point out the necessity for a third law.

2. How far must a body fall to acquire a velocity of 1 foot per second, and how long will it take to acquire that velocity?

3. Explain how a train is guided round a curve. Find the horizontal pressure on the rails when a 20-ton engine runs at 50 miles per hour on a curve of a mile radius.

4. Trace the effects, as to change of temperature, molecular state, and volume, as heat is steadily applied to a pound of very cold ice; stating the number of units of heat required for each stage of the operation.

5. Enuntiate Kepler's Laws, and point out Newton's deductions from each.

6. Define an Image, as formed by any optical instrument. Point out the distinction between real and virtual images, and explain why an image can never be brighter than the object.

7. State the laws of Boyle and Charles; and apply them to show how the temperature of a mass of air must be altered so as to keep its pressure unchanged while it is allowed to expand.

8. Define the capacity of a body for heat and for electricity; and give instances of common phenomena depending on either of these.

9. When a cylindrical jar is immersed mouth downwards in water, the water rises in it to a very small extent, but as the depth to which it is plunged increases, the water rises higher. Explain this, and calculate at what depth it will be three-fourths full of water.

10. State the laws of the composition of any number of velocities. Show that there is only one point within a triangle, such that velocities represented in magnitude and direction by the lines drawn from it to the angles would, if generated simultaneously, leave the body at rest.

11. Mention the more striking analogies between light and radiant heat.

12. Define a Musical Note. In what respects may two notes differ, and upon what physical circumstances can these differences depend?

ASTRONOMY.

Time allowed: 2 hours.

1. Account for the phenomenon of *Twilight*. The day of the year being given, how would you determine the places on the earth's surface at which twilight lasts all night?

2. Define the terms—*Right Ascension*, *Declination*, *Terrestrial Latitude*, and *Longitude*, *Celestial Latitude*, and *Longitude*.

3. Explain the important function performed by a clock in an observatory. In what respects, as to the rate of going, and the time indicated, does an astronomical clock differ from one employed for measuring civil time? How may an error existing in the rate of going of an astronomical clock be detected?

4. Describe Hadley's sextant, and explain its use, and its adjustments.

5. What is meant by the *Precession of the Equinoxes?* To what physical causes is it attributable?

6. From what astronomical phenomena is it proved that the Moon is an opaque solid, and that its light is derived from the Sun?

7. State the argument in favour of universal gravitation derivable from the Moon's motion.

8. Distinguish between the Heliocentric, and Geocentric, positions of a planet.

9. From what discrepancy between calculation and observation has it been inferred that the passage of light through space is not instantaneous?

10. Show that the apparent orbit of a planet A relatively to a planet B is the same as that of B relatively to A but turned, in its plane, through two right angles.

LINEAR PERSPECTIVE.

Time allowed: 1 hour.

[These problems had to be worked to a scale of half an inch to the foot, the distance of the spectator from the picture being, in each case, 12 feet, and the horizon 5 feet above the ground plane. The lines by which each problem was solved appeared on the paper sent up to the Examiner.]

1. A CIRCULAR slab of stone (or short right cylinder) lies upon the ground plane on one of its plane faces, the centre of which is 2 feet on the left of the centre of vision, and 4 feet from the picture line. The diameter of the slab is 6 feet, and its thickness 3 feet. Give its perspective representation.

2. Draw a diameter of the upper face of the slab, vanishing to the right at 45 degrees with the picture; produce this diameter 1 foot towards the picture. Let this produced diameter be a rod, and represent it by a strong pencil line.

3. Across this rod, at right angles to it, 6 inches from the stone slab, draw a second rod 8 feet long, running into the ground plane at an angle of 30° with it, and vanishing below the horizon.

IMITATIVE COLOURING

Place before the Candidate, on white table-cloth, or napkin, an apple, pear, or other fruit in a light sufficiently distinct to cast a well-defined shadow on the cloth.

The Candidate should make a study representing the fruit and its cast shadow not less than six inches in its longest dimension, and may be allowed two hours or more, the time employed to be stated on the study.

DRAWING FROM MEMORY.

Time allowed. 1½ hour.

1. Make a drawing, from memory, of a pair of painter's steps.

These must contain at least eight steps, and are to be supposed to stand open, cords connecting the back legs with the front.

2. Draw also an ordinary garden watering-pot with a rose spout.

Each of these objects should be represented in such a position as to exhibit most completely its form and construction.

MUSIC.

Time allowed: 2 hours.

[Credit was given for clear writing of the Music.]

1. What is the meaning of Major and Minor as applied to the two modes?

2. Give a table of the dissonant intervals, with their inversions.

3. Give the Italian equivalents for—very slow, with agitation, gracefully, heavily, gradually quickening the time, little by little.

4. Harmonize in open score and four parts this figured bass :—

5. Give examples of false relation, of similar, oblique, and contrary movements.

9. What are the roots of these chords ?—

7. Give a list, in chronological order, of the chief composers of Opera and Oratorio.

CHAPTER X.

HIGHER, OR UNIVERSITY EDUCATION: WOMEN'S COLLEGES, AND UNIVERSITY TEACHING AS APPLIED TO WOMEN'S EDUCATION. GIRTON COLLEGE—NEWNHAM HLAL—UNIVERSITY COLLEGE, BRISTOL—ALEXANDRA COLLEGE—QUEEN'S COLLEGE—BEDFORD COLLEGE, CHELTENHAM LADIES' COLLEGE.

I HAVE now considered, as fully as space and circumstances will permit, and I trust in a way that may be productive of some practical advantage to the reader, the Secondary Education of Girls; or, as we may say, their education up to the period of their leaving school, at the age of 18. I propose in this chapter to point out the opportunities, within reach of women in England, of obtaining Higher, or University instruction; in other words, of continuing their education after the age of 18 has been attained. In general, "if a girl learns anything more than what school teaches her, she learns by herself from books, under the disadvantages of having no one to guide her study, no means of testing her progress, no goal or external reward to look forward to; above all, no oral teaching either to convey knowledge to her, or to excite that intellectual ardour which is so much more precious than any quantity of knowledge—more precious, as Lessing says, than the passive possession of truth itself. Hence almost all women have to remain content with what school has taught them, picking up more or less from books according to their acuteness, but without the means of following out any study systematically, since they have not been so much as taught how to study."* A great and beneficial change has taken place in the general system of English female education since the foregoing was written. Better schools have been established, in which girls are now taught with clearness and efficiency "how to study"; and it can no longer be said, that means are unprovided, by which they may follow out systematically at the end of their school course, any branch of knowledge for which, during their school years, they have discovered special aptitude Many of the public and intercollegiate Lectures of the Universities of Cambridge and London, heretofore only delivered to male students, are now open to women. University College, London, has for some time past accorded them facilities for attending its classes; and the extension of University teaching, generally, has provided them with opportunities for obtaining readily, and at no great expense, instruction of a higher kind which, prior to the year 1870, women did not enjoy.

The establishment of GIRTON COLLEGE, near Cambridge, in the year 1872–3, may be said to have given the first impetus in this country to the application of University teaching to women's education For some years previously, however, a movement had been afoot in England, having for its object the improvement of female education. The promoters of that movement in the first place directed their efforts toward securing the countenance and support of the two senior Universities, chiefly by persuading them to listen to arguments in favour of admitting girls to their local examinations. An experiment in this direction was made, and found to succeed. Cambridge in 1865, and Oxford at a later date, granted permission to female candidates to attend these examinations; but the maximum limit of age was fixed, as we have noticed, at eighteen. No inducement was forth-

* Mr. Bryce's Report to the Schools Inquiry Commission.

coming to girls to continue their studies after that age. The boys had the Universities to look forward to; the girls, as yet, could find no educational goal to strive for. It was felt by the advocates of the higher education of women, that something more was needed to place young Englishwomen on a level with their brothers as regards opportunities of acquiring knowledge. At Oxford and Cambridge residence is required, under a system of instruction and discipline for a certain period, by those who aspire to be graduates of the University. In order to give women an opportunity of fulfilling similar conditions of residence, it was determined to found a College for them, to be connected as closely as possible with the University of Cambridge.

Girton College was the outcome of this resolution. The institution was begun in very humble fashion. A house was hired at Hitchin, about thirty miles from Cambridge, and some of the best tutors connected with the University promised, as an experiment, to give the students who should join the new College the benefit of their tuition. "In October, 1869, six women came together at Hitchin and entered upon their new and arduous undertaking. They were but slightly acquainted with even the elements of classics and mathematics, and to their inexperience the modest requirements of the 'Little-go' had a formidable aspect. After a year of somewhat anxious work, a little band of five went up to Cambridge for this, their first, University examination, the Examiners having consented to look over their papers and report upon them according to the University standard. This crisis was successfully passed, and two years later one of the same students was examined in the papers set for the Mathematical Tripos, and her work was pronounced to be such as would have entitled an undergraduate to a place in the Second Class.

In February, 1873, two other students were similarly examined in the papers set for the Classical Tripos and declared to be deserving of Honours. Meanwhile a field of sixteen acres was purchased in the parish of Girton, about two miles from Cambridge, and a College building fitted to accommodate twenty-one students was erected. This building is one side of a proposed quadrangle. The funds required for it were raised by loans on mortgage and by public subscription. While the building was in progress undergraduates and dons made it a favourite goal of their afternoon ramble, and many a brick was laid by these as a token of their goodwill. In 1872 the institution was incorporated under the name of Girton College. In October, 1873, the occupation of the new building began, and since then the interest of Cambridge in her foster-child has been more generous than ever." *

The prospectus of the College sets forth that it "is designed to hold, in relation to girls' schools and home teaching, a position analogous to that occupied by the Universities towards the public schools for boys. The students' fees are fixed on such a scale as to secure that, the building having been provided, the institution shall be self-supporting." Since the opening of the institution seventy students have been enrolled, and have been in residence for longer or shorter periods. The academical year is approximately thus divided:—Michaelmas Term, beginning about the middle of October, eight weeks; Lent Term, beginning about the end of January, eight weeks; Easter Term, beginning in April, eight weeks. The charge for Board, Lodging, and Instruction, is 35*l.* per Term, paid in advance.

* 'An Interior View of Girton College, Cambridge,' by an American Lady, sometime a Student of the College. Printed for the London Association of Schoolmistresses, 1876.

This sum covers the whole of the College charges. Candidates for admission are required to pass an entrance examination as follows:—

PART I. PRELIMINARY.

1. The principles and practice of Arithmetic.

2. English Grammar, with questions on the construction of sentences and meanings of words.

3. Physical and Political Geography.

4. English History. Some period (of about fifty years) since the accession of the Tudors, the period to be chosen by the Candidate.

N.B.—A general knowledge of the leading facts of English History is required.

5. English Composition.

6. Scripture History.* (The New Testament.)

PART II. OPTIONAL SUBJECTS.

Every Candidate is also required to satisfy the Examiners in two of the following subjects, of which one must be a language. No Candidate will be examined in more than five.

1. Latin. Easy passages for translation from Latin into English, and easy English sentences for translation into Latin, with questions on Grammar.

2. Greek. An easy passage of Attic Greek for translation into English, and easy English sentences for translation into Greek, with questions on Grammar.

3. French.

4. German.

5. Algebra. Addition, Subtraction, Multiplication, and Division of Algebraical Quantities, Fractions, Square and Cube Roots, Simple and Quadratic Equations, Permutations and Combinations, Arithmetical and Geometrical Series, Variation, Ratio and Proportion, Scales of Notation and the Binomial Theorem.

A knowledge of Algebra up to and including Simple Equations, will enable a Candidate to pass in this subject.

6. Geometry. Euclid, Books I.–IV., VI., and XI., Props. 1–21.

A knowledge of Books I.–III. will enable a Candidate to pass in this subject.

---

* In case of objection, this subject is not required.

7. Trigonometry, up to and including the solution of Triangles.

The elementary parts of Conic Sections treated *either* geometrically *or* analytically. (No Candidate will be examined in both methods.)

It may be remarked that candidates who have passed the following examinations are excused from passing the entrance examination of Girton College, viz.:—

(*a*) The Matriculation Examination of the University of London.

(*b*) The Examination of the Oxford and Cambridge Schools Examination Board.

(*c*) The Cambridge Examination for Senior Students.

(*d*) The Oxford Examination for Senior Students.

(*e*) The Durham Examination for Senior Students.

(*f*) The "Honour Certificate" Examination of the University of Edinburgh.

(*g*) The Cambridge Higher Local Examination.

With regard to the Course of Instruction followed at Girton College, I do not think that I could do better than print the following letter bearing upon the point, addressed by the Treasurer of the institution to one of its Local Secretaries:—"We are hearing continually" (writes the Treasurer) "of an impression that the distinguishing characteristic of Girton is, that everyone who comes must try for a University degree, and even, it is sometimes added, for honours. This impression is entirely contrary to fact, and, as it is calculated to frighten away women who might be glad to become students, and also to discourage support on the ground of its being an unreasonable requirement, it is important in the interests of the College that it should be dispelled. No student as such, apart from special conditions attached to certain scholarships, is, or ever has been, required to take any University examination, or to try for any kind of certificate. They choose their own course. If they choose to try for 'Degree examinations,' we do our best to obtain the opportunity for them on the same conditions as those which the University imposes on undergraduates. We think it essential that the conditions should be the same, and that no indulgence should be claimed for our students on the ground of their being women, either in the form of exemption from the preliminary examinations which all candidates for Degrees are required to pass, or in any other way. But whether they take University examinations or not is entirely optional. If they decide not to take them, they make their own choice among the various subjects included in our Course of Study, and their work is tested by an examination held at the end of each year, the results of which are reported to our committee. This is no new feature. It has been the principle of the College from the beginning, and not only the theory, but the practice. Since the first year there never has been a time during which we have not had one or more students in residence studying without any reference to University examinations.

"It is easier to contradict such a misapprehension as this, than to give a clear idea of what Girton really is. We are told sometimes that it is impossible to understand it without seeing it; and it is also quite possible to see it without understanding it. But I will mention two or three points in which it differs, I believe, from any other place of education for women. First, there is the Entrance Examination. This puts a hindrance in the way of those whose early education has been so defective as to leave them unprepared for advanced studies. It effectually checks rapid growth in numbers, but we are satisfied that it works well. The examination is by no means severe, and the Candidates who have failed to pass were certainly not fit to enter upon a course of higher education.

"Then as to the nature of the teaching given at the College, which is perhaps its most important distinction. This, though it goes by the name of Lectures, is very different from the sort of teaching usually understood by that term. It is given to very small classes, in which the students ask as well as answer questions. We consult the Lecturers as to whether the instruction can best be given to a class or individually, and in some subjects, especially mathematics, the differences in the stage of progress and manner of working are such as to make it desirable that it should be to a great extent individual. In a place like ——, where the inevitable drawbacks as well as the special advantages of Lectures must be well known, it will be understood that even when the Lecturer and the subject are the same, the number and the quality of his class make a great difference in the nature of his teaching. I do not mean that very small classes and individual teaching must always be best, but they seem necessary, with the very wide range of subjects which the extension of knowledge has introduced, and while women are, so to speak, all at sixes and sevens as to their previous education, if the instruction is to be thoroughly effective, and every student is to have a fair chance of doing her best. We have now the great advantage of having resident teachers —our own old students—who are able to give an amount and a kind of help which we could scarcely expect from the Lecturers. It has already been most valuable, and we expect to find it even more so." *

The ordinary course of study at Girton College comprises the following subjects:—viz. Divinity, Modern Languages (English, French, and German), Mathematics, Moral Science, Natural Science, History, Vocal Music. Arrangements are made for holding examinations of the students and certifying proficiency. A Certificate, called "a Degree Certificate," is conferred upon any student whose proficiency has been certified to the satisfaction of the College, accord-

* A Letter addressed to one of the Local Secretaries of Girton College. By Miss Davies. London. 1875.

ing to the standard of any examinations qualifying for the B.A. Degree of the University of Cambridge, provided that such student has fulfilled, so far as in the judgment of the College may be practicable, all the conditions imposed for the time being by the University on candidates for Degrees.

A Certificate, called a "College Certificate," is conferred upon any student who has passed, to the satisfaction of the College, Examinations similar in subjects and standard to those qualifying for the B.A. Degree of the University of Cambridge, the following deviations being permitted; the substitution of French and English or German and English for Latin or for Greek; the substitution of English, French, and German for both Latin and Greek; the omission, in case of objection, of the Theological part of the Examinations.

Speaking generally, about half of the students at Girton College look forward to being Teachers; not Governesses, but Teachers and Head-mistresses in Schools. The Endowed Schools for Girls established, or in course of being established, under the authority of the Endowed Schools Commission, will doubtless look to Girton for their Head-mistresses, while in turn they will prepare students for her. In the scheme for one of these schools—St. Paul's, London* —not yet in operation, 700*l.* a year is provided for girls from the school to pursue their education at institutions of superior learning; and at least a share of this will probably be spent at Girton. It is satisfactory to be able to state, that in one or two of the school prospectuses which have come under my notice in course of preparing this book, it is set to the credit of a Teacher that she holds the Girton College Certificate, much the same as to a Master's when he has taken University Honours.

There are certain Scholarships in gift of the College, as

* See Note at the end of Chapter IV.

follows :—A Scholarship, of the value of 100*l.* a year for three years, being a year's proceeds of an Oxford Fellowship, given by R. S. Wright, Esq., Fellow of Oriel College, Oxford, and two Scholarships of the value respectively of 60*l.* and 40*l.* a year for three years, given by the Goldsmiths' Company. An Entrance Exhibition of the value of fifty guineas a year for three years, beginning October, 1879, will be awarded in connection with the Entrance Examination of March, 1879, to a lady whose means are inadequate to cover the whole cost of her College education, preference being given to one engaged in, or preparing for, the profession of teaching. Mrs. Russell Gurney has recently signified her intention of presenting to Girton College the sum of 1000*l.* for the foundation of an Entrance Scholarship. The name of Russell Gurney will be attached to the scholarship in memory of the Right Hon. Russell Gurney, who was one of the earliest and most valued friends of the College.*

Connected with the University of Cambridge is another collegiate institution for promoting the Higher education of Women, known as NEWNHAM HALL. It was opened in October, 1875, for the reception of students coming from a distance to attend the Lectures for Women at Cambridge. Soon after these Lectures were started in January, 1870, students began to be attracted from various parts of the country by the educational advantages thus offered. In October, 1871, Miss A. J. Clough, a lady well known as an earnest advocate of the claims of women to higher educa-

* The Court of the Clothworkers' Company, whose interest in the cause of the higher education of women has long been conspicuous, have just agreed to raise from 50 to 80 guineas per annum the three Exhibitions granted by the Company in 1873 for "ladies of limited means intended for the profession of teaching" at Girton College, and the Exhibition to be competed for next June will be of the value of 80 guineas per annum, and tenable for three years.

tional advantages, took charge of a house in which five students entered. The number had increased at Easter 1874 to twenty-six, and it was thereupon decided to build in the immediate neighbourhood of Cambridge a house capable of supplying adequate accommodation for the Principal and thirty students. To carry out this object the Newnham Hall Company was formed in the spring of 1874, and a site of two and a half acres having been secured at Newnham, just outside the town of Cambridge, the building was commenced shortly afterwards, and it was completed and opened in October, 1875. The Rules and Terms of Admission to Newnham Hall are as follows:—

No student is admitted under the age of seventeen.

Students are required to give references satisfactory to the Principal, and no student is permitted to come into residence without the approval of the Principal.

Students are expected to give three months' notice before leaving. Failing this they are liable to be charged for the ensuing term, subject to the discretion of the Principal.

The Principal may require any student to withdraw who, in her opinion, is not profiting by the course of study at Cambridge.

The charges for board and lodging, per term of eight weeks, are 20 guineas for ordinary students, and 15 guineas for students who are allowed by the Council to enter at the reduced charges.* These payments are to be made in advance.

The payment for instruction varies slightly, according to the line of study taken up, but rarely exceeds four-and-a-half guineas per term. Moreover, grants are made from a special fund to promising students of scanty means.

The Academic year, from October to June, is divided into three terms, corresponding to the terms of the Cambridge University.

No examination is compulsory on students either on admission or later. Instruction is given by the Women's Lectures Association of Cambridge, through its Lecturers,

* About half the students are received at the reduced charges. They are expected to give some evidence of intellectual qualification.

in the following subjects:—viz. Divinity, History, English Literature, Arithmetic, Greek, Latin, French, German, and various branches of Mathematics, Moral Science, and Natural Science. The students also attend the Public Lectures of the University of Cambridge, more than two-thirds of which are now open to women, and they have likewise permission to avail themselves of the teaching of the Professors of Natural Science and access at times to the Natural Science Museums and Laboratories. The Principal of Newnham Hall has kindly sent me the following information:—"Our students," she writes, "usually pass in two or three Groups of the Cambridge Higher Local Examination,* and, then, those who remain take up some of the subjects of study which prepare them for one of the University examinations. They have been allowed to have the papers of the 'Final examination' informally, and their answers have been looked over by the examiners who, generally, give an informal certificate to those who are successful." In this connection it is interesting to remark, that students of Newnham Hall have been recently examined in the papers of the Mathematical, Natural Science, and Historical Tripos, and they all attained such a standard as would have entitled them to honours. Among those ladies who have completed their studies at Newnham, four are Head-mistresses, and thirteen are Assistant Mistresses in Girls' Public Day-schools, and several are private teachers.

As regards Scholarships and Exhibitions within reach of students from Newnham Hall, the Committee of the Association for promoting the Higher Education of Women in Cambridge, offer annually several Exhibitions to the best candidates in the "Higher Local Examination." By the aid of donations from the Drapers' Company, and from several private donors, they offer, for success in each of the

* The Regulations are given in Chapter XII.

five principal groups, an Exhibition tenable for one year, and they also offer one of 50*l.*, tenable for two years, given by the Clothworkers' Company for general success. The Committee also offer an Exhibition, tenable for two years, for success in the Senior Local Examination for girls under eighteen, held annually in December. They make it a condition of receiving these Exhibitions that those who gain them should attend two courses of Lectures in Cambridge during each term of the year following election, and (if not residents in Cambridge) they recommend that they should reside at Newnham Hall.

The Council of Newnham Hall have at their disposal two Scholarships to be held by students residing in the Hall. One of these, founded by the liberality of the Goldsmiths' Company, is a Scholarship of 50*l.*, tenable for two years, to be awarded annually for success in the Cambridge Higher Local Examination. The other, called the Birmingham Scholarship, has been founded by a donor who wishes to be anonymous; the endowment consists of the dividends on ten shares of the Newnham Hall Company, which are held in trust for this purpose.

Among other institutions offering Higher Instruction to Women, UNIVERSITY COLLEGE, BRISTOL, requires notice. This college is intended to supply for persons of either sex, above the ordinary school age, the means of continuing their studies in Science, Languages, History, and Literature, and, more particularly, to afford appropriate instruction in those branches of Applied Science which are employed in the Arts and Manufactures. It has no buildings at present providing lodging for students; but those coming from a distance may learn of suitable accommodation on application to the Principal (Alfred Marshall, Esq., M.A., *Late Fellow of St. John's College, Cambridge*) through the secretary of the College. Instruction is given to the students by means of the Day and Evening Lectures of the Professors. The course of study useful to women comprises the following subjects:—viz. Arithmetic, and Elementary Mathematics; Mathematics (Advanced course); Natural Philosophy; Geometrical Drawing; Geology; Botany; Political Economy; Law; Modern History; English Literature; Greek and Latin; Ancient History and Literature; French; and German. The fees for Day Lectures generally are 5*l.* 5*s.* for each course for three Terms; 4*l.* 4*s.* for two consecutive Terms; 3*l.* 3*s.* for the first or second Term solely; 2*l.* 2*s.* for the third Term. Exceptions to this rule will be found in the College Calendar. The fees for Evening Lectures are 7*s.* for one Term; 10*s.* 6*d.* for two Terms; 15*s.* for three Terms; and in classes in which one hour of instruction only is given per week, 8*s.* for two Terms. In addition to the above fees, an entrance fee of 7*s.* for each course for the Day Lectures is required of all *unregistered* students; but not of those who have at any time paid the *registration fee* of 1*l.* 1*s.* For the Evening Lectures there is charged an entrance fee of 1*s.* for each course.

The Terms begin and end as follows:—First Term begins the first week in October and ends the middle of December; Second Term begins about the middle of January and ends the first week in April; Third Term begins about the fourth week in April and ends the first week in July.

The Clifton Association for the Higher Education of Women offers four or more Scholarships of 15*l.* to 50*l.* each for competition among female students, who have signified their intention of entering at the College.

ALEXANDRA COLLEGE, DUBLIN, differs somewhat from the institutions already named, in that it receives pupils as early as the age of fifteen. But its methods of instruction and course of study are equally adapted to the requirements of ladies above that age, and therefore it can claim to be ranked among Colleges for Women. It was founded in the year 1866, for the purpose of supplying defects in the existing system of education for women of the upper and middle classes—of affording an education more sound, more solid, more systematically imparted, and better tested than was at that time to be obtained in Ireland. The College was established on a self-supporting basis, was set on foot by subscriptions from those more actively interested in the experiment, and has been sustained solely by the fees of the students, who at present number 251. The College is governed by a Visitor and Council, who have the financial control and the final decision on all matters. The Committee of Education consisting of the Professors (most of whom are either Fellows of Trinity College, or Professors in the University) engaged in the instruction of the higher classes of the College, have the control of the educational arrangements. The officers are, a Principal who has a seat in the Council, Vice Principal, a Bursar and Secretary, a Lady Superintendent, and Assistant Ladies.

Instruction is given to the Higher Classes of the College (with which, only, we are concerned in this chapter) principally by means of Lectures delivered by appointed Professors. The subjects of these Lectures as set forth in the College Calendar are as follows:—Algebra and Geometry; Arithmetic; Drawing; English Language and Literature; French Language and Literature; German Language and Literature; Geography, Physical, Political, and Historical; Greek; History, Ancient and Modern; Italian Language and Literature; Languages (Comparative Study of); Latin Language and Literature; Music, Vocal and Theoretical, the Pianoforte and the Science of Harmony; Natural Science:—Botany, Geology, and Zoology; Philosophy:—

Mental, Moral, and Natural; Theology:—History of the Christian Church.

The religious instruction is given in accordance with the doctrines of the Church of England and Ireland, but attendance on these classes is perfectly optional to the student.

The manner of instruction in the Language classes is that of advanced exercises in composition, *viva voce* questioning, reading of authors. In the Literature classes it is carried on by means of prelections and taking of notes, &c. In Science, by lecture, demonstration, and experiment.

Attendance on a two years' course of study with examinations conducted by printed questions and written answers four times during the course, is required from the candidates for the Certificates which the College grants.

These examinations take place in the College under the care of the Lady Superintendent, two hours being allowed to the answering of each paper of ten questions. The answers are sent to the teachers, by whom they are examined and marked to a fixed standard, and at the end of each two years' course the papers of the candidates for Certificates are submitted to independent examiners, who sign the Certificates conjointly with the teachers.

Following is the table of College Fees:—

STUDENTS TAKING SEVERAL CLASSES—
COMPOUNDERS.

All fees to be paid in advance by Term or Half-Session.

	Single Term.		Session.
Students not taking Instrumental Music ..	£5 0 0	or	£14 0 0
Students taking Instrumental Music	8 0 0	,,	21 0 0

Compounders paying 5*l.* the Term, or 7*l.* by the Half-Session, may choose five classes meeting twice a week.

Compounders paying 8*l.* the Term, or 10*l.* 10*s.* by the Half-Session, may choose five classes meeting twice a week, in addition to Science of Harmony, Calisthenics, and Instrumental Music.

	Single Term.		Session.
Any additional classes, each	£1 0 0	or	£2 10 0

Students taking the Course of Instruction recommended by the Committee of Education :—

	Session.
Senior Course—Six classes meeting twice a week	£16 0 0
Junior Course— ditto ditto	14 0 0

STUDENTS TAKING ONE, TWO, OR THREE CLASSES—NON-COMPOUNDERS.

All fees to be paid in advance.

	Single Term.		Session.
Students taking one subject, the class meeting twice a week	£1 12 6	or	£4 10 0
Students taking one subject, the class meeting once a week	1 1 0	,,	3 0 0
Students taking two subjects, class meeting twice a week	3 0 0	,,	8 0 0
Students taking two subjects, class meeting once a week	1 10 0	,,	4 0 0
Students taking three subjects, class meeting twice a week	3 15 0	,,	10 10 0
Students taking four subjects, class meeting twice a week	4 10 0	,,	13 0 0
Music, Instrumental, and Science of Harmony	3 0 0	,,	8 0 0
,, Vocal (Solo Singing) and Science of Harmony	3 0 0	,,	8 0 0

Instruction in Instrumental Music is given only to students who take at least two additional Literary or Scientific subjects.

Instruction in Vocal Music is given only to Students who take at least one additional Literary or Scientific subject.

The classes for SCIENCE OF HARMONY are obligatory to all Students of Music.

The class for PERSPECTIVE is free to all Students of Drawing.

Students are not lodged within the college buildings. Those coming from a distance are provided with board and lodging: (1) at The Residence House, 5, Earlsfort Terrace, Dublin, under control of the Lady Resident, Miss Hutchins; (2) at 18, Adelaide Road, Dublin, under control of Miss

Johnston, Lady Assistant of Alexandra College. The Residence Fees are as follows :—

At the First :—	
For the Session (or academic year)	£55
Paid by Half-Session in advance.	
Half-Session	27 10*s.*
At the Second :—	
For the Session (or academic year)	50
Paid by Half-Session in advance.	
Half-Session	25
Term	18

These charges are exclusive of the College Fees.

The College Terms are as follows :—MICHAELMAS TERM begins the Fourth Week in September; LENT TERM begins the Second Week in January; EASTER TERM begins the Week after Easter Sunday.

A large number of Exhibitions and Scholarships are tenable in the College as follows :—

The Archbishop of Dublin Exhibitions, two in number, of 10*l.* a year each, and Ten other Exhibitions of the like annual value founded by various persons interested in the institution. The "Trinity College Scholarship" of 25*l.* tenable for one year, the gift of the Board of Trinity College, Dublin, open to candidates under the age of eighteen. The "National Union Scholarship" of 25*l.* tenable for one year, the gift of the National Union for Promoting the Education of Women. A Scholarship of the value of 40*l.*, giving free education for two years in the College, founded by the Governesses' Association. Two "Stearne Scholarships" of the value of 20*l.* tenable for one year. The "Provost's Scholarship" of the value of 25*l.* tenable for one year. The regulations and subjects of examination for these several Scholarships and Exhibitions are to be found in the Alexandra College Calendar.

QUEEN'S COLLEGE, LONDON (43 and 45, Harley Street), "for the general education of ladies," as its prospectus advertises, "and for granting certificates of knowledge," although, like Alexandra College, it admits pupils at an early age, is strictly entitled to rank as a collegiate institution for the higher education of women. It was established in the year 1848, and was incorporated by Royal Charter five years later. It enjoys the distinction of being governed by a Council, composed of persons of considerable eminence in their respective walks of life; and it has a body of "Honorary Fellows," and an influential committee of "Acting Lady-Visitors," all of which serves to show, that Queen's College has deserved well of the public in the past, and has claims upon its further support and consideration. The College admits pupils at the age of fourteen to what is called the "four years' course"; providing, as well, a "Higher Course of Instruction" for students above the age of eighteen. "It is intended (recites the prospectus) that students preparing for the first B.A. examination of the University of London should receive through the Lectures given in this course the assistance they may require." Following are the subjects on which at present Lectures by Professors are delivered: *—Church History; Botany; English Language; French Literature; Greek; Mathematics (Algebra from Quadratic Equations onwards); Physiology; Political Economy; Roman History. The Fees are 1*l.* 1*s.* for each course of ten lectures, or 5*s.* for a single lecture. A large number of Scholarships and Exhibitions are tenable in the College, but they seem for the most part to be limited to pupils who have entered for the "four years' course," and who are under the age of sixteen. Among the Lecturers at the College are Professors Bentley and Henry Morley, the

* See the Appendix.

Rev. J. Llewelyn Davies, M. Kastner, Mrs. E. Bovell Sturge, M.D., Mrs. Henry Fawcett, &c.

Bedford College, London (8 and 9, York Place) is an institution similar to the above. It was founded in 1849, and received a charter of incorporation in 1869. Like Queen's College, it admits pupils at the age of fourteen; but its "college classes;" apart from the school, provide instruction of a higher kind, useful to students above the age of eighteen who may desire "to matriculate and graduate at the University of London." Students, known to the Bedford College authorities as "Regular Students," who are not less than eighteen years of age, "who shall have diligently attended the classes for not less than three sessions, and who shall have passed with credit the examinations of those several classes, will receive the diploma of 'Associate of Bedford College.'" There are several Scholarships tenable in the College, limited, however, to pupils who have passed through the school course as "Regular Students." Among the Professors and Teachers of the College are Professors Beesly and Seeley, Rev. A. W. Milroy, Mr. Sonnenschein, M. Roulier, Miss Gertrude Martineau, &c.

The Cheltenham Ladies' College. Attention has been already sufficiently directed to this institution under the head of Secondary Education. It remains to be said, that its "First Division," which is attended by many adult students, several of whom have recently passed (with Honours) the Higher or Women's Examinations of London, Oxford, or Cambridge, strictly entitles the College to rank with the other institutions mentioned in this chapter. Special courses of lectures, as well as classes for Logic, Greek, and the Higher Mathematics, are provided for the students of the First Division. Among the Lecturers attending the College are Professor Nichol (English Literature), Professor Rowley (History), Professor Letts (Chemistry), Professor Barrett (Sound), Rev. T. Webb, F.R.A.S. (Astronomy).

THE CITY OF LONDON COLLEGE (8, City Road, Finsbury Square), likewise affords higher instruction to students above the age of eighteen. It is partly a school and partly a college, organized very much on the same plan as the institutions which have just been noticed.

This chapter would not be, within its scope, complete, unless some reference were made to an institution which advances the cause of Higher female education by means of its admirable series of Lectures open both to women and men. I refer to the Queen-Square College (29, Queen Square, London). This handbook is chiefly designed for the use of persons of the upper Middle-class (as its title page sets forth), or of persons who may reasonably be expected to spend from 40*l.* to 100*l.* a year on a daughter's education. But I have in writing the book never lost sight of the possibility that it might fall into the hands of others to whom such an annual expenditure would present a serious difficulty. I have been compelled, however, to draw the line at a certain standard of school, otherwise I might have had to include within the design of my work all educational institutions that admit girls to their classes, beginning at Board Schools and ending with Ladies' Colleges. To have done so would have been to have at once departed from the course which I had mapped out for myself when I first sat down to write this handbook. It seems to me, however, while carefully adhering to my original plan, that I am not precluded from calling attention in its pages to any institution which welcomes to its classes students who are fairly well-to-do, and those not so prosperous in a worldly sense. The Queen-Square College appears to me to be an institution of the kind. Though primarily intended for the working-classes, it is open to all without distinction of class, and at present there are persons of all ranks of life receiving instruction from its teachers. The main object for which the institution was founded, was that it should be a college for working-women, to afford them the opportunity of gaining a higher culture, rather than a mere advancement in life. In 1874 it was determined that the college classes should be open both to male and female students. Girls are admitted at fifteen, and young men at seventeen years of age, and it is gratifying to learn that there has never been any difficulty in carrying on this system of mixed education. The College affords instruction in Mathematics; Language and Literature; Physical Science; Politics; Law; History and Art. The teaching is gratuitous, and the fees are very low. The admission to the College is only 2*s.* a year, and a mere trifle is exacted for admission to the classes.

CHAPTER XI.

HIGHER, OR UNIVERSITY EDUCATION—*continued.* UNIVERSITY, AND OTHER HIGHER TEACHING OPEN TO WOMEN.

It has been remarked in the foregoing chapter that more than two-thirds of the Public Lectures of the University of Cambridge are open to Women. This privilege, in the case of many of these lectures, has been long enjoyed by customary indulgence. It has now been formally granted by twenty-nine Professors, subject to such regulations as the University may from time to time think fit to make in the matter.* Following is a list of the Professors referred to:—

Prof. G. M. Humphry, M.D.	Anatomy.
,, W. Wright, LL.D...	Arabic.
,, E. H. Palmer, M.A.	Arabic (*Lord Almoner's*).
,, The Rev. Churchill Babington, B.D.	Archæology (*Disney*).
,, J. C. Adams, M.A.	Astronomy (*Lowndes'*).
,, C. C. Babington, M.A.	Botany.
,, G. D. Liveing, M.A.	Chemistry.
,, E. C. Clark, LL.D.	Civil Law (*Regius*).
,, The Rev. J. B. Lightfoot, D.D.	Divinity (*Lady Margaret*).
,, The Rev. J. J. S. Perowne, D.D.	Divinity (*Hulsean*).
,, The Rev. C. A. Swainson, D.D.	Divinity (*Norrisian*).
,, The Rev. B. F. Westcott, D.D.	Divinity (*Regius*).
,, Sidney Colvin, M.A.	Fine Art.
,, T. M. Hughes, M.A., F.R.S. ..	Geology (*Woodwardian*).
,, The Rev. B. H. Kennedy, D.D. ..	Greek.

* Four College Courses of Lectures are open to women, namely, Mr. Vine's on the Physiology of Plants, at Christ's College, Mr. Oscar Browning's at King's College, on Italian History, Mr. Prothero's on Roman and English History, Mr. Welldon's on Cicero's Academics.

PROF.	THE REV. THOS. JARRETT, M.A.	Hebrew.
,,	J. E. B. MAYOR, M.A.	Latin.
,,	W. LL. BIRKBECK, M.A.	Law (*Downing*).
,,	SIR W. G. G. V. VERNON HARCOURT, M.A., Q.C., M.P...	International Law.
,,	J. STUART, M.A.	Mechanism and Applied Mechanics.
,,	PETER W. LATHAM, M.D.	Medicine (*Downing*).
,,	W. H. MILLER, M.D., F.R.S. ..	Mineralogy.
,,	J. A. SEELEY, M.A.	Modern History.
,,	SKEAT..	Early English.
,,	THE REV T. R. BIRKS, M.A... ..	Moral Philosophy.
,,	JAMES DEWAR, M.A.	Natural Philosophy (*Jacksonian*).
,,	H. FAWCETT, M.A., M.P.	Pol. Economy.
,,	A. CAYLEY, M.A.	Pure Mathematics.
,,	E. B. COWELL, M.A.	Sanskrit.

In addition to those of the University Professors, Lectures on the following subjects, delivered under the auspices of the "Association for Promoting the Higher Education of Women in Cambridge," by some of the resident members of the University engaged in academic teaching, are open to ladies who have attained the age of seventeen years, viz. :—

Divinity..	V. H. STANTON, M.A., Fellow of Trinity College.
English History ..	G. W. PROTHERO, M.A., Fellow and Lecturer of King's College.
Early English Language and Literature.	PROFESSOR SKEAT.
English Literature	R. C. JEBB, M.A., Professor of Greek in the University of Glasgow. H. SIDGWICK, M.A., Prælector of Trinity College.
Arithmetic	W. H. H. HUDSON, M.A., Lecturer and late Fellow of St. John's College.
Latin	R. D. HICKS, M.A., Fellow of Trinity College.
Latin Composition	J. E. NIXON, Esq., Fellow and Lecturer of King's College.
Greek	R. D. ARCHER-HIND, M.A., Fellow and Lecturer of Trinity College.

Ancient Philosophy	H. Jackson, Esq., Fellow and Prælector of Trinity College.
German	H. J. Wolstenholme, Esq.
French	L. Boquel, Esq.
Algebra, Advanced	Professor Cayley.
Geometry and Astronomy.	N. M. Ferrers, M.A., Fellow and Tutor of Gonville and Caius College.
Algebra and Trigonometry.	A. F. Torry, M.A., Fellow of St. John's College.
Conic Sections ..	C. Smith, M.A., Fellow and Tutor of Sidney Sussex College.
Statics and Dynamics.	W. Garnett, M.A., Fellow of St. John's College.
Logic	J. N. Keynes, B.A., Fellow of Pembroke College.
Political Economy	J. S. Nicholson, B.A., Scholar of Trinity College.
Moral Sciences ..	H. Sidgwick, M.A., Prælector and late Fellow of Trinity College.
	J. Ward, M.A., Fellow of Trinity College.
	Professor Seeley.
History and Political Philosophy.	B. E. Hammond, M.A., Fellow and Lecturer of Trinity College.
	E. S. Thompson, M.A., Fellow and Lecturer of Christ's College.
Chemistry	P. T. Main, M.A., Fellow and Lecturer of St. John's College.
Zoology	G. T. Bettany, M.A., Gonville and Caius College.
Harmony and Thorough Bass.	G. M. Garrett, Mus.D., Organist of St. John's College, and of the University Church.

This scheme of Lectures (including those of one lady, Miss Crofts, on English History) embraces the subjects included in the Cambridge Higher Local Examination (see Chapter XII.), together with more advanced teaching in the different subjects of the University course for students who have passed this Examination. A list of the Lectures for each academical year, with the days and hours of their delivery, is published annually; and supplementary notices of such changes and additions as may be found desirable are published at the commencement of Term. These lists and notices, together with tickets for the Lectures, may be obtained at *Macmillan & Co.'s*, 1, Trinity Street, Cambridge.

The Fee for a single course of Lectures is generally speaking 21*s*., in the case of Lectures that prepare for Group A (see p. 189), and Modern Languages; in other cases 31*s*. 6*d*. Students preparing for Group E (see p. 192) may, if they like, compound for all their Fees by paying 15*l*. 15*s*. per annum in three instalments of 5*l*. 5*s*. each term.

Persons under the age of seventeen will be admitted to the Lectures under certain circumstances, upon special application being made on their behalf, stating their ages and qualifications. Such application is not required in the case of girls who have passed the Senior Local Examinations, or who have distinguished themselves in the Junior Local Examinations. All persons attending the Lectures are required to reside in some house approved by the Committee of the Ladies' Lectures Association. Inquiries respecting the accommodation available in Cambridge for lady-students may be addressed to Miss Clough, *Newnham Hall*, or to Miss Kennedy, the *Elms*, *Cambridge*. In addition to Newnham Hall, *Norwich House*, under the superintendence of Madame Rasche, is now open for the reception of ladies attending the Cambridge Lectures.*

FUND FOR TEACHERS, &c.

A fund has been formed for the purpose of assisting persons of scanty means, desirous of attending the Lectures

* It is interesting to learn, from the last issued Report of the "Association for Promoting the Higher Education of Women in Cambridge," that the number of students attracted to the University by the Lectures for Women was larger in the academical year 1877–8 than in any previous year. The attendance averaged 68 for the three terms. The total number of students who attended the lectures of the Association was, on the average of the three terms, 127; while the average number of classes attended by each was 2½.

at Cambridge, especially those preparing for the profession of education. This fund, which is limited in amount, is employed chiefly in lending sums, without interest, to students likely to profit by the lectures of the Ladies' Association, to enable them to pay their lecture fees, and to purchase the necessary books.

Any person wishing to obtain assistance from the fund should communicate with Mrs. Bateson, *St. John's Lodge.* All applications should be accompanied by a statement in writing of the applicant's circumstances together with whatever evidence can be given of her intellectual qualifications.

Mrs. Bateson will inform applicants of the terms on which the loan is made.

It has been decided to continue the Classes hitherto held at UNIVERSITY COLLEGE, LONDON, in connection with the "London Ladies' Educational Association" during the session 1878–79, in addition to others, as College Classes to which only ladies are admitted. At the same time there will be in future a considerable increase in the number of Classes open to both men and women.

University College now offers to Women education in all subjects taught in the two Faculties of Arts and Laws, and of Science. Whether they attend separate or mixed classes, they become regular students; and all honours attained through examination will in future be awarded by the College. Among the PRIZES and SCHOLARSHIPS now open to Women entering at University College are three, "Andrew's Entrance Prizes" of 20*l.* each—one for classics; one for two of the three subjects, Mathematics, Physics, Chemistry; one for three languages—(*a*) English; (*b*) either Latin or Greek; (*c*) French or German or Italian.

Following is a summary of the Classes to which Women are admitted:—

A.—SPECIAL CLASSES FOR WOMEN ONLY.

SUBJECTS.	LECTURERS.	FEES.
GREEK (Advanced and Elementary Course).	Prof. The Rev. W. Wayte, M.A.	4*l.* 4*s.* for the Session; 1*l.* 11*s.* 6*d.* for a Term.
ENGLISH LANGUAGE AND LITERATURE.	Prof. Henry Morley.	For the Session, from 3*l.* 3*s.* to 5*l.* 5*s.*; for the Term, from 1*l.* 1*s.* to 2*l.* 2*s.* Teachers' Evening Class: Fee for the Session or any part of it, 1*l.* 1*s.*
FRENCH LANGUAGE AND LITERATURE.	Prof. Ch. Cassal, LL.D.	For the Session, from 1*l.* 1*s.* to 3*l.* 3*s.*; for a Term, 1*l.* 11*s.* 6*d.*
GERMAN LANGUAGE AND LITERATURE.	Prof. Friedrich Althaus, Ph.D.	For the Course, 2*l.* 2*s.*; for a Term, 1*l.* 11*s.* 6*d.*
ARITHMETIC	Prof. Olaus Henrici, Ph.D., F.R.S.	For the Course, 1*l.* 11*s.* 6*d.*; for a Term, 1*l.* 13*s.*
MATHEMATICS (Elementary).	Ditto	For the Session, 6*l.* 6*s.*; for a Term, 2*l.* 12*s.* 6*d.*
PHYSICS	Prof. G. Carey Foster, B.A., F.R.S.	For the Session (for two Terms), from 3*l.* 13*s.* 6*d.* to 6*l.* 6*s.*; for a Term, 2*l.* 2*s.*
CHEMISTRY (Elementary).	C. A. Bell, B.A., M.B.	Fee, 4*l.* 4*s.*
BOTANY (Elementary) ..	Prof. E. Ray Lankester, M.A., F.R.S.	For the Course, 5*l.* 5*s.*; Perpetual, 7*l.* 7*s.*
PHYSIOLOGY AND HISTOLOGY.	Prof. J. Burdon Sanderson, M.D., LL.D., F.R.S.	Fee, 3*l.* 3*s.*
HYGIENE AND PUBLIC HEALTH.	Prof. W. H. Corfield, M.A., M.D.	For the Course, 2*l.* 2*s.*; for the Term, from 1*l.* 1*s.* to 1*l.* 11*s.* 6*d.*
CONSTITUTIONAL HISTORY OF ENGLAND.	Prof. J. W. Willis Bund, M.A., LL.B., Barrister-at-Law.	Two Courses: for both Courses, 2*l.* 2*s.*; for either Course, 1*l.* 11*s.* 6*d.* For a Term: for both, 1*l.* 11*s.* 6*d.*; for either, 1*l.* 1*s.*

B.—CLASSES OPEN TO BOTH MEN AND WOMEN.

SUBJECTS.	LECTURERS.	FEES.
LATIN	Prof. Alfred Goodwin, M.A.	For the Session, 3*l.* 3*s.* to 6*l.* 6*s.*; for the Term, from 1*l.* 11*s.* 6*d.* to 2*l.* 2*s.*
GREEK	Prof. The Rev. W. Wayte, M.A.	For the Session, from 4*l.* 4*s.* to 8*l.* 8*s.*; for a Term, from 1*l.* 11*s.* 6*d.* to 3*l.* 3*s.*
SANSKRIT	Prof. Ernst Haas, Ph.D.	For the Session, from 5*l.* 5*s.* to 8*l.* 8*s.*; for a Term, from 2*l.* 2*s.* to 3*l.* 3*s.*
HEBREW	Prof. The Rev. D. W. Marks.	For the Session, 4*l.* 4*s.*; for a Term, 1*l.* 11*s.* 6*d.*
ENGLISH LANGUAGE AND LITERATURE.	Prof. Henry Morley.	For the Session: for one Lecture a week, 3*l.* 3*s.*; for two Lectures a week, 5*l.* 5*s.* For a Term: for one Lecture a week, 1*l.* 1*s.*; for two Lectures a week, 2*l.* 2*s.* Perpetual to all the English Lectures, 12*l.* 12*s.*
FRENCH LANGUAGE AND LITERATURE.	Prof. Ch. Cassal, LL.D.	For the Session, from 3*l.* 3*s.* to 6*l.* 6*s.*; for the Term, from 1*l.* 1*s.* to 2*l.* 12*s.* 6*d.*
GERMAN LANGUAGE AND LITERATURE.	Prof. Friedrich Althaus, Ph.D.	For the Session, from 2*l.* 2*s.* to 6*l.* 6*s.*; for a Term, from 1*l.* 11*s.* 6*d.* to 2*l.* 12*s.* 6*d.*
ITALIAN	Prof. Cav. Girolamo Volpe.	For the Session, from 2*l.* 12*s.* 6*d.* to 4*l.* 4*s.*; for a Term, from 1*l.* 1*s.* to 1*l.* 11*s.* 6*d.*
ANCIENT AND MODERN HISTORY.	Prof. E. S. Beesly, M.A.	Two Courses: Fee for both, 2*l.* 2*s.*

SUBJECTS.	LECTURERS.	FEES.
PHILOSOPHY OF MIND AND LOGIC.	Prof. G. C. Robertson, M.A.	For the Session, 6*l.* 6*s.*; for the Term, from 2*l.* 2*s.* to 3*l.* 3*s.*
POLITICAL ECONOMY ..	Prof. W. Stanley Jevons, LL.D., M.A., F.R.S.	For the Course, 3*l.* 3*s.*; for either Term, 2*l.*.2*s.*
MATHEMATICS	Prof. Olaus Henrici.	For the Session, from 5*l.* 5*s.* to 6*l.* 6*s.* ; for a single Term, 2*l.* 12*s.* 6*d.*
PHYSICS	Prof. G. Carey Foster, B.A., F.R.S.	For the Session, from 6*l.* 6*s.* to 8*l.* 8*s.* ; for a Term, from 2*l.* 2*s.* to 3*l.* 13*s.* 6*d.*
GEOLOGY AND MINERALOGY.	Prof. The Rev. T. G. Bonney, M.A., F.R.S.	For the Course, from 3*l.* 3*s.* to 4*l.* 4*s.* ; for the Term, from 1*l.*1*s.* to 1*l.* 11*s.* 6*d.*
ELEMENTARY BIOLOGY	Prof. E. Ray Lankester, M.A., F.R.S.	Fee, 3*l.* 3*s.*
ROMAN LAW..	Prof. W. A. Hunter, M.A., Barrister-at-Law.	For the Session, 6*l.* 6*s.*; for a single Term, 2*l.* 12*s.* 6*d.*
CONSTITUTIONAL LAW	Prof. J. W. Willis Bund, M.A., LL.B., Barrister-at-Law.	For the Course, 6*l.* 6*s.*; for a single Term, 2*l.* 12*s.* 6*d.*
DEPARTMENT OF THE FINE ARTS.	Slade Professor, A. Legros.	For the General Course: for the Session, 19*l.* 19*s.* ; for each Term, 7*l.* 7*s.*

During the first term succeeding the introduction of the new regulation (from October to Christmas, 1878) the number of women in regular attendance on the University College classes was 225. Of these 72 were in the Fine-Art School, which has been open to women since its first establishment.

The remaining 153 were in attendance upon the classes open to women only, and the so-called mixed classes. As a general rule, mixed classes are confined to subjects attended by the more advanced students, as will be remarked from a perusal of the foregoing list; but the arrangements are based more on experience than theory, and have thus far answered perfectly. The ladies have a Common-Room of their own, for use between lectures, and are entering quietly and unaffectedly into the College life. They are already establishing amongst themselves a College Debating Society. It appears that in the mixed classes there is no more difficulty found in fellowship of study among men and women than at lectures of the Royal or the London Institution; and the whole system is so simply accepted, that the fear of a failure in readiness to translate aloud or answer questions, among the members of mixed classes, has proved groundless. There can be no doubt, however, that the maintenance of classes to which only men or only women are admitted will have to remain part of the system. In some cases a mixed class would be too large; in other cases a separate class meets a particular demand.

At EDINBURGH, classes for Women above the age of seventeen are held under the auspices of the "Edinburgh Ladies' Educational Association" (117, George Street). Lectures are delivered by Professors of the University of Edinburgh. The course of instruction includes English Literature, Mathematics, Economic Science, Moral Philosophy, Latin and Greek, and the Theory and Practice of Education.

Fees, for each Course *2l. 2s.*, except for that on the Theory and Practice of Education, which is *3l. 3s.* Examinations in the subjects of the classes are held and various

Prizes and Certificates given. Pass Certificates and Honour Certificates are granted by the University of Edinburgh in connection with these Lectures.

The GLASGOW Association for the Higher Education of Women (Miss Galloway, Hon. Secretary, 59, Bath Street), has organized Courses of Lectures for ladies (to be delivered by Professors of the University and others) Tutorial Classes, and a system of Instruction by Correspondence for ladies living in Glasgow and the country; and it has instituted a Diploma for students who have successfully passed through its classes. The Lectures on Domestic Economy by Miss Mungeam appear to be deserving of special notice.

It offers Bursaries to be competed for by girls in Glasgow and the West of Scotland at the University Local Examinations.

It has also made arrangements with the London Society of Arts for holding Examinations and giving Certificates in theory and practice of music, in connection with the Association, and classes in preparation for the theoretical part of these examinations are now held in Glasgow.

The organization, by the ALEXANDRA COLLEGE (Dublin) Committee of Education, of a course of Saturday Lectures, held in the Museum Building, Trinity College, has greatly enlarged the usefulness of Alexandra College in respect of Higher Education. It is worthy of remark, that upwards of 300 ladies and gentlemen have attended these lectures each year.

The Council of the COLLEGE OF PRECEPTORS (42, Queen Square, Bloomsbury, W.C.), in the year 1873, instituted a Professorship (the first which has been established in this country) of the *Science and Art of Education*, as a special subject of instruction; and a training Course of Lectures and Lessons for Teachers, extending over the whole year, under the direction of competent Lecturers, is now in full operation and attended by a large and increasing class of students. As affording a good illustration of the scope of these Lectures and of their practical usefulness to teachers, or to those who may intend to become teachers in schools, the following synopsis of a course recently delivered at the Rooms of this College by Mr. J. G. Fitch (one of H.M.'s Inspectors of Schools, and late Assistant Commissioner under the Endowed Schools Act) may prove useful to the reader.*

The object of this course was, generally, to point out the conditions of success, in the management and discipline of a school; and in particular, to investigate, as far as time allowed, the methods of teaching the ordinary subjects included in the routine of secondary instruction.

Lecture I. dealt with "*Reasons for studying Method*," and discussed the following points:—Skilled teaching—how far dependent on experience, and how far on natural gifts and aptitude. The training of a Teacher. His special qualifications. His attainments. His habits of study. His Assistants. How to distribute their duties, and to economize their time. Classification.

Lecture II. had reference to "*The Schoolroom*," and considered:—Its furniture and surroundings. Books and appliances. Ventilation. Lighting. Registers of attendance and progress. School bookkeeping. Libraries. Museums. Collections of objects of local or scientific interest.

Lecture III. took up the matter of "*Discipline*," and dwelt upon such matters as:—Mechanical drill. Personal influence. The art of obtaining attention and obedience, and of keeping them. The moral

* Lectures to Teachers will be delivered during the year 1879 at the rooms of the College (42, Queen Square, Bloomsbury), by G. Croom Robertson, M.A., Professor of Logic and Mental Philosophy in University College, London; J. M. D. Meiklejohn, M.A., Professor of Education in the University of St. Andrews; and by J. G. Fitch, M.A.,

habits to be fostered in school life. Rewards and punishments. Recreation.

Lecture IV. was upon "*The Memory*," and discussed:—How this faculty operates, and how it should be trained. When and what to learn by heart. Oral teaching. Lecturing. Collective teaching. The sympathy of numbers. Book work. Home Lessons.

Lecture V. was upon the "*Art of Examining*," and gave attention to (i.) Written Examinations—how to set a paper of questions, and to estimate the answers. (ii.) *Vivâ voce* interrogation—when and why necessary. How to make questioning efficient as an instrument of teaching as well as of testing.

Lecture VI. was upon the "*Art of Reading*"—The various systems of teaching it. Early exercises. Spelling—oral and written. Distinct articulation, and intelligent expression. Various devices for securing them.

Other Lectures were upon the following subjects:—"The Teaching of Language"; "English Language and Literature"; "Writing, Counting and Computation considered as Mechanical Arts"; "Mathematics"; "Geography and History"; and "The Teaching of Natural Science."

The Fee for the course was 1*l.* 1*s.*

Courses of Weekly Lectures and Classes, open to persons of both sexes, are held at various places under the auspices of the "LONDON SOCIETY for the EXTENSION of UNIVERSITY TEACHING." The session usually extends from October to April. The following list of subjects and Lecturers for the session 1878–79 will serve to give the reader an idea of the facilities for Higher Instruction afforded to students by the above-named Association, the address of whose Secretary (Mr. Ernest Myers) is at 22, Albemarle Street, W.

I. At the MEDICAL COLLEGE, LONDON HOSPITAL, Whitechapel Road, E.:—

1. *Physiology:* J. MCCARTHY, M.B. Lond.; Wednesday, October 2, and following Wednesdays.

2. *England in the Middle Ages:* S. R. GARDINER, M.A., Christ Church, Oxford; Friday, October 4, and following Fridays.

3. *Political Economy:* J. BONAR, B.A., Balliol College, Oxford; Tuesday, October 1, and following Tuesdays.

In these three Courses the Lectures will be at 8.15 P.M.

II. In HOXTON. *Geology:* R. D. ROBERTS, B.A., Clare College, Cambridge; Friday, November 1, and following Fridays, at 8.15 P.M.

III. BAYSWATER (Hyde Park College, 115, Gloucester Terrace, W.). *English Literature*, 1661–1731 A.D. (*Dryden and the Essayists; English Literature in the lifetime of Daniel Defoe*): E. ARBER, F.S.A., Lecturer in English Literature, University College, London; Tuesday, November 12, and following Tuesdays, 3 P.M.

A Course of *Constitutional Law* by Mr. H. H. CUNYNGHAME, St. John's College, Cambridge, to begin in January.

IV. At PUTNEY (South-west London College, Putney Hill). *Geology:* R. D. ROBERTS, B.A., Clare College, Cambridge; Thursday, October 31, and following Thursdays, 8 P.M.

V. At WIMBLEDON (Wimbledon Lecture Hall). *Heat:* O. J. LODGE, D.Sc. Lond.; the date, beginning in November, to be further advertised.

All the Lectures are followed by an hour of Class-teaching for those who desire it, and written answers to questions are looked over by the Lecturer.

Tickets for admission to these Courses (including both Lectures and Classes) may be got from the Hon. Secretaries or Agents of the Local Committees of the Society in each district. Their addresses are:—I., at 42, New Street, Stepney, E.; II., at 38, Brownswood Road, Green Lanes, South Hornsey; III., at 86, Queen's Gate, S.W.; IV., at 8, Gordon Terrace, Putney, S.W.; and V., at 12, Ridgway Place, Wimbledon, S.W.

The Price of a Ticket for Division I. is 5*s*. for 12 weeks' teaching (or 9*s*. for 24); II., 7*s*. for 16 weeks; III., 21*s*. for 12; IV., 25*s*. for 16; V., 21*s*. for 12; reductions being made in certain cases. In Divisions I. and II. the first Lectures in each Course are free.

It is, perhaps, unnecessary to remind the reader that the SOUTH KENSINGTON SCIENCE SCHOOLS afford instruction to students (female as well as male) in Chemistry, Physics, and Applied Mechanics. Fees, 3*l*. 3*s*. to 6*l*. 6*s*. the course. Admission to Laboratory practice only by special permission.

Further general information may be obtained from the Secretary, Science and Art Department, South Kensington.

Ladies are admitted to the Lectures, but not to the Laboratory, of the SCHOOL OF PHARMACY of "the Pharmaceutical Society of Great Britain" (Bloomsbury Square, W.C.). The subjects of these Lectures are Chemistry and Pharmacy, and Botany and Materia Medica. The Lecturers are, as to the first two branches of science, Professor Redwood, Ph.D., F.I.C., F.C.S., and, as to the last two, Professor Bentley, M.R.C.S. Eng., F.L.S. The exclusion of Women from the Laboratory practice of the School, of course, prevents their obtaining from the Society's Professors instruction in practical Chemistry. The Pharmaceutical Society offers less inducement, therefore, to female students to attend its lectures than that already afforded by the Cambridge "Association for Promoting the Higher Education of Women." Through the courtesy of the authorities, ladies attending the Cambridge lectures have hitherto been permitted to work in the laboratory of St. John's College, Cambridge.

It may be mentioned in connection with this subject that a chemical laboratory is being erected (if it is not already completed) at Newnham Hall, which will be available, under certain conditions, for students of the above-named Association.

Arrangements have been made, with the sanction of the Council of KING'S COLLEGE, London, for a system of lectures, to be conducted for the present at 5, Observatory Avenue, Kensington, with the object of providing systematic instruction for ladies in the higher branches of knowledge. The various courses are conducted by the Principal and Professors of the College in the following subjects:—Scripture and Church History; Logic and Moral Philosophy; History,

Ancient and Modern; English, Latin, French, German; Mathematics, and Experimental Science. Examinations are held after each course, for those who desire to obtain certificates. The Women's Education Union are co-operating in the scheme, and the organization has been entrusted to an influential committee of ladies and gentlemen, on which the local clergy are represented.

The Lectures at the BIRKBECK INSTITUTION (Southampton Buildings, Chancery Lane, W.C.), to which ladies are admitted, deserve mention as being of a class tending to promote the cause of higher education.

CHAPTER XII.

HIGHER OR UNIVERSITY EDUCATION—*concluded.* UNIVERSITY AND OTHER EXAMINATIONS DESIGNED TO TEST THE ATTAINMENTS OF WOMEN ABOVE THE AGE OF EIGHTEEN.

HAVING passed through a course of Higher Instruction under the direction of Professors of the Universities, the student might reasonably be expected to inquire, what are the means within her reach of testing her progress and attainments? The two senior English Universities, the University of London, and the Universities of Edinburgh, Dublin, and St. Andrews afford such opportunity through their system of Higher-Local and Degree Examinations. The older Universities do not, it may be remarked, admit Women to Degrees in their several faculties of Arts, Divinity, Law, Medicine, and Music, as residence within the University is, in their case, an indispensable condition of such admission. The University of London, however, has within the last few months thrown open all its Degrees to Women.

Under a Statute passed by Convocation November 10th, 1875, the Delegates of Local Examinations for the UNIVERSITY OF OXFORD are charged to hold every year an Examination by which the attainments of women over eighteen years of age may be tested. For the purposes of this Examination the Delegates have the same powers and are charged with the same duties as those which have been assigned to them in respect of the Examination of younger persons.

It will be useful to note the nature and requirements of this Higher Examination of the University of Oxford. The "Examination of Women over eighteen years of age" in 1879 commences on Monday, May 26th, and will consist of a Preliminary Examination and a Further Examination. Candidates who satisfy the Delegates in the Preliminary Examination may proceed to the Further Examination at once, or may postpone this Further Examination to a subsequent year. No Candidate will be admitted to the Further Examination unless she has passed the Preliminary or some other Examination accepted by the Delegates as equivalent.

Following are the Regulations for the year 1879:—

I. The Preliminary Examination.

Every Candidate will be required to satisfy the Delegates in

1. English Composition.
2. Any two of the following languages: (*a*) Latin; (*b*) Greek; (*c*) French, or Italian; (*d*) German.
3. Arithmetic.
4. (*a*) Euclid, Books I. and II., or (*b*) Algebra to simple equations inclusive.

In all the Exercises attention must be given to spelling, punctuation, and correctness of expression.

The books to be prepared in Latin and Greek for 1879, are,

LATIN: Cæsar, Bell. Gall., V., VI., Virgil, Æneid, II.
GREEK: Euripides, Medea. Xenophon, Hellenics, II.

Candidates will be expected to answer questions on the Grammar of the Languages selected, and to translate a piece of easy English into Latin, French, *or* Italian, and German, as the case may be.

II. The Further Examination

will consist of a Pass Examination, and an Examination for Honours.

1. The Pass Examination will consist of Six Sections, viz.:—

(*a*) Languages. (*b*) Ancient History. (*c*) Modern History. (*d*) Mathematics. (*e*) Physical Science. (*f*) Logic and Political Economy.

Candidates will not satisfy the Delegates until they pass, at the same Examination, in Section A and in one at least of the other sections, but Candidates who have so passed, may offer any two or more of the other sections at a subsequent Examination.

In Section A the Examination will be in the same languages as those prescribed for the Preliminary Examination, but will be of a higher character. Candidates will be required to pass in two languages.

The books to be prepared in Latin and Greek are

LATIN.—Livy, XXI., XXII. Virgil, Æneid, VI.

GREEK.—Herodotus, V. Æschylus, Prometheus Vinctus.

A *vivâ voce* Examination in the Modern Languages *for such as desire it* will be held in Oxford and at such other large centres as the Delegates may appoint. This will comprise writing from dictation, reading aloud, and conversation. Candidates who satisfy the Examiners in this portion of the Examination as well as in that conducted on paper, will have a special note to that effect added to their Certificates.

In Section B Candidates must satisfy the Delegates in the general outlines of Greek History from B.C. 510 to the death of Alexander the Great, and of Roman History from the beginning of the First Punic War to the accession of Nerva, and must show an accurate knowledge of one of the following periods :—

GREEK HISTORY. 1. From the outbreak of the Peloponnesian War to the peace of Antalcidas. 2. From the accession of Philip of Macedon to the death of Alexander.

ROMAN HISTORY. 1. From the beginning of the second Punic War to the destruction of Carthage. 2. From the death of Sulla to the death of Augustus.

In Section C Candidates must satisfy the Delegates in the general outlines of English History, from the accession of Henry II. to the Revolution of 1688, and show an accurate knowledge of one of the following periods :—

1. The period of the Hohenstaufen, A.D. 1152-1268. 2. French history, from the death of Francis II. to the death of Henry IV. 3. The accession of Charles I. to the Revolution of 1688.

In Section D Candidates must satisfy the Delegates in

1. Algebra, including quadratic equations and the simplest properties of Ratio and Proportion. 2. Euclid, Books I.-IV. 3. The elements of Mechanics, including the properties of matter, the composition and resolution of forces, centre of gravity, the simple machines and the application of virtual velocities to them, the laws of motion, the laws of falling bodies, and the motion of projectiles.

In Section E Candidates must satisfy the Delegates in the elements of 1. PHYSICS ; 2. CHEMISTRY. They will also be permitted to offer for Examination the elements of 3. BIOLOGY ; 4. GEOLOGY.

1. PHYSICS.—Candidates will be examined in (1) Mechanics and in one at least of the following subjects, viz.: (2) Heat; (3) Light and Sound; (4) Magnetism and Electricity. The extent to which these subjects will be required is represented by their treatment in Ganot's 'Elementary Treatise on Physics,' or Deschanel's 'Elementary Treatise on Natural Philosophy,' translated by Professor Everett.

2. CHEMISTRY.—Candidates will be examined in this subject to the extent represented by Roscoe's 'Lessons in Elementary Chemistry,' to page 289.

There will also be a practical Examination, which will comprise the analysis of single substances, and such elementary exercises as are included in Harcourt and Madan's 'Exercises in Practical Chemistry.'

3. BIOLOGY.—Candidates will be examined in—

(1) The Elements of General Biology to the extent represented by Huxley and Martin's 'Elementary Biology.'

(2) Botany to the extent represented by Bentley's 'Manual of Botany,' Book I., and Book II. chaps. i. and ii., together with a knowledge of the leading structural and physiological characters of the following classes of the Vegetable Kingdom, viz.: (1) Algæ; (2) Fungi; (3) Lichenes; (4) Characeæ; (5) Musci; (6) Filices; (7) Lycopodiaceæ; (8) Coniferæ; (9) Phanerogamia, *a.* Monocotyledones, *b.* Dicotyledones.

(3) Animal Physiology to the extent represented by Huxley's 'Elementary Lessons in Physiology,' and Huxley's 'Introduction to the Classification of Animals.'

There will also be a practical Examination in which Candidates will be required to dissect and describe plants and parts of plants, and such common animals as are given in Huxley and Martin's 'Elementary Biology.'

4. GEOLOGY.—Candidates will be examined in this subject to the extent represented by Sir C. Lyell's 'Student's Elements of Geology.'

There will also be a practical Examination in which Candidates must show an acquaintance with the general characters of the more common rocks and fossils.

Candidates who pass in Section E may offer any two of the four subjects on a future occasion.

In Section F Candidates must satisfy the Delegates in

1. The Elements of Logic to the extent represented by Whateley's 'Elements of Logic' (omitting the Appendices); and Jevons's 'Elementary Lessons in Logic' (omitting chapters xxii. and xxiii.).
2. The Elements of Political Economy to the extent represented by Adam Smith's 'Wealth of Nations,' Books I. and II.

III. The Honours Examination.

The Examination for Honours will include eight sections, and Candidates may offer to be examined in one or any two of these sections at the same Examination. Candidates will be divided into three classes in each section, according to their merits, and the names in each class will be placed in alphabetical order. The Delegates will assign the highest classes to such only as pass with great distinction. The eight sections will be—

1. English. 2. Latin and Greek. 3. German, French, Italian, and Spanish. 4. Mathematics, Pure and Mixed. 5. Ancient History, with Latin and Greek Texts. 6. Modern History, with Original Texts. 7. Philosophy. 8. Physical Science.

1. English.—Papers will be given on English Literature from Chaucer to Pope, and on the philology and growth of the English Language. The following authors must be specially studied :—

Chaucer, The Prioresses Tale ; The Clerkes Tale (Skeat) ; The Prologue ; The Knightes Tale (Morris).
Piers the Plowman (Clarendon Press Series).
Sackville, Poems.
Hooker, Ecclesiastical Polity, Book I.
Shakspeare, Macbeth ; Hamlet ; Richard II. ; Tempest.
Milton, Minor Poems.
Sir T. Browne, Religio Medici.
Bacon, Essays ; Advancement of Learning.

2. Latin and Greek.—This Examination will consist of composition in these languages, of papers on the philology and grammar of the languages, and of unprepared passages for translation into English. Papers will also be set on the following books, which must be specially studied.

Latin.

Virgil, Georgics ; Æneid, I.–VI.
Horace, Odes ; Epistles ; Ars Poet.
Cicero, Pro Murenâ ; Pro Sestio ; with Part II. of Watson's Select Letters.
Pliny, Letters.

Greek.

Homer, Odyssey, I.–XII.
Sophocles, Antigone ; Electra ; Œd. Rex. ; Œd. Coloneus.
Euripides, Medea ; Alcestis ; Bacchæ ; Hecuba.
Demosthenes, De Coronâ ; and Æschines in Ctesiphontem.

3. German, French, Italian, and Spanish.—Candidates must offer German and one at least of the other three languages. The Ex-

amination will consist of composition in the languages offered; of papers on the philology and grammar of these languages; and of unprepared passages for translation into English. Papers will also be set on the following books, which must be specially studied.

GERMAN.

Wackernagel, Deutsches Lesebuch, 3r. Theil 1te Band ('Proben der Deutschen Prosa seit 1500 bis 1740').
Schiller, Wallenstein (Prolog; Wallenstein's Lager; Die Piccolomini; Wallenstein's Tod); Wilhelm Tell.
Goethe, Faust, Part I.; Gedichte (Lieder, Gesellige Lieder).
Lessing, Nathan der Weise; Laocoon.

FRENCH.

Joinville, Mémoires.
Molière, Le Misanthrope; Les Femmes Savantes; Les Précieuses Ridicules; Le Bourgeois Gentilhomme.
Corneille, Le Cid; Racine, Athalie; Voltaire, Mérope.
Sainte Beuve, Causeries de Lundi, vol. ix.

ITALIAN.

Dante, Inferno; Vita Nuova.
Petrarca, Trionfi.
Alfieri, Filippo; Saul; La Congiura dei Pazzi.
Villari, Vita di Savonarola.

SPANISH.

Poema del Cid (Sanchez, Poesias Castellanas).
Calderon, El principe constante; El magico prodigioso; Darlo todo y no dar nada; Fineza contra fineza.
Cervantes, Don Quijote, Part II.
Solis, Historia de la conquista de Méjico.

The Certificates issued to the Candidates will specify the languages in which they have gained distinction.

A *vivâ voce* Examination in the Modern Languages *for such as desire it*, will be held in Oxford and at such other large Centres as the Delegates may appoint. This will comprise writing from dictation, reading aloud, and conversation. Candidates who satisfy the Examiners in this portion of the Examination as well as in that conducted on paper, will have a special note to that effect added to their Certificates.

Candidates who pass in this Section may offer any two of the selected languages on a future occasion.

4. MATHEMATICS.—Pure and Mixed. Papers will be set in—

PURE MATHEMATICS.

Algebra.
Trigonometry, Plane and Spherical.
Pure Geometry, and the Elements of Analytical Geometry.
The Elements of Differential and Integral Calculus.

MIXED MATHEMATICS.

Mechanics.
Hydrostatics.
The Elements of Optics.
The Elements of Astronomy.

5. ANCIENT HISTORY, &c.—Papers will be set on Greek History from the earliest times to the death of Demosthenes, B.C. 322, and on Roman History from the earliest times to the death of Domitian. The following modern authors are recommended for study :—in Greek History, Grote, Curtius, Boeckh (Public Economy of Athens); in Roman History, Mommsen, Ihne, Merivale (Romans under the Empire). Candidates must offer in addition the following books, from the text of which passages will be set.

Livy, I.–X.
Tacitus, Annals.
Herodotus.
Thucydides, I.–VII.

6. MODERN HISTORY, &c.—Papers will be set on (1) the History of England, including Constitutional History, to the Accession of Queen Victoria; (2) one of the following special periods of History, both English and Foreign, to be known accurately, viz.: From the Great Charter to the Accession of Edward IV. with Joinville, Matthew Paris (1235–1259), and Froissart. *Or*, From the Accession of Edward IV. to the death of Elizabeth, with Bacon's Henry VII., Cavendish's Wolsey, and Philip de Commines. Passages for explanation and translation will be set from the text of these authors.

The following books are recommended for study :—

I. ON ENGLISH HISTORY. (1) Constitutional History :—Stubbs' Select Charters and Constitutional History; Hallam's Middle Ages and Constitutional History; May's Constitutional History. (2) General History :—Lappenberg's Anglo-Saxon and Anglo-Norman Kings, with Freeman's Old-English History; Lingard's History of England, from Henry II.; Ranke's English History. For the Hanoverian period no books are recommended, but Candidates are required to supplement their study of Hallam and May by an adequate knowledge of the continuous political history. This head of examination must be taken to include the social and literary history, and the history of the growth of the English Colonies and Dependencies.

II. ON THE SPECIAL PERIODS (in addition to the books named above). (1) Milman's Latin Christianity; Hallam's Middle Ages; Coxe's House of Austria; Michelet's Histoire de France. *Or* (2) Robertson's Charles V.; Coxe's House of Austria; Ranke's History of the Popes and History of Germany during the period of the Reformation; Roscoe's Life of Lorenzo de' Medici and Life of Leo X.; Sismondi's Histoire des Français.

7. PHILOSOPHY.—In this Section general papers will be set. Candidates must also offer at least two of the following groups of books, which must be specially studied. Passages will be set from the text of the books selected. If only two groups be offered (4) may not be combined with either (2) or (5).

(1) Aristotle, Nicomachean Ethics; Elementa Logices Aristoteleae (Trendelenburg).

Plato, Protagoras, Georgias, Philebus, Theaetetus, Phaedo, and Euthydemus.

(2) Bacon, Novum Organon.

Descartes, Discours de la Methode.

Spinoza, Tractatus de Intellectus Emendatione.

Locke, Essay on the Human Understanding.

Leibnitz, Nouveaux Essais Philosophiques.

(3) Berkeley, Treatise on the Principles of Human Knowledge; Alciphron; An Essay towards a New Theory of Vision.

Hume, Treatise of Human Nature.

Kant, Prolegomena zu einer jeden künftigen Metaphysik; Grundlegung zur Metaphysik der Sitten.

(4) Sir W. Hamilton, Lectures on Logic and Metaphysics.

Mansel, Prolegomena Logica.

Mill, Logic; Examination of the Philosophy of Sir W. Hamilton.

(5) Mackintosh, Introduction to Ethical Philosophy.

Butler, Preface and Three Sermons on Human Nature, with the Dissertation on Virtue.

Bentham, Treatise of Legislation, by Dumont, translated by Hildreth: Introduction (Principles of Legislation); Civil Code, Parts i., ii.; Penal Code, Parts i., ii.

Mill, Utilitarianism.

Sidgwick, Methods of Ethics.

A general acquaintance with the History of Philosophy will be required, and Candidates will also be expected to show a more detailed knowledge of the periods and branches of philosophy specially represented by the groups of authors offered.

8. PHYSICAL SCIENCE.—Candidates must show an acquaintance with one or more of the following subjects, viz.: 1. Physics. 2. Chemistry. 3. Biology. 4. Geology.

1. PHYSICS. Candidates must show an accurate general knowledge of Physics; they will also be allowed to present themselves for a more detailed Examination in one or more of the following branches of Physics, viz.: (1) Sound; (2) Heat; (3) Light; (4) Electricity and Magnetism. For the highest honours a Mathematical treatment of these subjects will be required.

2. CHEMISTRY. Candidates must show an acquaintance with the following subjects: (1) Chemical Physics; (2) Inorganic Chemistry; (3) Organic Chemistry; (4) General and Theoretical Chemistry.

There will also be a practical Examination which will comprise (5) The Qualitative Analysis of Inorganic Substances; (6) The Quantitative Analysis of Inorganic Substances. The use of books will be allowed to Candidates in the Practical Examination.

3. BIOLOGY. Candidates must show an acquaintance with the general principles of Physics, Chemistry, and Biology.

They must also present themselves for a more detailed examination in one or more of the following branches of Biology, viz.:—(1) Physiological Botany; (2) Systematic Botany; (3) The Physiology of Animals; (4) The Comparative Anatomy of Animals.

There will also be a practical Examination in which Candidates will be required to show by dissection that they possess an intimate knowledge of the subject or subjects selected.

4. GEOLOGY. Candidates must show an acquaintance with the general principles of Physics, Chemistry, and Geology (including Physical Geography).

They must also present themselves for a more detailed examination in one at least of the following branches of Geology, viz.:—(1) Petrology; (2) Palæontology.

There will also be a practical Examination in Petrology and in Palæontology, in which Candidates offering either of these subjects will be required to show an intimate knowledge, in the former subject with the structure of Rocks, in the latter with the general structure and classification of Animal and Vegetable Life.

RUDIMENTS OF FAITH AND RELIGION.

A separate Certificate will be given to Candidates who satisfy the Delegates in this subject. Candidates may offer themselves for examination in this subject either at the same time with their Further Examination or on any subsequent occasion. They may be examined in the following subdivision of the subject:—

I. HOLY SCRIPTURES.—The Historical and Prophetical Books of the Old Testament, the Holy Gospels, the Acts of the Apostles, and the Epistle to the Hebrews.

II. THE BOOK OF COMMON PRAYER.—The Morning and Evening Services, the Litany, the Office for the Holy Communion, together with the Outlines of the History of the Prayer Book.

Candidates who satisfy the Delegates in I. only will receive a Certificate for Holy Scripture. Those only will receive a Certificate for the Rudiments of Faith and Religion who satisfy the Delegates in both I. and II.

Candidates may offer, in addition, the Greek Text of the books selected from the New Testament, and, if they satisfy the Delegates in it, will have the fact noted on their Certificates.

Candidates may be examined at any of the places appointed for the Local Examination of Girls, with consent of the Local Secretary.

The Fees payable will be for the Examination in Preliminary Subjects, or in the Rudiments of Faith and Religion, 2*l.*; and 2*l.* 10*s.* for the Pass Examination, and for each Section of the Examination in Honours.

The UNIVERSITY OF CAMBRIDGE holds annually a "Higher Local Examination," which is open to Women who have completed the age of eighteen years. In 1879 this Examination will commence on Monday, June 16th, and following are the Regulations relating to it:—

1. Every one admitted to Examination will be required to pay a fee of forty shillings. After a Candidate has passed in any group, the fee in any subsequent year will be twenty shillings.

2. *Honour Certificates.* (*a*) A Candidate who satisfies the Examiners in group A and in elementary Arithmetic, and in two of the groups R, B, C, D, E, obtaining a First or Second Class in two of these six groups, will receive an Honour Certificate.

(*b*) A Candidate who has obtained a First, Second, or Third Class in the Local Examinations for Seniors, and obtains a First or Second Class in two of the groups R, A, B, C, D, E, will receive an Honour Certificate.

3. *Ordinary Certificates.* A Candidate who satisfies the Examiners in group A and in elementary Arithmetic and in two of the groups R, B, C, D, E, will receive a Certificate to that effect.

4. Candidates may take the paper in Arithmetic and the various groups in which they wish to be examined either in the same year or in

different years. If a Candidate passes in any group, or in Arithmetic, though not in all the work necessary for a Certificate, this will be recorded and will count towards a Certificate in any subsequent year.

5. Candidates may be examined a second time in any group with a view to obtaining a higher Class in that Group. An ordinary Certificate may by this means be converted into an Honour Certificate.

6. The Candidates who pass with credit in each group will be placed alphabetically in two Honour classes. Those who pass to the satisfaction of the Examiners, yet not so as to deserve Honours, will be placed alphabetically in a third class. The names of those who request that their names may not appear will not be published. If a Candidate is specially distinguished in particular parts of the Examination, the fact will be notified by endorsement on the Certificate. After the Examination, notice of the result will be sent to each Candidate through the Local Secretaries.

A schedule of books recommended by the Syndicate is appended to each group. But it is to be understood that such schedules are not intended to limit the studies of the Candidates or the range of questions in the papers set by the Examiners. The works marked with an asterisk are suitable to the more advanced Students. The last edition is always meant where the contrary is not expressed.

Candidates who have passed in group A in 1878 *or previous years will be allowed to obtain a Certificate by passing in any one of the groups R, B, C, D, E, in* 1879, *notwithstanding the new Regulations requiring two of these groups.*

Subjects of Examination.

Group R.

A knowledge of the Scripture subjects and of one of the three books of Butler, Hooker, Paley, will be required to enable a Candidate to pass in this group. For a First or Second Class a knowledge of at least one other of the three books will be required in addition.

Old Testament: The two Books of Samuel; [1] Psalms i.–xli.

New Testament: St Mark; the first Epistle to the Corinthians, and Acts xvi.–xix. inclusive. Credit will be given for a knowledge of the original Greek.

Butler, 'Analogy,' Introduction and Part I. Hooker, 'Of the Laws of Ecclesiastical Polity,' Preface and Bk. I. Paley, 'Horæ Paulinæ,' chapters i.–v.

The following will be found useful books of reference for students in

[1] This will be repeated for June, 1880.

this group :—Blunt, 'Scriptural Coincidences.' Smith, 'Dictionary of the Bible.' Stanley, 'Lectures on the Jewish Church.' Stanley, 'Sinai and Palestine.' Westcott, 'On the Canon.'

GROUP A.

A knowledge of the first two of the subjects 1, 2, 3, 4 will be required to enable a Candidate to pass in this group. For a First or Second Class, a knowledge of one at least of the remaining two will be required in addition.

1. ENGLISH HISTORY. Part 1, not exceeding one-third of the paper, will consist of questions on the general History of England. Part 2 will consist of questions on the special period A.D. 1588–1660 inclusive. A knowledge of Geography, so far as it bears on this subject, will be expected. Candidates must pass in both parts of the paper.

2. ENGLISH LANGUAGE AND LITERATURE (selected books).

   a. Chaucer: 'Man of Law's Tale'; 'Pardoner's Prologue and Tale'; 'Second Nun's Tale.'

   b. Shakspeare: 'As You Like It.' Milton: 'Paradise Lost,' Bks. X. XI.

   c. Bacon: 'Advancement of Learning,' Book I.

No Candidate will be allowed to answer questions on more than two of the subjects *a*, *b*, *c*.

The paper will consist of questions on the language as well as the subject-matter of the selected books.

3. ENGLISH LANGUAGE.

   The papers will consist of (1) passages for translation into modern English from the books mentioned in the subjoined schedule, (2) passages for translation into modern English from other books, (3) questions on grammar and philology.

   Sweet's 'Anglo-Saxon Reader,' sections iv.–xii. inclusive. 'Specimens of Early English,' from 1298–1393, ed. Morris and Skeat, sections xii., xiii., and xv.

4. ENGLISH LITERATURE.

   This paper will contain general questions on English Literature, relating especially to the Elizabethan and Jacobean periods. The answers required will be for the most part of the nature of Essays.

The following will be found useful books of reference for Students in English Language and Literature :—Bosworth, 'Smaller Anglo-Saxon Dictionary.' Marsh, 'Lectures on the English Language,' edited by

N

W. Smith. Morris, 'Historical Outlines of English Accidence,' Morley, 'First Sketch of English Literature.' Craik, 'Manual of English Literature and the English Language.' Hallam, 'History of Literature,' so far as relates to English writers, 'Grammar of Shakspere.'

GROUP B.

A knowledge of one of the five languages will enable Candidates to pass in this group. For a First or Second Class a knowledge of two will be required.

1. LATIN. 2. GREEK.

The papers will consist of (*a*) passages for translation into English from the books mentioned in the subjoined schedule, and questions on the language and subject-matter of the books, (*b*) passages for translation into English from other books, (*c*) passages of English prose for translation.

No Candidate can pass in either of these languages without satisfying the Examiners in (*b*) : and no Candidate can obtain honours without satisfying the Examiners in (*b*) and (*c*).

1. Virgil, Æneid IX., X. Horace, Odes IV. Tacitus, [1] Hist. I. and II., 1–50.

2. Euripides, [1] Iphigenia Aulica, [1] Iphigenia Taurica. Plato, Phædo, Crito, Apology.

3. FRENCH. 4. GERMAN. 5. ITALIAN.

The papers will consist of (*a*) passages for translation into English taken from the best authors, (*b*) questions on grammar and philology, (*c*) questions on the history of the language, and on the selected period of literature, viz. for French, A.D. 1650–1700; for German, A.D. 1750–1800; for Italian, A.D. 1300–1350, (*d*) a passage of an English author for translation. The passages for translation from the French will not be taken from authors earlier than A.D. 1600, except in cases of short sentences selected for illustration of the history of the language. No Candidate can pass without satisfying the Examiners in (*a*) and (*d*).

In the papers in French and Italian, the connection between these languages and Latin will be included; but a knowledge of Latin will not be required.

The following will be found useful books of reference :—

3. Brachet, 'Historical French Grammar.' Littré, 'Abridged French Dictionary.' Brachet, 'Etymological French Dictionary.' Geruzez, 'Histoire de la Littérature Francaise.'

4. Eve, 'Short German Syntax.' Gostwick and Harrison, 'Outlines

[1] These subjects will be repeated for June, 1880.

of German Literature.' Becker, 'Schulgrammatik der deutschen Sprache.' Vilmar, 'Geschichte der deutschen Nationallitteratur.'

5. Monnier, 'L'Italie est-elle la Terre des Morts?' Chambers, 'Italian Literature.' Ambrosoli, 'Manuele della Letteratura Italiana.'

In this group Max Müller's 'Lectures on the Science of Language,' First Series, will be found useful. In the Second Series, Lectures i., v., vi., xii. may be read.

GROUP C.

A knowledge of the first three subjects will be required to enable a Candidate to pass in this group. For a First or Second Class, a knowledge of two at least of the remaining six will be required in addition.

1. ARITHMETIC. [N.B. No Candidate can obtain a Certificate who does not pass in Part I (elementary) of this paper, except in the cases provided for in paragraph *2b* on p. 187. Both parts of the paper are necessary for the mark of distinction in Arithmetic.]
2. EUCLID, Books I., II., III., IV., VI., and XI. to Prop. 21 inclusive.
3. ALGEBRA, the elementary parts; namely, the Rules for the Fundamental Operations upon Algebraical Symbols, with their proofs; the solution of Simple and Quadratic Equations and of Problems producing such Equations; Arithmetical and Geometrical Progression, Permutations and Combinations, the Binomial Theorem and the Principles of Logarithms.
4. The elementary parts of Plane Trigonometry, so far as to include the solution of Triangles.
5. The simpler properties of the Conic Sections, treated either geometrically or analytically.
6. The elementary parts of Statics, including the equilibrium of Forces acting in one plane, the properties of the Centre of Gravity, the laws of Friction, and the Mechanical Powers.
7. The elementary parts of Astronomy, so far as they are necessary for the explanation of the more simple phenomena.
8. The elementary parts of Dynamics, including the laws of Motion, Gravity, and the Theory of Projectiles.
9. Elements of the Differential and Integral Calculus.

Hamblin Smith, 'Algebra.' *Todhunter, 'Algebra for the use of Colleges and Schools.'

Hamblin Smith, 'Trigonometry. Todhunter, 'Trigonometry.'

Todhunter, 'Mechanics for Beginners.'

Lockyer, 'Lessons in Elementary Astronomy.' Airy, 'Lectures on Astronomy,' delivered at Ipswich.

Besant, 'Geometrical Conic Sections.' Taylor, 'Geometrical Conic Sections.' Puckle, 'Elementary Treatise on Conic Sections.'

Todhunter, 'Differential and Integral Calculus.'
Williamson, 'Differential and Integral Calculus.'

GROUP D.

A knowledge of one of the three subjects will enable a Candidate to pass in this group. For a First or Second Class, a knowledge of two will be required.

1. POLITICAL ECONOMY. 2. LOGIC.

3. Constitutional History of England. A part of the paper, not exceeding one-third, will have special reference to the period from 1603 to 1660.

1. Mill, 'Political Economy.' *Cairnes, 'Logical Method of Political Economy.' *Adam Smith, 'Wealth of Nations' (McCulloch's edition), i. 1–5, 10, iii., iv., v.

2. Jevons, 'Elementary Lessons in Logic,' Lessons 1–22. Fowler, 'Inductive Logic.' Mill, 'Logic.'† Thomson, 'Outlines of the Laws of Thought.'

Omitting the following: Book I., ch. iii. (except § 1); Book II., ch. iv.–vii.; Book III., ch. v. § 9 and note, ch. xiii., ch. xviii., ch. xxiii., ch. xxiv. (except § 1, 2); Book V., ch. iii. § 3–6; Book VI., ch. ii.

3. Hallam, 'Constitutional History of England'; Stubbs, 'Constitutional History of England.'

GROUP E.

A knowledge of one of the six subjects will enable a Candidate to pass in this group. For a First or Second Class, a knowledge of two of them will be required. No Candidate will be examined in more than three in any one year.

1. BOTANY. 2. GEOLOGY and PHYSICAL GEOGRAPHY. 3. ZOOLOGY. 4. CHEMISTRY (theoretical and practical). 5. PHYSICS. 6. PHYSIOLOGY.

1. Oliver, 'Elementary Botany.' Balfour, 'Manual of Botany,' or Maxwell Master's edition of Henfrey's 'Elementary Course.' *Sachs, 'Text-Book of Botany.'

2. Lyell, 'The Student's Elements of Geology.' Lyell's 'Principles of Geology.' Tenth Edition, ch. i.–xxxiii. and xliv.–xlix. *Nicholson, 'Palæontology.' Huxley, 'Physiography.'

3. S.P.C.K. 'Manual of Zoology' (elementary). Nicholson, 'Manual of Zoology.' Huxley, 'Introduction to the Classification of Animals,' and 'Anatomy of Vertebrated Animals.' Huxley, 'Invertebrata.' *Flower, 'Osteology of the Mammalia.' *Rolleston, 'Forms of Animal Life.'

4. Miller, Prof. W. A., 'Introduction to the Study of Inorganic

Chemistry.' Roscoe, 'Lessons in Elementary Chemistry.' Fownes, 'Manual of Chemistry.' Armstrong, 'Organic Chemistry.' *Miller, Prof. W. A., 'Elements of Chemistry.'

5. Balfour Stewart, 'Elementary Physics.' Ganot's or Deschanel's 'Physics.' *Maxwell on 'Heat,' ch. i.–viii. and xvi.–xviii. inclusive.

6. Huxley, 'Elementary Lessons in Physiology.' Foster, 'Text-Book of Physiology,' Books I., II., III., and Appendix; students may omit the small print. *Frey, 'Histology,' translated by Barker.

GROUP F.

1. THEORY of MUSIC.

Proficiency in this subject will not count towards a Certificate, but will be notified on the Certificate in cases where the Candidate obtains one.

PRIZES and SCHOLARSHIPS open to FEMALE CANDIDATES at the Cambridge "Higher Local Examination":—

With a view to meeting the actual expenses of examination of Women who are engaged in tuition as a profession, or are preparing for that profession, the sum of 5*l.* each will be given by the Syndicate to the five Candidates fufilling these conditions who are placed highest in order by the Examiners in June, 1879.

The Association for promoting the Higher Education of Women announce five Exhibitions of 35*l.* each, for one year, one for success in each of the Groups A, B (two languages at least, of which one must be Latin or Greek), C, D, E; also a Scholarship of 50*l.* for two years, given by the Clothworkers' Company, for the best qualified among the Candidates whose resources are inadequate to defray the expenses of residence in Cambridge; † one of 50*l.* for two years, given by the Goldsmiths' Company; and one of 50*l.* a year for two years, given by the Drapers' Company, for those who are preparing for the profession of teaching. The recipients are expected to proceed to Cambridge and to conform to the conditions of residence and attendance at lectures laid down by the Association. The recipient of the Goldsmiths' Scholarship must reside at Newnham Hall. Further information can be procured on application to H. SIDGWICK, Esq., Trinity College, Cambridge.

Candidates for the above gratuities or for the Exhibitions must give

---

† See note at foot of p. 150.

notice *in writing* to the Local Secretary at the centre at which they are to be examined before the end of the Examination.

A prize of 5*l.* is offered by a private donor for the best Candidate in Religious Knowledge.

A New Supplemental Charter was in 1878 granted to the UNIVERSITY OF LONDON empowering the Senate to admit Women to graduate in its several Faculties of Arts, Science, Law, Medicine, and Music. Female Candidates are now admitted to the Matriculation Examination of the University (the "General Examination for Women" being superseded, see Chapter VIII.), and, after the required interval, are admissible to the First Degree Examination in either of the Faculties.

With a view to the special encouragement of female candidates desiring to go through a regular Academical Course, the Trustees of the Gilchrist Educational Trust have instituted two Exhibitions, one of 30*l.*, the other of 20*l.*, per annum, tenable for two years, to the female candidates who pass highest in the Honours Division at the Matriculation Examination; and two Exhibitions, one of 40*l.*, the other of 30*l.* per annum, tenable for two years, to the Female Candidates who pass highest at the First B.A. Examination (provided that they obtain in the first case two-thirds, and in the second three-fifths, of the total number of marks), to assist them in pursuing their studies at some Collegiate Institution approved by the Trustees; with the further reward of a Gold Medal of the value of 20*l.* (or of a Book-Prize of the same value) to the Female Candidate who passes highest at the Second B.A. Examination, if she obtains not less than two-thirds of the total number of marks. These rewards are quite independent of those granted by the University, and may be held in conjunction with them. Further particulars may be obtained by application to the Registrar of the University, London, W.

It seems unnecessary to print here at length the whole of the Regulations of the University of London relating to Degrees in Science, Law and Medicine.* We need only to deal with those examinations for which women are, for the present at least, most likely to enter. These are the First and Second B.A., and the First B.Mus. Examinations.

Following are the Regulations which refer to each :—

FIRST B.A. EXAMINATION.

Candidates for the Degree of Bachelor of Arts are required to have passed the Matriculation Examination (see Chapter VIII.). The first B.A. Examination takes place annually, and commences on the third Monday in July. No candidate (with the exception of such as have obtained Honours at the Matriculation Examination in the preceding January) will be admitted to this examination within one Academical Year of the time of her passing the Matriculation Examination; nor will any candidate be admitted unless she can produce a satisfactory certificate of Good Conduct.

The Fee for the First B.A. Examination is 5*l.* No Candidate will be admitted to the Examination unless she shall have previously paid this Fee to the Registrar. If, after payment of her Fee, a Candidate withdraws her name, or fails to present herself at the Examination, or fails to pass it, the Fee will not be returned to her; but she will be allowed to enter for any *two* subsequent First B.A. Examinations without the payment of any additional Fee, provided that she give notice to the Registrar at least *fourteen days* before the commencement of the Examination; such notice, in respect to the privilege aforesaid, being considered equivalent to entry.

The Examination is conducted by means of Printed Papers; but the Examiners are not precluded from putting, for the purpose of ascertaining the competency of the Candidates to pass, *vivâ voce* questions to any Candidate in the subjects in which they are appointed to examine.

Candidates will be examined in the following subjects :—

MATHEMATICS.

ARITHMETIC.

The ordinary Rules of Arithmetic.
Vulgar and Decimal Fractions.
The Rule of Three, and its applications.

---

* The subject of the Medical Education of Women is referred to in a following chapter.

Simple and Compound Interest.
Present Value, Discount, and Annuities.
Extraction of the Square Root.
Nature and Use of Logarithms.

ALGEBRA.

The ordinary Rules of Algebra.
Reduction and Manipulation of Algebraical Fractions.
Ratio, Proportion, and Combination.
Permutations and Variations.
Arithmetical and Geometrical Progressions.
Simple and Quadratic Equations.
Determination of Common Factors.

GEOMETRY.

The Relations and Properties of similar Rectilinear Figures.
The Elementary Properties of the Plane, including those of the Angles made by Planes with right lines and with each other.
The Elementary Properties of the Sphere, including those of the Great and Small Circles on the Surfaces of Spheres.
The Mensuration of the Simpler Plane and Solid Figures, including that of the Circle, the Sphere, the Cylinder, and the Cone.
Elements of Co-ordinate Geometry in Rectangular and Polar Co-ordinates, as far as the Equations and Properties of the Right Line and Circle.

TRIGONOMETRY.

The different Measurements of Angles, and the Ordinary Relations of their Trigonometrical Ratios.
The Elementary Formulæ connecting the Trigonometrical Ratios of two or more Angles.
The Solution of the several cases of Plane Triangles, including the determination of their Areas.
The determination of the Heights and Distances of Inaccessible Objects.

CLASSICS.

THE LATIN LANGUAGE.

Two Latin subjects, one in prose, the other in verse; to be selected two years previously by the Senate from the works of the undermentioned authors: *—

---

* The Latin Subjects for 1879 and 1880 are—
For 1879:—*Horace*, Satires; and *Cicero*, De Divinatione, Book II.
For 1880:—*Virgil*, Georgics, Books II. and III.; and *Tacitus*, Annals, Book I.

Virgil, The Eclogues; or two Books of the Georgics; or two Books of the Æneid.

Horace, The Odes; or the Satires; or the Epistles.

Cicero, One of the Orations; or one Book from any of the Philosophical or Rhetorical Works.

Livy, One Book.

Tacitus, One Book of either the Annals or the Histories.

HISTORY.

History of Rome to the Death of Augustus.

The papers in Latin and Roman History shall contain passages of the specified Authors, with simple passages of Latin from books not previously named, to be translated into English; short passages of English to be translated into Latin;* and questions in Grammar, History, and Geography.

GREEK.

One Book either of Homer or of Xenophon, to be selected two years previously by the Senate; together with easy questions in Grammar.†

THE ENGLISH LANGUAGE, LITERATURE, AND HISTORY.

Writing out the substance of a paragraph previously read by the Examiner; the Grammatical Structure of the Language; Composition; other special subjects to be defined two years previously.‡

History of England to the end of the Seventeenth Century.

---

* Grammatical correctness in the rendering of English into Latin is imperatively necessary.

† The Greek Subjects for 1879 and 1880 are—
For 1879:—*Homer*, Iliad, Book XXIV.
For 1880:—*Xenophon*, Cyropædia, Book VIII.

‡ The English Subjects for 1879 are—
History of English Literature from 1548 to 1603.
Spenser: Faerie Queen, Book I.
Morris and Skeat: Specimens of Early English; Part II. (Clarendon Press Series): Introduction and Sections I.–XI. (both inclusive).
Shakspeare: Othello.

The English Subjects for 1880 are—
History of English Literature from 1649 to 1700.
Milton: Paradise Regained.
Shakspeare: Coriolanus.
Skeat: Specimens of English Literature.

THE FRENCH OR THE GERMAN LANGUAGE.

Translation into English with Questions in Grammar.

Candidates will not be approved by the Examiners unless they have shown a competent knowledge in

1. Latin, and Roman History;
2. Greek;
3. English Language, Literature, and History;
4. Mathematics;
5. Either the French or the German Language.*

On Saturday morning at nine o'clock in the week following the examination, the Examiners will publish a List of the Candidates who have passed, arranged in two divisions, each in alphabetical order. And a Pass Certificate signed by the Registrar will be delivered to each Candidate who shall apply for it, after the report of the Examiners has been approved by the Senate.

SECOND B.A. EXAMINATION.

The Second B.A. Examination takes place once in each year, and commences on the Fourth Monday in October.

No Candidate will be admitted to this Examination within one Academical Year of the time of her passing the First B.A. Examination, unless she shall have previously taken the Degree of B.Sc.; nor will any Candidate be admitted unless she can produce a satisfactory Certificate of Good Conduct.

The Fee for the Second B.A. Examination is 5*l.* No Candidate will be admitted to the Examination unless she shall have previously paid this Fee to the Registrar. If, after payment of her Fee, a Candidate withdraws her name, or fails to present herself at the Examination, or fails to pass it, the Fee will not be returned to her; but she will be allowed to enter for any *two* subsequent Second B.A. Examinations without the payment of any additional Fee, provided that she give notice to the Registrar at least *fourteen days* before the commencement of the Examination; such notice, in respect to the privilege aforesaid, being considered equivalent to entry.

The Examination is conducted by means of Printed Papers; but the Examiners are not precluded from putting, for the purpose of ascertaining the competence of the Candidates to pass, *viva voce* questions to any Candidate in the subjects in which they are appointed to examine.

Candidates will be examined in the following subjects:—

---

* Candidates can obtain credit for only One of these Languages.

MECHANICAL AND NATURAL PHILOSOPHY.

The following subjects are to be treated Experimentally, and also Mathematically so far as the subjects of the First B.A. Examination are applicable to them.

STATICS.

Elementary Statics, including the Resolution of Forces, the Mechanical Powers, the Centre of Gravity, and simple cases of Equilibrium of bodies or systems of bodies under the action of Gravity.

DYNAMICS.

Elementary Dynamics, including the Laws of Motion and Propositions required for determining the Rectilinear Motion of a body whether free or along inclined planes.

Direct Impact of Spheres.

Motion of Projectiles, and the simpler cases of motion round Centres of Force.

Elementary Propositions relating to Mechanical Work.

HYDROSTATICS, HYDRAULICS, AND PNEUMATICS.

Elementary Propositions respecting the nature, transmission, and intensity of Fluid Pressure; and the Conditions of Equilibrium of Floating Bodies.

Nature and simple properties of Elastic Fluids; and the Pressures produced by them.

Specific Gravity, and modes of determining it.

The Common Pump and Forcing-Pump.

The Hydrostatic Press.

The Barometer.

The Air-Pump.

The Steam-Engine.

OPTICS (Geometrical).

Laws of Reflexion and Refraction; Reflexion at plane mirrors; Reflexion at spherical mirrors, and Refraction through lenses, the incident pencils being direct.

Separation of Solar Light into rays of different colours; Description of the Solar Spectrum. Description of the Eye; Simple Optical Instruments; Camera Obscura; Reflecting and Refracting Telescopes.

ACOUSTICS.

Nature of Sounds; mode of Propagation; Musical Tones, and simple propositions respecting them.

OPTICS (Physical).

Fundamental Hypotheses of the Undulatory Theory respecting the Origin and Propagation of Light.

General explanation of Interferences; formation of Newton's Rings, with descriptions of simple experiments which elucidate the effects of Interference.

Polarized Light, with the description of simple experimental modes of producing it.

ASTRONOMY.*

Systems of Great Circles to which the positions of the Heavenly Bodies are referred.

Principal phenomena depending on the Motion of the Earth round the Sun, and its Rotatory Motion round its own axis.

General description of the Solar System.

General Explanation of Lunar and Solar Eclipses.

THE FRENCH OR THE GERMAN LANGUAGE.

Translation from English into French or German.

CLASSICS.

THE GREEK AND LATIN LANGUAGES.

One Greek subject and one Latin Prose subject, to be selected two years previously by the Senate from the works of the following authors:†—

Homer, Six Books.
Æschylus, One Play.
Sophocles, One Play.
Euripides, One Play.
Herodotus, One Book.
Thucydides, One Book.

---

* The Mathematical treatment of this subject will require the application of the elements of Spherical Trigonometry; viz.: Circles of the Sphere—Measures of the sides and angles of Spherical Triangles—Supplemental Triangle.

† The Classical Subjects for 1878, 1879, and 1880 are—

For 1878:—*Demosthenes*, Orations against Lacritus and Dionysodorus; *Tacitus*, Annals, Book VI.

For 1879:—*Euripides*, Hippolytus; *Cicero*, De Oratore, Book I.

For 1880:—*Sophocles*, Antigone; *Tacitus*, Histories, Book III.

Plato, Apology of Socrates, and Crito.

Xenophon, Two Books, from any of his larger works.

Demosthenes, One of the longer or three of the shorter Public Orations; or two of the Private Orations.

Cicero, One of the Orations; or one Book from any of the Philosophical or Rhetorical works.

Livy, One Book.

Tacitus, One Book of either the Annals or the Histories.

HISTORY.

History of Greece to the Death of Alexander.

The Papers in Classics will contain passages of the specified Authors, with simple passages of Greek from books not previously named, to be translated into English; short passages of English to be translated into Latin;* and Questions in Grammar, History, and Geography.

LOGIC AND PSYCHOLOGY.†

Names, Notions, and Propositions.

Syllogism.

Induction and subsidiary operations.

The Senses.

The Intellect.

The Will, including the Theory of Moral Obligation.

Candidates will not be approved by the Examiners unless they have shown a competent knowledge in

1. Classics.
2. Grecian History.
3. Mechanical and Natural Philosophy.
4. Either the French or the German Language.‡
5. Logic and Psychology.

On Saturday morning at nine o'clock in the week following the examination, the Examiners will publish a List of the Candidates who have passed, arranged in Two Divisions, each in alphabetical order.

A Certificate under the Seal of the University and signed by the Chancellor will be delivered at the Public Presentation for Degrees to each Candidate who has passed.

---

* Grammatical correctness in the rendering of English into Latin is imperatively necessary.

† The extent of acquirement expected in Logic and Psychology is such as may fairly be attained by a course of instruction in a Class during the year preceding examination.

‡ Candidates can obtain credit for only One of these Languages.

EXAMINATION FOR THE DEGREE OF BACHELOR OF MUSIC (B.MUS.).

Candidates for the Degree of Bachelor of Music are required to have passed the Matriculation Examination.

FIRST B.MUS. EXAMINATION.

The First B.Mus. Examination takes place once in each year, and commences on the Second Monday in December.

No Candidate will be admitted to this Examination unless she shall have passed the Matriculation Examination (or taken one of the equivalent Degrees) at least Ten Months previously: nor will any Candidate be admitted unless she can produce a satisfactory Certificate of Good Conduct.

The Fee for this Examination is 5*l.* No Candidate will be admitted to the Examination unless she shall have previously paid this Fee to the Registrar. If, after payment of her Fee, a Candidate withdraws her name, or fails to present herself at the Examination, or fails to pass it, the Fee will not be returned to her; but she will be allowed to enter for any *two* subsequent First B.Mus. Examinations without the payment of any additional Fee, provided that she give notice to the Registrar at least *fourteen days* before the commencement of the Examination; such notice, in respect to the privilege aforesaid, being considered equivalent to entry.

Candidates will be examined in the following subjects:—

- The relations between Musical Sounds and the Vibrations of Sonorous Bodies, as affecting the *pitch* of the sounds.
- The simpler properties of Stretched Strings, and the Sounds produced by them. Compound Vibrations. Nodes.
- The nature of Harmonics.
- The general theory and simpler phenomena of Compound Sounds.
- The theoretical nature and values of Musical Intervals.
- The theoretical construction of the Modern Scales.
- Temperament.
- Melody. Time. Rhythm.
- The theoretical nature of Consonance and Dissonance as determined by Helmholtz.
- The principles of the Construction of Chords.
- The History of Music, in so far as it relates to the growth of Musical Forms and Rules.

The Examination will be conducted by Printed Papers, and extends over Two Days; in the Morning from Ten to One, and in the Afternoon from Three to Six.

Candidates will not be approved by the Examiners unless they have shown a competent knowledge in each of the foregoing subjects.

On Saturday morning at nine o'clock in the week following the examination, the Examiners will publish a List of the Candidates who have passed, arranged in Two Divisions, each in alphabetical order. And a Pass Certificate signed by the Registrar will be delivered to each Candidate who applies for it, after the Report of the Examiners has been approved by the Senate.

SECOND B.MUS. EXAMINATION.

The Second B.Mus. Examination takes place once in each year, and commences on the Third Monday in December.

Every Candidate for this Examination will be required to have passed the First B.Mus. Examination at least One Year previously: she will also be required to produce a satisfactory Certificate of Good Conduct.

The Fee for this Examination is 5*l.* No Candidate will be admitted to the Examination unless she shall have previously paid this Fee to the Registrar. If, after payment of her Fee, a Candidate withdraws her name, or fails to present herself at the Examination, or fails to pass it, the Fee will not be returned to her; but she will be allowed to enter for any *two* subsequent Second B.Mus. Examinations without the payment of any additional Fee, provided that she give notice to the Registrar at least *fourteen days* before the commencement of the Examination; such notice, in respect to the privilege aforesaid, being considered equivalent to entry.

Every Candidate for this Examination is required to transmit to the Registrar, at least *one calendar month* before the commencement of the Examination, a *Musical Exercise*, clearly and legibly written in the proper clefs, of such length as to occupy from twenty to forty minutes in performance, and fulfilling the following conditions:—

(*a*) It must be a Vocal Composition to any words the writer may select.

(*b*) It must contain real five-part Vocal Counterpoint, with specimens of imitation, canon, and fugue.

(*c*) It must have accompaniments for a quintett String Band.

The Candidate will be required to make a solemn declaration that the Exercise is entirely her own unaided composition.

If the Exercise be approved by the Examiners, the qualifications of the Candidate will be further tested by an Examination in the following subjects:—

Practical Harmony and Thorough Bass.

Counterpoint, in not more than five parts, with Canon and Fugue.

Form in Musical Composition.

Instrumentation, so far as is necessary for understanding and reading a full score.

Arranging for the Pianoforte, from an instrumental score.

A critical knowledge of the full scores of such standard Classical Compositions as shall be announced beforehand.

The Candidate may also be examined, at the discretion of the Examiners, on points in her own Exercise.

No reference to any Musical Instrument will be allowed during the Examination, unless specially directed by the Examiners.

The Examination will be in part conducted by Printed Papers, and will be in part *vivâ voce;* and will extend over Three Days.

Candidates will not be approved by the Examiners unless they have shown a competent knowledge in all the foregoing subjects.

Although technical skill in performance will constitute no part of the qualification for this Degree, any Candidate may offer to be examined in

(α) Playing at sight from a five-part Vocal Score.

(β) Playing an Accompaniment from a figured bass.

Any Candidate otherwise approved will obtain a distinguishing mark for merit in either or both of these particulars.

On Saturday Morning at Nine o'clock in the week following the examination, the Examiners will publish a List of the Candidates who have passed, arranged in Two Divisions, each in alphabetical order.

The Musical Exercise of each Candidate who has passed will be deposited in the Library of the University.

A Certificate, under the Seal of the University and signed by the Chancellor, will be delivered at the Public Presentation for Degrees to each Candidate who has passed.

In the Local Examination Scheme of the UNIVERSITY OF EDINBURGH provision is made for granting Honour Certificates to Women under the age of twenty years who have passed the requisite examination. The Regulations having reference to this examination, known as the "Honour Certificate Examination," have been already given in proper order in Chapter VIII. It may be remarked that the standard is the same as that required of male students matriculating at the University of Edinburgh.

The Honour Certificate, in case of indicating that the holder has passed in Latin, Greek, and Mathematics, may be presented by a student at the time of his entrance to the University, and is accepted by the Professors in the Faculty of Arts as evidence of qualification to attend the higher classes in these subjects. This applies, of course, only to male students; but the fact is here mentioned so that the reader may form an idea of the educational value of the certificate referred to.

As has been already pointed out (Chapter VIII.), the UNIVERSITY OF DUBLIN undertakes three examinations, which may be attended in succession at intervals of one or more years, by women, as follows:—(1) The First or Junior Examination; (2) The Second or Intermediate Examination; (3) The Third or Senior Examination. There are no limits of age prescribed for Candidates for the Second and Third, and the maximum limit for the First is eighteen years. It is improbable that a Candidate would enter for the third examination unless she had passed the second or some examination equivalent to it; I have therefore not thought it necessary to print here the regulations relating to the Senior Examination. The Local Examination Scheme of the University of Dublin would seem, indeed, mainly to apply to those students who have availed themselves of its working during their school course.

The UNIVERSITY OF ST. ANDREWS grants a Certificate of attainments in Arts, with the title of L.A. (Literate in Arts), to all Women who pass the requisite examination, wherever they may have received their education. The following are the conditions of examination:—

I. In each subject there will be a Pass and an Honour Standard.

II. The subjects will, for the most part, be limited to those taught

O

in the University; but History, and the French, German, and Italian languages and literatures have been added.

III. The standard of attainment both for Pass and Honours will be the same as that required for the M.A. Degree in the subjects included in the University curriculum; and in the subjects not at present included in the curriculum, an analogous standard will be aimed at.

IV. Any Candidate who passes in four subjects (one at least being a language), or gains Honours in any one subject, and passes in two more (one of the three being a language), will receive the title of Literate in Arts (L.A.). It is believed that such a title will be of great use to women who propose to become teachers, as being equivalent to a diploma or licence to teach in the subjects in which they have passed or taken honours.

V. One subject may be taken in each year; and should the Candidate pass, this pass will count towards the title for the next year.

VI. The present centres are London, Halifax, and St. Andrews. Such other centres as may be afterwards fixed by the Senatus will be announced to intending Candidates. The next Examination will begin on Tuesday, 10th June, 1879, at Ten o'clock; and those who intend to become Candidates are requested to send in their names, with the subjects in which they wish to be examined, to Professor Knight, the University, St. Andrews, on or before 31st March, 1879.

VII. The Fee to be paid by Candidates coming up to be examined for the first time will be Two Guineas; but this Fee will be allowed to cover two years or periods of Examination; and such Candidates as have already passed a University Local Examination will be required to pay a Fee of only One Guinea. The Fee to be sent with application.

VIII. Candidates who obtain the title of L.A. will be required to pay an additional Fee of Three Guineas.

SUBJECTS OF EXAMINATION AND BOOKS RECOMMENDED TO BE READ.

1. ENGLISH LANGUAGE AND LITERATURE. — (*a*) History and Structure of the English Language. (*b*) Minto's Characteristics—prose and verse. (*c*) Morris and Skeat's Early English, vol. ii. (*d*) Chaucer's Knightes Tale (Clarendon Press Edition). (*e*) Bacon's Advancement of Learning, Books I. and II. (Clarendon Press). (*f*) Shakspeare's Hamlet (Clarendon Press).

2. LATIN LANGUAGE AND LITERATURE.—(*a*) Livy, Book IX. (*b*) Virgil, Æneid, X. (*c*) Cicero, Pro Lege Manilia. (*d*) Unseen passage. (*e*) Questions in Grammar. (*f*) Prose Composition. (*g*) Questions in Roman History and Antiquities.

3. GREEK LANGUAGE AND LITERATURE.—(*a*) Odyssey, Book VI.

(*b*) Herodotus, Book I. (*c*) Sophocles, Antigone. (*d*) Questions on Grammar. (*e*) An easy passage to be turned into Greek. (*f*) Questions in Greek History.

4. FRENCH LANGUAGE AND LITERATURE.—(*a*) Brachet's Historical Grammar. (*b*) Geruzez's Littérature Française. (*c*) Taine's Histoire de la Littérature Anglaise, vol. i. (*d*) Pascal's Pensées (first half). (*e*) Molière's Tartuffe. (*f*) Racine's Athalie. (*g*) Composition. (*h*) Questions in Grammar.

5. GERMAN LANGUAGE AND LITERATURE.—(*a*) Goethe's Faust, Part. I. (*b*) Lessing's Laocoon, i.–xiii. (*c*) Goethe's Iphigenie. (*d*) Schiller's Marie Stuart. (*e*) Grammar and Composition.

6. ITALIAN LANGUAGE AND LITERATURE.—(*a*) Dante's Inferno, i.–xvii. (*b*) Tasso's Gerusalemme, cantos i. and ii. (*c*) Manzoni's I promessi Sposi. (*d*) Hallam's History of Literature in Europe, Part I., chaps. ii. and iii. (*e*) Grammar and Composition.

7. COMPARATIVE PHILOLOGY.—(*a*) Max Müller's Lectures (First Series). (*b*) Peile's Primer. (*c*) Whitney's Life and Growth of Language (International Series).

8. HISTORY. — (*a*) Gibbon's Decline and Fall, chaps. liii.–lxxi. (*b*) Bryce's Holy Roman Empire. (*c*) Macaulay's History, first twelve chapters. (*d*) Green's Short History of the English People.

9. EDUCATION.—(*a*) Herbert Spencer on Education. (*b*) The Candidate must also bring up some standard work on the history or on the method of instruction in French or in German. (*c*) Currie on Common School Education. (*d*) Shirreff's Intellectual Education.

10. LOGIC AND METAPHYSICS.—(*a*) Whately's Logic. (*b*) Mill's Logic, Books III. and IV. (*c*) Hamilton's Reid's Intellectual Powers and Editor's Dissertations. (*d*) Locke's Essay, Books II. and IV. (*e*) Schwegler's History of Philosophy, sections i.–xxiv.

11. MORAL PHILOSOPHY.—(*a*) Plato's Philebus (Jowett). (*b*) Zeller's Plato and the Older Academy, chaps. i., iv., v., vi., x., xi., xii. (*c*) Aristotle's Nicomachean Ethics, Books I.–IV. (*d*) Kant's Theory of Ethics (Abbott), or Kant's Metaphysic of Ethics (Semple).

12. POLITICAL ECONOMY.—(*a*) Smith's Wealth of Nations, Books I., II., III. (*b*) Fawcett's Manual of Political Economy. (*c*) Senior's Political Economy.

13. MATHEMATICS.—(*a*) The First Four and the Sixth Books of Euclid. (*b*) Algebra as far as Quadratic Equations inclusive. (*c*) Elements of Trigonometry and Conic Sections.

14. NATURAL PHILOSOPHY. — (*a*) Parkinson's Mechanics. (*b*) Deschanel's Physics. (*c*) Herschel's Astronomy (smaller edition).

15. CHEMISTRY.—(*a*) Cooke's First Principles of Chemical Philosophy. (*b*) Galloway's First and Second Steps. (*c*) Miller's Chemistry.

16. MINERALOGY.—(*a*) Nicol's Mineralogy. (*b*) Brush's Determinative Mineralogy. (*c*) Dana's Mineralogy.

17. PHYSIOLOGY.—(*a*) Huxley's Elementary Lessons in Physiology. (*b*) Bennet's Text-book of Physiology. (*c*) Kirke's Hand-book of Physiology. (*d*) Dalton's Treatise on Human Physiology.

18. BOTANY.—(*a*) Balfour's Outlines. (*b*) Brown's Manual. (*c*) Hooker's Students' Flora of the British Isles. (*d*) Baker's Botanical Geography.

19. ZOOLOGY.—(*a*) Nicholson's Manual. (*b*) Rolleston's Forms of Animal Life. (*c*) Huxley's Elementary Lessons in Physiology. (*d*) Huxley and Martin's Elementary Biology.

20. GEOLOGY, PHYSICAL GEOGRAPHY, AND PALÆONTOLOGY.—(*a*) Juke's Manual of Geology. (*b*) Lyell's Elements of Geology. (*c*) Page's Advanced Text-book of Geology. (*d*) Nicholson's Life-History of the Earth. (*e*) Page's Advanced Text-book of Physical Geography.

Examinations in Hebrew, Biblical Criticism, Church History, and the History of Doctrines will also be held, should Candidates in these subjects present themselves. A list of the Books to be read in each of these subjects may be obtained on application to the Convener, Professor Knight.

HONOURS.

As a guide to those Candidates who may desire to take Honours in one or more of the above subjects in future years, the following catalogue of the subjects prescribed for 1879 is appended.

HONOURS SUBJECTS (1879).

1. ENGLISH LITERATURE.

   (1) Sir P. Sidney's Apologie for Poetrie. (2) Shakspeare's Tempest and Macbeth. (3) Milton's Paradise Lost, Books I. and II. (4) Johnson's Lives of Pope and Dryden. (5) Wordsworth's Critical Prefaces, with Book I. of the Excursion.

2. LATIN LITERATURE.

   (1) Tacitus, Annals, Books I., II., III., IV. (2) Plautus, Captivi. (3) Lucretius, Book V. (4) Virgil, Æneid, Books X., XI., XII. (5) Passages from Latin Authors not prescribed. (6) Latin Composition. (7) Questions on History, Philology, and Antiquities.

3. GREEK LITERATURE.

   (1) Homer, Odyssey, I.–VI. (2) Herodotus, Books I.–V. (3) Æschylus, Prometheus. (4) Sophocles, Antigone and Trachiniæ. (5) Plato, Republic, Books II., III. (6) Prose Composition.

4. French Literature.

The same as for the Ordinary Certificate; only a severer examination, especially in translating from English into French.

5. German Literature.

(1) Schiller's Gedichte. (2) Goethe's Aus Meinem Leben. (3) Vilmar's Geschichte der Deutschen Literatur; in addition to Ordinary Certificate.

6. Italian Literature.

(1) Dante, Divina Commedia, Purgatorio, Cant. 28–33; Paradiso, Cant. 1–17. (2) Goldoni, Commedie Scelte. (3) Vasari, Vita di Giotto, Brunelleschi, Lionardo da Vinci. (4) Macchiavelli, Istorie Florentine, Libr. 7, 8. (5) Capponi, Storia della Republica di Firenze, 2nda edizione, Tom. 1mo. (6) Translation at sight from authors not prescribed. (7) Composition. (8) Questions on Literature from Villari's History of Italian Literature, and Burckhardt's Renaissance in Italy.

7. Comparative Philology.

(1) Max Müller's 2nd volume on the Science of Language. (2) Peile's Latin and Greek Philology. (3) Papillon's Manual of Comparative Philology: in addition to the subjects for the Ordinary Certificate.

8. History.

(2) Hallam's Middle Ages. (2) The whole of Gibbon's Decline and Fall: in addition to the subjects for Ordinary Certificate.

9. Education.

(1) Marcel's Language as a Means of Mental Culture; or, (2) Schräder's Erziehung Unterrichts Lehre; or, (3) Hanschmann's Fröbel, die Entwickelung, &c.; or, (4) Write a Thesis on the best methods of teaching some one School subject—to contain not less matter than is equal to 32 pages of printing (octavo). The Thesis to be sent in at least twenty-eight days before the date of Examination.

10. Logic and Metaphysics.

In addition to the subjects for the Ordinary Certificate: (1) Berkeley's Principles of Human Knowledge. (2) H. Spencer's Principles of Psychology.

11. Moral Philosophy.

(1) Plato's Republic. (2) Aristotle's Nicomachean Ethics. (3) Spinosa's Ethics. (4) Butler's Sermons. (5) Kant's Metaphysic of Ethics.

12. Political Economy.

In addition to the subjects for Ordinary Certificate: (1) Mill's Principles of Political Economy. (2) Cairnes' Essays in Political Economy.

13. Mathematics.

(1) Algebra, Todhunter's Larger Work. (2) Trigonometry, Todhunter's Larger Work; Spherical Trigonometry, Todhunter, Chapters I.–VIII., inclusive. (3) Theory of Equations, Todhunter's Theory of Equations, Chapters I.–XIII., inclusive, omitting II. and XI. (4) Geometry of the Conic Sections—for the purely Geometrical treatment, Besant; for the Analytical, Salmon, Chapters I.–XIII., inclusive, with the easier parts of XIV., XV., and XVI. (5) Some knowledge of the properties of Determinants will be expected (Todhunter's Theory of Equations, Chapters XXV., XXVI., and XXVII. (6) The Elements of Analytical Geometry of Three Dimensions. (7) The Elements of the Differential and Integral Calculus as based on the Doctrine of Limits. *N.B.*—The Candidates will be tested as much as possible for soundness of elementary knowledge; extensive reading is of secondary importance.

14. Natural Philosophy.

Prof. Swan will indicate, on application, a course of reading in the following books:—

(1) Thomson and Tait's Elements of Natural Philosophy. (2) Tait and Steele's Dynamics. (3) Todhunter's Statics. (4) Routh's Rigid Dynamics. (5) Newton—three sections. (6) Parkinson's Optics. (7) Lloyd's Lectures on the Undulatory Theory of Light. (8) Airy's Tract on Light. (9) Balfour Stewart on Heat. (10) Clerk Maxwell on Heat. (11) Deschanel's Natural Philosophy.

15. Chemistry.

Any one of the three following subjects:—(1) The Lighting, Heating, Ventilating, and Disinfecting of Houses. (2) The Chemistry of Foods. (3) Mineral or Commercial Analysis.

16. Mineralogy.

One or other of the following:—(1) The modes of occurrence, and recognition of the natural products utilized in the Arts. (2) British Minerals and Ores.

17. Physiology.

(1) Carpenter's Human Physiology (8th edition, by Power). (2) Dr. Austin Flint's Physiology of Man. (3) Frey on the Histology and Histo-Chemistry of Man.

18. BOTANY.

(1) Vegetable Organography. (2) Vegetable Physiology. (3) Classification and Characters of the chief divisions of the Vegetable Kingdom. (4) Geographical Distribution of Plants. (5) An Elementary knowledge of the Geological Distribution of Plants. *Books recommended:*—(1) Brown's Manual of Botany. (2) Balfour's Class-Book of Botany.

19. ZOOLOGY.

(1) The General Principles of Zoological Science. (2) The Morphology and Physiology of the Orders of the Animal Kingdom, with the distribution of these in space and time. *Books recommended:*—(1) Nicholson's Manual of Zoology. (2) Huxley's Comparative Anatomy of the Invertebrata, and Comparative Anatomy of the Vertebrata.

20. GEOLOGY AND PHYSICAL GEOGRAPHY.

(1) The more important facts in Physical Geography which bear upon Geology (the constitution of the globe, the distribution of dry land and sea, mountains, volcanoes, earthquakes, phenomena of denudation, &c.). (2) The chief facts of Physical Geology (structure and formation of the crust of the earth, aqueous, volcanic, plutonic, and metamorphic rocks, divisional planes of rocks, folds, contortions, faults, unconformability, &c.). (2) The characters, divisions, and succession of the Geological formations of Great Britain, and the more important fossils by which they are distinguished. *Books recommended:*—(1) Huxley's Physiography. (2) Lyell's Elements of Geology. (3) Nicholson's Ancient Life-History of the Earth.

21. HEBREW.

(1) Psalms I.-XLI.; and Hosea, Amos, and Micah.

22. BIBLICAL CRITICISM—N.T.

(1) Wescott on Canon of New Testament—Introduction to the Gospels. (2) Discussions on the Authenticity of Fourth Gospel. (Godet's, Luchardt's, Sam. Davidson's, Bleek's (N.T., Eng. Tran., Vol. I.) Works are recommended; also, Supernatural Religion.) (3) Critical Exposition of the Three Synoptic Gospels, and of the Epistle to the Hebrews. N.B.—Candidates must have a *sound Grammatical* knowledge of Greek, and must have studied *critically* the prescribed portions of the Greek Testament.

23. CHURCH HISTORY.

(1) Scripture History. (2) Controversies in the fourth and fifth

centuries regarding the nature and person of Christ. (3) The causes and principles of the Reformation in the sixteenth century.

24. THEOLOGY.

(1) Müller's Christian Doctrine of Sin, Books I. and II. (2) Archbishop Thomson's Bampton Lectures on the Atonement. (3) Anselem's Cur Deus Homo; or, Bull's Defensio Fidei Nic., Sect I., II., cap. 1–8; or, Dorner's Doctrine of the Person of Christ, V. Div. 1st and 2nd Epochs. (4) Dr. Hill's Lectures, Book III.

General Note to Scientific Subjects.

With regard to these subjects, it is to be understood that the works quoted are intended simply as guides for study; and the Examination will, as far as possible, be conducted so as to test the practical knowledge of the Candidate.

CHAPTER XIII.

THE HIGHER EMPLOYMENT OF WOMEN. TEACHING:—SALARIES OF HEAD MISTRESSES IN ENDOWED SCHOOLS —TRAINING COLLEGE FOR HIGHER GRADE TEACHERS—COLLEGE OF PRECEPTORS' DIPLOMAS—TEACHERS' REGISTRATION BILL.

THERE are few questions of the day which have attracted more general attention, or provoked more ample and earnest discussion than that relating to the Employment of Women. The practical importance of this subject is daily forcing itself upon the notice of hundreds of ladies who are compelled from one cause or another to support themselves. I have elected to consider it in this chapter, chiefly in relation to the opportunities which may be open to women of obtaining employment, after receiving such an education as has been sketched in this handbook. The subject is not inappropriate, it seems to me, to a work of the kind, and may fitly follow the matter of the preceding chapters.

The question of women's employment, and, especially, of what may be termed their higher employment (to which alone I shall direct my attention) is one, about which, considerable controversy has arisen, even among those most willing to yield to women the fullest measure of liberty in entering into educational competition with men. I am not disposed to add one to the number of the controversialists by advocating here any particular line of work for a woman to engage in after she has completed her education. Were I to venture upon such a course this book, instead of affording me the guidance that I hope to receive from it by and by, would too surely prove a source of perplexity. A vast aggregate of opinion—too vast and conflicting, indeed, for me ever to attempt to grapple with—would certainly be opposed to mine in whatever views I might entertain as to those employments which, according to my way of thinking, should, and those which should not, be thrown open to women. To show what divergence of opinion obtains as to the kind of work which may be undertaken by an educated lady, let me give the following views upon this point offered by three of my friends. While discussing the purpose of my book with a gentleman who has devoted some attention to the practical side of women's employment, I asked, if he would suggest to me any remunerative occupations, besides those of which I might reasonably be expected to know, which he thought fitted for a lady of good education? His reply was, that he considered "Cookery" at present offered an excellent field for the display of a woman's abilities. Whereupon he proceeded to point out to me the several inducements which the art of Cookery offered to a woman of energy and talent. I applied to another friend of some experience, asking if he would bring to my notice any employments particularly suitable to ladies of education. He replied, that Domestic Service presented itself to his mind as a capital opening for "females of education and experience, gifted with tact," and, that so far from there being anything derogatory in the calling, he would have no objection to make one in the servants' hall—"with plenty to eat and to drink, and lots of leisure." Another friend suggested "Hospital Nursing" as affording fair prospects for women of culture and breeding, forgetting that, in order to become a hospital nurse, practical training, combined with other very special qualifications, is necessary. In fact, each of my friends suggested those very employments that a lady who had received such an education as has been sketched in this book would be least likely to enter upon. And they all ignored the fact, that education, thorough and complete, is ordinarily imbued with a loftier ambition than the cooking of omelettes and management of servants would imply, and that it generally seeks a wider and more congenial field for its employment than that contained within the four walls of a kitchen, albeit that kitchen may be conveniently placed in the inviting mansion of a lady of title.*

It is really astonishing to find what a low estimate is held by some persons of the value of female education. According to the views of not a few, women are only required to minister to the more selfish wants of men, and these satisfied, what need for woman's higher education? Women themselves are partly to blame for this seeming indifference to their intellectual endowments. As yet they have shown no particular vigour in overthrowing the old conservative notions, that the principal qualifications for refined life are to be clever at the piano, ready in the dance, prattling and fascinating in the drawing-room, deft at arranging things in the kitchen, and, above all, not too learned in literature, the arts, or sciences. A woman to bear her part well as "a lady" should be careful for nothing, in fact, but what is likely to make her pleasing in the eyes of men. Let all her efforts be directed toward securing their good opinion, and she may rest and be thankful, leaving "the morrow to take thought for the things of itself." Hence it too frequently arises, that, when a lady is compelled to make shift for herself, she lacks skill to discover, or even energy to prosecute, a scheme which might perchance place

* See an article in a recent number of a so-called "society journal," bearing the title of 'Vanity Fair,' wherein an "eminent writer" (I may explain that the term is copied from the pages of the periodical itself, and is evidently intended to denote the rank, and not the literary qualifications of the writer of the article), sets forth the various inducements that Domestic Service offers to gentlewomen.

her on the road to independence. She has received no special training—in the great majority of cases, no thorough education to stand in lieu of such training—and has been taught from a child to be dependent upon others; so that when the death of a father or husband throws her upon the world, she is to all intents and purposes helpless, and utterly unprepared to earn her own living. Then she listens to the suggestions of writers of her own sex—well-intentioned ladies who dabble in periodical literature to advertise their own freedom from more engrossing cares—to undertake those offices ordinarily reserved for the uneducated and uncultured classes. She pores over the advertisement columns of the daily Press, seeking an outlet for her untrained labour, and, in nine cases out of ten, pays the penalty of being swindled in her anxiety to sell that for which practically there is no demand. She wearies friends with oft-repeated applications to secure employment for her—where, or in what manner, she cares not—only to learn from painful experience that friends, like other people, are, for the most part, only disposed to help those who are in a position to help themselves. At length, as the only alternative to charity or destitution, she accepts of some humble position for which no particular qualifications are needed. In this she continues, may be supporting some dearly-loved child, presently to be left to the rude mercies of the world, until in sorrow she ends her days, bitterly condemning that pernicious principle which, in earlier life, led her to believe that the free co-operation of her sex in the industrial life of society is a thing to be shunned and overcome.

It is difficult to write altogether dispassionately of those who would make light of the efforts now being made to advance the cause of women's better education. It is still more difficult to bring oneself to speak calmly of the people who say that woman's chief mission is to cook, to sew, to sing, to play, to be always merry, and to look pretty. Have such persons, it may be asked, ever given a thought to the widespread misery that lies around them because of the too-frequent adoption of this most vicious creed? Within the circle of my own acquaintance, I know of instances where ladies, reduced by misfortune to a condition of dependence—ladies by birth and ladies by education, in so far that they were trained to believe that an all-round smattering of knowledge represents the proper standard of a "lady's" education—I know of instances, I repeat, where such women are little short of begging food. They have become so utterly unstrung by sudden reverse of fortune, and the discovery of their inability to undertake any kind of work which will bring in money, that, by degrees, they have sunk into a state of stoical indifference as to their condition, and have been brought to lie at the feet of friends for that bread which, if thoroughly educated, they should be capable of earning for themselves. If there be no other virtue in education, at least it has this one—it brings strength in the day of adversity. It enables men—and I should hope women, too, else this little book will have been written in vain—to bear themselves bravely, to brace themselves to action, to stand determined not to succumb, come what may, so long as strength and the power of thought shall be permitted them.

Circumstances and the duties of my calling have brought me much in contact with "ladies" having to earn their own living, and I have been greatly struck with the number of them who fail to obtain remunerative employment, because of their utter inability to perform any kind of skilled labour. Their previous training has been directed to no definite end but that of marriage, and beyond this point it has never been their business to look, until the day came which left them homeless. They had picked up a little of this and a little of that, could speak a little French and German, could draw a little, and play the piano a little, knew a little of one thing and a little of another; but not one single branch of knowledge had they learned thoroughly. To paraphrase an everyday expression, they were Joans of all trades and mistresses of none. They were ready, indeed, to undertake all kinds of work that might fall into their hands—literary work, drawing for the wood-engraver, translating for the publisher, designing for the manufacturer, painting for the potter, book-keeping for the merchant; and last not least, they were eager at once to enter upon the arduous business of imparting instruction to others, without so much as being able to advance the slightest testimony as to their fitness satisfactorily to undertake, leave alone to perform, either of these offices. Women should know, and doubtless they do know, only, when misfortune falls upon them, they are slow to recognize the fact, that employers require somewhat more than the mere *ipse dixit* of a person to testify to his or her competence to fulfil a certain function which he or she may be desirous of acquiring. "Produce to us evidence of your capability" is a very common request made by employers to applicants for work; "show us that you are able to do exactly what we require to be done, and we shall have no difficulty as to the rest." Let women who desire to obtain employment now, or who may have to seek it in the future, follow the example of most men who have to work: let them first of all seek out some occupation for which they have a special aptitude and liking, and let them use their utmost endeavours to fit themselves for that occupation. Let them disabuse themselves of the silly notion that it is unbecoming in ladies to educate themselves in any other branches of knowledge save those included in the absurd and misleading phrase—"female accomplishments." Let them strive earnestly for thoroughness in their studies, in whatever directions those studies may lead them. Let them aim at attaining a high standard of proficiency in their general work at college or school, and the utmost excellence that is permitted them in any department of knowledge to which they may elect to devote special attention, whether it be Literature, or Art, or Science, or Music, or the study of Languages, or any other parts of a liberal education. Then, should the day come when they are compelled to support themselves, they will find that they have capital to work upon. They will have received a sound general education to begin with, and, in reserve of that, they will have acquired a special qualification for certain kinds of work for which there is always some demand. Earnestness in the study of Literature, for instance, might pave the way to profitable occupation of a literary kind. Accuracy and thoroughness in the knowledge of Music must always be of considerable value. And so with respect to Art (Art, I mean, in its lesser divisions) and an intimate acquaintance with foreign Languages. Women must always be prepared to encounter the like difficulties that men experience in obtaining suitable employment at the very moment when it may be needed; but they will be infinitely better prepared to surmount those difficulties, if they have educated themselves upon the chance of having one day to meet them, than if they have devoted years of precious leisure only to frivolity and pleasure.

I remarked at the beginning of this chapter that I had no intention of constituting myself an advocate of any special lines of work suitable for women after they have completed their education. Those who may have followed me, then, in the hope that I was about to communicate something new concerning higher female employments will be disappointed. All that I propose here to do is to consider the facilities that may be within reach of women of placing themselves on the high-road that leads to profitable occupation. And first of all, with the reader's permission, I will deal with that most important and honourable profession of Teaching, for which women have great inherent advantages. Indeed, they may be called Nature's own teachers: * they are careful and persevering with young children, added to which, they are possessed of endless patience. At present, the majority of women take up teaching against their will, and, as it were, unexpectedly. Excepting a few enthusiasts or noble-hearted philanthropists, few women become teachers if they can avoid it.† And yet it is the profession of all others offering the greatest inducements to well-educated, well-trained women. To use a vulgar but oft-spoken expression, "there is money in it." As yet, parents are only just awakened to the necessity of insisting on a better system of education for girls; by and by, when that system has been perfected, and we have the same kind of instruction accorded them as is permitted to boys, the demand for properly-qualified schoolmistresses will be an hundred-fold greater than it is now. And even now the demand is in excess of the supply. "The demand for good teachers increases," writes the Principal of Newnham Hall, in her last report upon the progress of that institution. "We have very great difficulty in procuring the right sort of women to fill the vacancies at our school," writes another lady. "From many quarters comes the cry that, although the supply of male teachers fairly meets the present demand, qualified schoolmistresses are difficult to obtain, and even more difficult to retain," remarks a writer in the daily Press. "There is a lamentable dearth of properly-qualified candidates for the honourable office of schoolmistress, nor can some of the provincial school-boards obtain what they want on any terms," declares another cor-

* Report of the Schools Inquiry Commission on the Education of Girls.
† Ibid.

respondent of a London daily newspaper. Vacancies for well-informed teachers there are in plenty; but there are few properly qualified ladies to fill them. And why? Because women still persist in looking upon tuition as an occupation of a strictly provisional, intermediate, and temporary character, only to be resorted to from sheer necessity. If they continue to hold to this dishonouring view of an honourable calling, they must not be surprised to find that the salaries of female teachers remain low in comparison with those paid to male tutors, or that the office of governess does not increase in dignity, or secure that respect to which it is justly entitled. If ladies will but bring themselves to look forward to engaging in tuition as men look forward to obtaining masterships in the Public Schools, they would find that the profession of schoolmistress would soon attain to a rank the equal in importance of any profession which men seek to enter. That even under existing circumstances the profession is one not to be lightly esteemed for the pecuniary prospects it presents may be ascertained from a perusal of the annexed paper, kindly placed at my disposal by Miss Brough, the Secretary of the "Teachers' Training and Registration Society."*

* The Council of the Girls' Public Day School Company advertised in November, 1877, for three Head Mistresses for schools which the Company were about to open. Following is an extract from the particulars given in the advertisement:—"The emoluments of the Head Mistress will consist in each case of a fixed stipend of 250*l.* per annum, together with a capitation fee of 1*l.* for every pupil in the school above the number of one hundred up to two hundred, and of 1*l.* 10*s.* for every pupil above the number of two hundred up to three hundred."

Here is an extract from the advertisement columns of the *Daily News* of January 15, 1879:—"The King's Schools, Warwick.—The Managers of the Girls' School are prepared to receive applications for the office of Head Mistress of the Girls' School, which will be opened after Easter next. The Head Mistress will receive a stipend of 100*l.* a year, and a residence will be provided for her. She will also receive an annual capitation fee of 1*l.* per girl for every girl in the school."

GIRLS' SCHOOLS, WITH SPECIAL REGARD TO SALARIES OF HEAD MISTRESSES.

(As recommended by the Endowed Schools Commission.)

Name of School.	No. of Pupils.	Pupils' Fees.	Head Mistresses' Emoluments.				Pupils' Exhibitions.
			Fixed Salary.	Capitation Fee.	Minimum.	Maximum.	
*Ambleside, Westmoreland	60	3*l.* to 6*l.*	75*l.*	1*l.* to 3*l.*	135*l.*	225*l.*	.. ..
*Bedford—Town School	200	1*l.* 10*s.* to 4*l.*	100*l.*	10*s.* to 3*l.*	200*l.*	700*l.*	100*l.* a year.
*Bedford—High School	100	6*l.* to 10*l.*, 10*l.* to 20*l.* (above 12).	Not fixed	Not fixed	..	..	100*l.* a year.
*Bradford, York	..	6*l.* to 10*l.*	120*l.*	As may be fixed by Governors.	..	..	Not to exceed 120*l.* a year in all.
*Bristol—Red Maids	80 boarders	None	Not fixed	Not fixed	..	..	100*l.* a year.
*Bristol—Whitson's (two schools)	..	30*s.* to 3*l.*, 3*l.* to 5*l.*	50*l.*	Not fixed	..	..	.. ..
*Bristol—Colston's School	200	2*l.* to 4*l.*	50*l.*	15*s.* to 1*l.* 10*s.*	200*l.*	350*l.*	200*l.* a year.
*Burton-on-Trent	150	2*l.* to 5*l.*	50*l.*	15*s.* to	163*l.*	..	.. ..
Bow	200	3*l.* to 6*l.*	75*l.*	15*s.* to	225*l.*	..	100*l.* a year.
*Brentwood, Essex	100	2*l.* to 4*l.*	50*l.*	1*l.* to 2*l.*	150*l.*	250*l.*	.. ..
*Burlington, Westminster	No limit	2*l.* to 6*l.*	70*l.*	10*s.* to 1*l.* 10*s.*	..	..	100*l.* to 150*l.* a year.
*Cambridge, Cambridge	50 & boarders	5*l.* to 15*l.*	Not fixed	Not fixed.	..	..	Exemption from fees.
*Camden School, London	400	4*l.* to 8*l.*	75*l.*	15*s.* to 1*l.*	375*l.*	475*l.*	.. 200*l.* a year.
Clerkenwell (Brewers' Company), London.	300	3*l.* to 6*l.*	100*l.*	1*l.* to	400*l.*	..	Scholarships of 10*l.* each tenable at School, aggregating 30*l.*, tenable elsewhere.
*Dolgelly, Wales	80	2*l.* to 5*l.*	70*l.*	10*s.* to 1*l.* 10*s.*	110*l.*	190*l.*	50*l.* a year, tenable elsewhere.
†Dulwich—Alleyn's High School	250	8*l.* to 16*l.* above.	100*l.* to 150*l.*	1*l.* 5*s.* to 2*l.* 10*s.*	412*l.* 10*s.*	775*l.*	250*l.* after School has been open six years.
†Dulwich—Alleyn's Middle School	250	2*l.* to 5*l.*	50*l.*	7*s.* 6*d.* to 1*l.*	143*l.* 7*s.* 6*d.*	300*l.*	One-fourth of Capitation money.
*Exeter—Maynard's Girls' School	100	6*l.* to 15*l.*	100*l.*	3*l.* to 6*l.*	400*l.*	700*l.*	Exemption from fees.
*Exeter—Episcopal Middle School	..	2*l.* to 4*l.*	50*l.*	Not fixed, not less than $\frac{1}{3}$ tuition fees.	..	..	Exemption from fees.
*Great Crosby, Lancaster	About 100	5*l.* to 10*l.*	120*l.*	2*l.* to 4*l.*	320*l.*	520*l.*	.. ..
*Grey's Thurrock, Essex	75 & boarders	3*l.* to 5*l.*	50*l.*	1*l.* to	125*l.*	..	.. ..
*Grey Coat, Westminster	300	2*l.* to 4*l.*	80*l.*	10*s.* to 1*l.* 10*s.*	230*l.*	530*l.*	Exemption from fees.

*Hatcham, Surrey	200	2*l.* to 5*l.*	100*l.*	1*l.* to 2*l.*	300*l.*	500*l.*	About 900*l.* a year.
*Hoxton	300	2*l.* to 4*l.*	75*l.*	10*s.* to 1*l.* 10*s.*	225*l.*	525*l.*	About 300*l.* a year.
*Ilminster—High School—Somerset	100	10*l.* to 20*l.*	100*l.*	3*l.*	400*l.*	..	Exemption from fees.
*Ilminster—Town School	80	2*l.* to 5*l.*	50*l.*	1*l.*	130*l.*	..	.. ..
*Keighley, Yorkshire	..	4*l.* to 8*l.*	80*l.*	1*l.* to 2*l.*	..	..	Exemption from fees.
*Kingston-on-Thames, Surrey ..	150	2*l.* to 5*l.*	75*l.*	15*s.* to	187*l.* 10*s.*	..	.. ..
*Loughboro'—Burton Upper School	100	4*l.* to 8*l.*	100*l.*	1*l.* 10*s.* to 3*l.*	250*l.*	400*l.*	.. 40*l.* a year.
*March, Cambridgeshire	60	3*l.* to 6*l.* and 5*l.* to 8*l.*	75*l.*	1*l.* to	135*l.*	..	About 40*l.* (i. e. 80*l.* shared with boys).
*Newport	60	3*l.* to 6*l.*	60*l.*	1*l.* to	120*l.*	..	120*l.* a year rateably between boys and girls.
*North London Collegiate School	400	10*l.* to 24*l.*	100*l.*	2*l.* to 3*l.*	900*l.*	1300*l.*	.. 200*l.* a year.
*Newcastle-under-Lyne	100	4*l.* to 6*l.*; under 14, 2*l.* to 5*l.*	75*l.*	1*l.* to	175*l.*	..	Exemption from fees.
†Reading—Kendrick Schools ..	100	3*l.* to 5*l.*	Not fixed	Not fixed.	..	..	Exemption from fees.
*Roan Schools, Greenwich	300	3*l.* to 6*l.*	100*l.*	1*l.* to 2*l.*	400*l.*	700*l.*	About 250*l.* a year.
*Stamford—Browne's Middle School	100 & boarders	3*l.* to 8*l.*	100*l.*	2*l.* to 4*l.*	300*l.*	500*l.*	50*l.*
*St. Helen's, Lancaster	..	4*l.* to 8*l.*	100*l.*	2*l.* to 4*l.*	..	..	.. ..
*St. Giles', Cripplegate, London ..	250	2*l.* 10*s.* to 6*l.*	100*l.*	10*s.* to 1*l.* 10*s.*	225*l.*	475*l.*	.. 100*l.* a year.
*St. Clement's Danes, London ..	150	4*l.* 10*s.* to 8*l*	100*l.*	1*l.* to 3*l.*	250*l.*	550*l.*	.. 210*l.* a year.
*St. Martin's-in-the-Fields, London	150	2*l.* to 5*l.*	80*l.*	10*s.* to 1*l.* 10*s.*	155*l.*	305*l.*	.. 100*l.* a year.
†St. Paul's, London	300	20*l.* to 30*l.*	200*l.*	3*l.* to 6*l.*	1100*l.*	2000*l.*	.. 700*l.* a year.
Sir John Cass' Aldgate Schools ..	..	2*l.* to 4*l.*	100*l.*	1*l.* to	..	..	About 800*l.* a year.
Sir John Cass' Hackney Schools	250	4*l.* to 8*l.*	100*l.*	1*l.* 10*s.*	475*l.*	..	About 250*l.* a year.
*Totnes, Devon	80	3*l.* to 5*l.*	50*l.*	1*l.* 10*s.* to	170*l.*	..	.. ..
*Taunton—Somerset	..	3*l.* to 6*l.*	40*l.*	1*l.* to	..	..	Exemption from fees.
*Thetford	40	2*l.* to 5*l.*	75*l.*	1*l.* to 3*l.*	115*l.*	195*l.*	.. ..
*Thornton, near Bradford, York ..	50	1*l.* 10*s.* to 4*l.*	40*l.*	15*s.* to	77*l.* 10*s.*	..	.. ..
*Uffculme	..	6*l.* to 15*l.*	Not fixed	Not fixed.	..	..	Exemption from fees.
*Wallingford, Berkshire	50	2*l.* to 5*l.*	75*l.*	15*s.* to	112*l.* 10*s.*	..	Exemption from fees.
*Westminster, London	120	3*l.* to 5*l.*	100*l.*	1*l.* to 2*l.*	220*l.*	340*l.*	Exemption from fees.
*Warwick, Warwickshire	80	2*l.* to 4*l.*	100*l.*	15*s.* to	160*l.*	..	50*l.* tenable at School, 100*l.* elsewhere.
*West Ham (Sarah Bonnell), Essex	200	2*l.* to 5*l.*	60*l.*	1*l.* to 2*l.*	260*l.*	460*l.*	Exemption from fees.
*Wyggeston, Leicester	200	4*l.* to 8*l.*	100*l.*	1*l.* to 3*l.*	300*l.*	700*l.*	.. ..
*Wakefield, Yorkshire	100	6*l.* to 10*l.*	100*l.*	1*l.* 10*s.* to 3*l.*	250*l.*	400*l.*	140*l.* a year.

* The schemes for those schools marked with an asterisk have passed into law.

† The schemes for these schools have become law, but no steps have yet been taken to carry such schemes into effect. (See Note at foot of Chapter IV.)

The Society to which I am under obligation for the foregoing particulars is doing a good work in making provision for the Training and Registration of Teachers for Higher-grade schools. It has recently established a College * with the view of training ladies who have completed their school education for the profession of teaching.

The following is the course of study laid down for the Students, as stated in the prospectus of the College :—

COURSE OF STUDY.

Upper Division.

Theory and Practice of Education.

The Lectures on the *Theory of Education* will treat of the Characteristics of Childhood—mental, moral, and physical. *The Mind*—the mode and order in which the mental faculties are developed, and may best be trained, the faculties which are specially exercised by the study of different subjects. *Moral qualities*—manner in which the cultivation of good, and the repression of bad qualities may best be carried out. Methods which have been found successful in cultivation of obedience, diligence, love of order, &c.

Physical Education.—Use of drill and of regulated physical exercises; proper positions of the body while engaged in different studies; precautions to be observed in not overstraining the body; discussion of the question of punishments.

The advanced lectures on these subjects will show what modern thinkers and theorists have held, and how far practical teachers have been able to carry out their theories.

The *Practice of Education* will include lectures on Method, giving graduated courses of instruction for such subjects as reading, writing, arithmetic, geography, language, &c., and suggesting courses for advanced subjects. This plan will enable teachers to know the steps by which they ought to proceed, in order to make the subjects of instruction effective as instruments of education.

These lectures will be illustrated by Model Lessons, given by experienced teachers. In these lessons, the points to be noticed will be indicated by the lecturer. The students will receive instruction as to

* Temporary address :—Skinner Street, Bishopsgate Street, E.C.

what constitutes a good, and what a bad lesson; and they will be called upon both to teach, and to criticise (under proper direction) the teaching of others.

The attention of the students will also be called to the art of questioning, as an essential part of teaching; to the illustration of lessons by description and by drawing on the blackboard; to the proper uses to be made of maps, diagrams, objects, and other mechanical appliances.

The practice lessons given by the students will teach them how to manage classes of different sizes; and under the superintendence of the Mistress of Method, they will learn school organization, the making of time-tables, the assigning of work to assistants, &c.

In the lectures on the *History of Education*, accounts will be given of the theories and practice of the best known Educational Reformers; and it will be shown what is meant by the "systems" of Jacotot, Stowe, Pestalozzi, Fröbel, &c. It will also be discussed how far these systems are, and can be, adopted in England, and to what circumstances they are particularly applicable. The lectures to the advanced students will discuss special systems applied to the teaching of music, drawing, mathematics, and foreign languages.

Human Physiology and Hygiene will be considered with particular regard to the laws of health—the treatment of children, their common diseases, need for rest, for exercise, for fresh air, good food, &c.

With the view of preparing teachers to give these lessons in an orderly and methodical manner, a special course of Logic is provided.

MIDDLE AND LOWER DIVISIONS.

Theory and Practice of Education.
English Language and Literature.
History and Geography.
Mathematics.
Arithmetic.
Languages—
Greek, Latin, French, German.

Mental Science—
Logic and Laws of Health.
Political Economy.
Natural Science—
Physiology.
Botany.
Astronomy.
Physics.

Following are the Regulations which applied to candidates for admission to the College in January, 1879. They were required either to pass an Entrance Examination or to produce certificates of having passed one or other of the undermentioned examinations, viz. :—

FOR THE UPPER DIVISION.

The Oxford Further Examination.
Honours in the Cambridge Higher Local Examination.
The London Examination for Women.

FOR THE MIDDLE DIVISION.

The Oxford Preliminary Examination.
The Cambridge Higher Local Examination.
Honours in the Oxford or Cambridge Senior Local Examination.
Oxford and Cambridge Schools Examination.
First Class in the Pupils' Examination of the College of Preceptors.

FOR THE LOWER DIVISION.

Oxford or Cambridge Senior Local or other similar Examination.

The Entrance Examination was in the following subjects :—

(1) To read fluently and with good expression.
(2) To write a letter or essay on a given subject.
(3) Arithmetic.
(4) Physical and Political Geography of the British Empire.
(5) History of England, general outlines, with special questions on Tudor or Stuart period (*the period to be chosen by the candidate*).
(6) Any two of the following languages—Latin, Greek, French, or German.

FOR THE MIDDLE DIVISION AS ABOVE ; ALSO—	FOR THE HIGHEST DIVISION AS ABOVE ; ALSO—
Group A.—Literature.	
Johnson's Lives of Dryden and Pope.	Bacon's Essays.
Milton's Paradise Lost, Books III. and IV.	Shakspeare's Tempest.
Group B.—Mathematics.	
Euclid, Books I.–III.	Algebra.
Algebra — including quadratic equations.	Euclid, Books I.–VI.

Group C.—Languages.

Göthe's Lyrical Pieces.	Schiller's Death of Wallenstein.
Racine's Athalie.	Corneille's Cid.
Cæsar's Gallic War, Book I.	Cæsar's Gallic War, Books I. and II.
Xenophon's Anabasis, Book I.	Xenophon's Anabasis, Books I. and II.

*** Two only of these books were required.

Group D.—History.

Outlines of Roman History.	Outlines of Grecian History.
French History from the accession of Louis XIV. to 1800.	Hallam's Middle Ages.

Group E.—Mental Science.

Locke's Essay, Book III.	Logic.
Political Economy.	Political Economy.

Group F.—Natural Science.

Physiology. Botany, Astronomy, Physics. } Elementary Stage.	Physiology, Botany, Astronomy, Physics. } Advanced Stage.

*** Two of these subjects were required.

In connection with this subject of Teaching it may be mentioned that in June, 1877, a memorial was presented to the Universities of Oxford and Cambridge signed by a large number of influential persons, praying the Universities to establish an Examination for Teachers, and to grant diplomas to the successful candidates at these examinations. The memorial was favourably received by the Universities; and certain of the persons most interested in the experiment having been requested to draw up a draft scheme for the training and examination of Teachers by the Universities, a paper of suggestions was accordingly drawn up and submitted.

The whole question appears to be still under consideration; but the following Report of the "Teaching Memorials" Syndicate, of the University of Cambridge, will be read with interest by ladies who have in view hereafter to adopt Teaching as a profession :—

"The Syndicate appointed February 7, 1878, 'to consider the questions referred to in the Memorials published in the 'University Reporter' on the 2nd of November, 1877, and to report to the Senate whether it is expedient that measures should be taken by the University for the preparation and examination of Teachers,' beg leave to report that they have communicated with about a hundred and fifty persons engaged in, or specially interested in, Education, and have received numerous answers.

"They find a decided preponderance of opinion in favour of some kind of University action in the theoretical part of the training of teachers; with regard to University action in the practical part of the training they find less agreement.

"The Syndicate are prepared to recommend that lectures should be given, and an examination held by the University on the theory, history, and practice of Teaching, and that certificates of proficiency should be given by the University on the results of the examination.

"On the other hand, they do not think it desirable at present that the University should undertake the training of teachers in the practice of their profession.

"They are, however, of opinion that steps might be taken to ascertain the practical efficiency of the persons who have received certificates, and that their competence in teaching up to a certain standard might be attested by an additional certificate.

"The Syndicate hope to be able to present to the Senate before the conclusion of the Michaelmas term a scheme for the carrying out of these objects."

A general standard of proficiency for those who would enter upon the profession of Teaching is usefully indicated in the regulations for membership of the COLLEGE of PRECEPTORS. The reader may be reminded that this incorporation was instituted "for the purpose of promoting sound learning, and of advancing the interests of education, especially among the Middle Classes, by affording facilities to the Teacher for acquiring a knowledge of his profession, and by providing for the periodical session of a competent Board of Examiners, to ascertain and give certificates of the acquirements and fitness for their office of persons engaged or desiring to be engaged in the education of youth." The College admits women, not being under eighteen years of age, to ordinary membership who have passed either of the following examinations, viz :—

(*a*) Matriculation, and all Higher Examinations in any University of Great Britain, Ireland, or the Colonies.

(*b*) Examinations for Diplomas at Foreign Universities.

(*c*) Foreign State Examinations for Licenses to Teach.

(*d*) The "Senior Local Examinations" held by the Universities of Great Britain.

(*e*) The Examinations for the "First-Class Certificates" of the College of Preceptors.

(*f*) The Examinations recognized by the General Medical Council as exempting candidates from the Preliminary Literary Examinations of the various medical corporations.

(*g*) The examinations held by the Committee and Council on Education for Government Certificates.

Candidates who are not able to produce certificates of having passed one or other of the above-mentioned examinations, are required to pass an examination in all the subjects required for the "Diploma of *Associate*" (see below) excepting the Theory and Practice of Education.

The College of Preceptors is empowered by Charter to grant Diplomas to Teachers. These Diplomas are of three grades; viz. *Associate*, *Licentiate*, and *Fellow*. The qualifications required for the grade of *Associate* are somewhat higher than those required by the Committee of Council for Certificated Teachers of the First Class; and those for the grades of *Licentiate* and *Fellow* correspond as nearly as possible to those required for an Ordinary Degree and for an Honour Degree in Arts, respectively, at the principal Universities of Great Britain and Ireland. A distinctive feature of the Examinations for these Diplomas is, that in all cases the "Theory and Practice of Education" is an obligatory subject for each grade.* Following are the general regulations and subjects of examination for the Diplomas granted by the College.

EXAMINATION FOR DIPLOMAS.

General Regulations.

The Examinations of Teachers are held half-yearly—viz. in the Midsummer and Christmas vacations.

All Candidates, previously to being admitted to the examinations, are required to produce such testimonials of character and practical ability in teaching as the Dean shall consider satisfactory. Candidates for the *Associateship* must give evidence of having had at least one year's experience in teaching, or of having attended the Training Course for Teachers at the College for one year, and of having obtained a satisfactory Certificate from the Professor; Candidates for the *Licentiateship*, of having had two years' experience; and Candidates for the *Fellowship*, of having had five years' experience, before they can be admitted to the Examination.

Candidates must give to the Secretary at least one month's notice of their intention to present themselves for examination, and must specify the subjects, and, when necessary, the Classical Authors, in which they wish to be examined.

Candidates are not required to pass in all the subjects for a Diploma at one examination.

Subjects of Examination.

For the Diploma of Associate.

1. The English Language, with special reference to its grammatical structure and history; and Outlines of English Literature.
2. English History, with special reference to the leading constitutional changes.
3. Geography, Political, Physical, and Mathematical.
4. Arithmetic.
5. The Theory and Practice of Education (see page 232).

And one at least of the following subjects:—

6. *a.* Classics or a Modern Foreign Language (see pages 234 and 236).
   b. Mathematics (see page 234).
   c. Science (see page 235).

---

* It is worthy of notice that Women at present form a large proportion of the candidates at the examinations for the diplomas of the College of Preceptors.

Additional Subjects.—Candidates may be examined, if they wish it, in the following:—1. Scripture History; 2. The Theory of Music (Instrumental or Vocal Music may be added); 3. Drawing (see page 236).

Women may substitute either the Theory of Music, or Drawing, for Algebra and Euclid.

Women who have passed the examinations for women held by the Universities of Great Britain and Ireland, are exempt from examination in all the above subjects, excepting the Theory and Practice of Education.

Persons who have passed the examination for Government Certificates in the first or second division, taking the papers of the second year, are exempt from examination in all the above subjects, excepting the Theory and Practice of Education.

For the Diploma of Licentiate.

Subjects 1, 2, 3, and 4, as for the Associateship.

(Candidates who have already passed for the Associateship in these subjects need not be re-examined.)

5. The Theory and Practice of Education (see page 233).

Two of the following subjects, viz.:—

6, 7. {
- Classics (see page 234).
- Modern Foreign Languages—two at least (see page 236).
- Mathematics (see page 234).
- Science (see page 235).

Additional Subjects.—Candidates may be examined in the same additional subjects as for the Associateship.

Women may substitute the Theory of Music, or Drawing, for Mathematics.

Women who have passed the examinations for women held by the Universities of Great Britain and Ireland, and obtained Special Certificates of higher proficiency in two subjects at least, are exempt from examinations in all the above subjects, excepting the Theory and Practice of Education.

For the Diploma of Fellow.

Subjects 1, 2, 3, and 4, as for the Licentiateship.

(Candidates who have already passed in these subjects for the lower Diplomas need not be re-examined.)

5. The Theory and Practice of Education (see page 233).

Three of the following subjects:—

6, 7, 8. {
- Classics (see page 234).
- Mathematics (see page 235).
- Modern Foreign Languages—two at least (see page 236).
- Science (see page 235).

Additional Subjects.—Candidates may be examined in the same additional subjects as for the lower Diplomas.

Women who have passed the examinations for women held by the Universities of Great Britain and Ireland, and obtained Special Certificates of higher proficiency in four subjects at least, are exempt from examination in all the above subjects, excepting the Theory and Practice of Education.

Classification of Candidates.

A Class List, containing the names of the successful Candidates, will be published in the 'Educational Times of February and August in each year. In the English Language and Literature, English History, Geography, Arithmetic, and the "additional subjects," no Candidate will pass who obtains less than one-half the maximum of marks allotted to the subject. In the other subjects, separate papers will be set for each grade of Diploma, and Candidates will be classed accordingly. No Candidate will pass in these subjects who obtains less than two-fifths of the maximum of marks.

Candidates who obtain four-fifths of the maximum of marks allotted to any subject, will be classed as having passed in honours in the subject, and the same will be specified in their Diplomas.

Fees.

Associateship.—One guinea for each Examination for which the Candidate is entered, and one guinea when the Diploma is granted.

Licentiateship.—One guinea for each Examination for which the Candidate is entered, and two guineas when the Diploma is granted.

Fellowship.—One guinea for each Examination for which the Candidate is entered, and five guineas when the Diploma is granted.

I.—Subjects of Examination in the Theory and Practice of Education.

1. *Associateship.*

Candidates must give evidence of having been at least one year engaged in tuition, or of having attended the Training Course for Teachers at the College of Preceptors for one year, and of having obtained a satisfactory Certificate from the Professor.

Text Books Recommended:—(1) The Principles and Practice of Common School Education. By J. Currie, A.M. (2) Lessons in Elementary Physiology. By Professor Huxley, F.R.S. (3) Manual of Mental and Moral Science. By Professor Bain, LL.D. Part I. [Mental Science published separately, price 6*s.* 6*d.*]

(1.) The Elements of Mental and Moral Science. Definition and Division of Mind:—*Intellect*—Association by Contiguity, Association by Similarity, Compound Association, Constructive Association, Abstraction and Generalization. *Feeling*—Classification of Emotions. *Will*—Primitive Elements of Will, Growth of Voluntary Power, Control of Feelings and Thoughts, Formation of Habits. (Bain, Introduction, chap. i.; Book II., chaps. i.–v.; Book III., chaps. i., ii.; Book IV., chaps. i.–iii., and ix.)

(2.) Animal Physiology, with special reference to its application to the Laws of Health and to Physical and Mental Education. (Huxley.)

(3.) Lesson-giving and Criticism of Methods.—(Currie, Parts II. and III.) The Candidate will be required—

(*a*) To draw out a sketch of a lesson on some assigned subject.

(*b*) To suggest and discuss cases of difficulty in teaching and discipline, and to propose and criticise methods.

2. *Licentiateship.*

Candidates must give evidence of having been at least two years engaged in tuition.

Text Books.—As for the Associateship, with Elementary Lessons in Logic, Deductive and Inductive, by Professor Jevons, F.R.S.

(1.) Elements of Mental and Moral Science, as for the Associateship.

(2.) Outlines of Logic, in its application to Education. (Jevons.)

(3.) Physiology, as for the Associateship, with special reference to the Physiology of Health and Disease.

(4.) Lesson-giving and Criticism of Methods, as for the Associateship; with a thesis on the life, character, methods, and influence of some distinguished educator, to be selected by the Candidate; or a description of the organisation and methods of some school of repute, derived from personal inspection and examination.

3. *Fellowship.*

Candidates must give evidence of having been not less than five years engaged in tuition.

(1.) Mental and Moral Science, including Logic.—An advanced knowledge.

(2.) Physiology.—An advanced knowledge.

(3.) *Government of a School*, including Lesson-giving, and School organisation in all its departments.

(4.) *History of Education and Educational Methods*, with studies of distinguished Educators, English and Foreign; and a description and discussion of the methods and organisation of Schools and Colleges of note at home and abroad.

II.—Classical Subjects.

1. *Associateship.*

Any one of the following authors :—

Cæsar, B. G. I.–III. Virgil, Æn. I.–III. Sallust, Catilina.

With simple Latin Prose Composition, and, at the option of the Candidate, the Rudiments of Greek with St. John's Gospel.

2. *Licentiateship.*

Any one of the Latin, and any one of the Greek authors following :—

Livy, XXI. and XXII. ; Cicero, De Senectute ; Horace, Odes.

Xenophon, Anab. I.–IV. ; Euripides, Medea ; Homer, Iliad, I.–III.

With Latin Composition, and, at the option of the Candidate, any book of the Greek Testament.

3. *Fellowship.*

One prose and one poetical author in Latin, and the same in Greek, selected from the following :—

Livy, XXI.–XXV. ; Cicero, Pro Lege Manilia ; Virgil, Georgics ; Horace, Satires and Epistles.

Demosthenes, De Corona ; Thucydides, I. and II. ; Sophocles, Œdipus Rex ; Aristophanes, Nubes.

With any book of the Greek Testament, at the option of the Candidate, and Greek and Latin Composition.

N.B.—All Candidates in Classics will be expected to answer questions in grammar, geography, &c., arising out of the passages in which they are examined, and to show a thorough acquaintance with the history of the period.

III.—Mathematical Subjects.

1. *Associateship.*

Arithmetic.

The first four books of Euclid, with deductions.

Algebra, including Quadratic Equations.

2. *Licentiateship.*

Arithmetic and Algebra.

Euclid, Books I.–VI. and XI. to Prop. xxi., or the subjects thereof.

Plane Trigonometry, with the Theory of Logarithms.

Conic Sections ; including the Equations to the Circle, the Straight Line, and the Conic Sections referred to rectangular coordinates.

3. *Fellowship.*

The following subjects in addition to those required for the Licentiateship :—

Higher Algebra, including the Theory of Equations.

Conic Sections ; treated by Pure or by Coordinate Geometry.

Spherical Trigonometry.

The Elements of the Differential and Integral Calculus.

IV.—Science Subjects.

1. *Associateship.*

Chemistry of the Non-metallic Elements.

With one of the following subjects :—

(*a*) Animal Physiology.

(*b*) Experimental Physics; including Heat, Electricity, and Magnetism.

(*c*) One of the following branches of Natural History :—1. Botany. 2. Zoology. 3. Mineralogy. 4. Geology.

(*d*) Elementary Natural Philosophy; including Statics, Dynamics, Hydrostatics, Hydraulics, Pneumatics, and Optics, so far as they can be treated by arithmetic, or by simple algebraical or geometrical methods.

2. *Licentiateship.*

Chemistry. A higher knowledge.

Animal Physiology. A higher knowledge.

With one of the following subjects :—

(*a*) Experimental Physics, as for the Associateship. A higher knowledge.

(*b*) A branch of Natural History, as for the Associateship. A higher knowledge.

Elementary Natural Philosophy, as for the Associateship. A higher knowledge.

3. *Fellowship.*

Inorganic Chemistry.

Animal Physiology. An advanced knowledge.

With one of the following subjects :—

(*a*) Experimental Physics, as for the Licentiateship. An advanced knowledge.

(*b*) A branch of Natural History, as for the Licentiateship. An advanced knowledge.

(*c*) Natural Philosophy and Astronomy, treated mathematically.

V.—Modern Foreign Languages.

1. *Associateship.*

Correct Pronunciation, tested by reading aloud.
General Knowledge of Grammar.
Translation of Prose into English.
Translation into the Foreign Language, &c.

2. *Licentiateship.*

Correct Pronunciation, tested by reading aloud and by conversation.
Thorough Knowledge of Grammar.
Translation of Prose and Verse into English.
Translation into the Foreign Language.

3. *Fellowship.*

The following subjects in addition to those required for the Licentiateship :—
Original Composition in the Foreign Language.
General Knowledge of the Literature of the Foreign Language.

VI.—Drawing.

(*a*) Every Candidate must make a fair copy of a subject in outline, and also a drawing from a group of common objects.

(*b*) Every Candidate must answer questions on Perspective, and show a satisfactory knowledge of the common rules necessary for drawing objects in Perspective.

(*c*) Oil and Water-colour Painting may be added at the option of the Candidate.

Candidates being Members of the College may be examined, and may obtain Certificates for Special Proficiency, in any of the foregoing subjects. The Fee for such Examination will be Two Guineas.

N.B.—In all the subjects of Examination, questions will be put on their application to the principles and methods of education.

Parliament, during the present session, will be asked, I understand, to give its consent to a Teachers' Registration Bill, the principal object of which is to secure for Teachers (masters and mistresses alike) a recognized professional status. This Bill (which will be brought in by Dr. Lyon

Playfair) has been provided by the Teachers' Association.* If the Bill should happen to become law there will be an additional incentive provided to women to devote themselves to Teaching as a distinct and honourable profession.

* Dr. Lyon Playfair is President of this Association. Among its vice-presidents and committee are included head masters, actual and past, of Rugby, Clifton, Marlborough, Shrewsbury, Charterhouse, Christ's Hospital, and Uppingham, besides assistant masters of Harrow and Merchant Taylors', and officers of the great modern schools attached to University and King's Colleges. Amongst its members are public and private schoolmasters and schoolmistresses resident in all parts of the United Kingdom.

CHAPTER XIV.

HIGHER EMPLOYMENT—*continued.* ART AND MUSIC: ART SCHOOLS—NATIONAL ART TRAINING SCHOOL—THE SLADE SCHOOL OF UNIVERSITY COLLEGE—STUDENTS OF THE ROYAL ACADEMY. THE ROYAL ACADEMY OF MUSIC.

THE last occasion on which the late Sir Francis Grant presided at the distribution of prizes to the students of the Royal Academy he remarked,—"one of these days it will become necessary to have a ladies' Academy." The observation was not passed in mere compliment, but by way of directing attention to the high position now attained by women in the department of painting. Several ladies had recently won prizes and medals in the open competition of the Academy, and the President considered that this circumstance called for special notice. Indeed Art is a field in which women have found lately that they can well hold their own. The water-colour galleries especially testify to the prominence that has been unanimously accorded to female art in this country. Among amateurs it is not found that ladies draw less cleverly or pleasantly than men. Their studies from the antique at the South Kensington Museum, and in other galleries, are not found to be wanting either in force or correctness. Merely considered as a profession, painting is surely happier and more enjoyable than some other occupations in which educated women at present engage; and it is well worthy their attention to study the ways by which efficient instruction in Art may be secured.

There are no less than 143 Schools of Art scattered

through the United Kingdom, each under the direction of instructors who have obtained one or more certificates of proficiency from the National Art Training School. London contains eleven of these schools, one of which, the Queen Square School, under the direction of Miss Gunn, has earned a reputation for thoroughness in teaching, second only to that which attaches to the schools of the Academy itself. Subsidiary to the foregoing are 724 art classes held at various places. These figures are sufficient to show that there is no lack of schools, elementary, secondary, and of higher grade, where women may procure instruction in the practice of Art and in the knowledge of its scientific principles. It may be useful to give here a list of Metropolitan District Schools of Art:—

1. The Female School of Art, 43, Queen Square, Bloomsbury.
2. City and Spitalfields, New Bishopsgate Ward Schools.
3. St. Thomas' Charterhouse, Goswell Road.
4. St. Martin's-in-the-Fields, Castle Street, Long Acre.
5. Lambeth, Miller's Lane, Upper Kennington Lane.
6. West London, 204, Great Portland Street.
7. North London, Sandringham Road, Kingsland.
8. Islington, 21, Cross Street.
9. Stratford, Maryland Point.
10. Westminster, St. Mary's, Hyde Place, Vincent Square.
11. Westminster Royal Architectural Museum.

These schools, and others of the same grade elsewhere, are open in the evening from 7 to 9 and there are Female Classes at most of them. Applications for admission, prospectuses, or any other information should be made at the school in each district.

The instruction given at the NATIONAL ART TRAINING SCHOOL (South Kensington) comprehends the following subjects:—Freehand, Architectural, and Mechanical Drawing; Practical Geometry and Perspective; Painting in Oil,

Tempera, and Water Colours; Modelling, Moulding, and Casting. The classes for Drawing, Painting, and Modelling include Architectural and other Ornament, Flowers, Objects of still-life, &c., the Figure from the Antique and the Life, and the study of Anatomy as applicable to Art.

In connexion with the Training School, and open to the public, classes, meeting separately, for male and female students are established; the studies comprise Drawing, Painting, and Modelling, as applied to Ornament, the Figure, Landscape and still-life. The fees charged on admission to these classes are as follow:—Fees for classes studying for five whole days, including evenings, 5*l.* for five months, and an entrance fee of 10*s.* Evening classes: Female school, 1*l.* per session, three evenings a week. Teachers in private schools or families are permitted to attend the day classes for not more than three months on payment of 1*l.* per month, without payment of the entrance fee.

No students are admitted to these classes until they have passed an examination in Freehand Drawing of the 2nd Grade. Examinations of candidates are held weekly at the commencement of each session, and at frequent intervals throughout the year. These examinations are held at the School on Tuesdays, at 10.30 A.M. and 6.45 P.M. Unsuccessful candidates cannot be re-examined until after a month's interval. Candidates who have already passed an Examination in Freehand Drawing are admitted on application to the Registrar, without further examination.

The Annual Sessions, each lasting five months, commence on the 1st of March and the 1st of October, and end on the last day of July and the last day of February respectively. Students who have passed the required examination may join the School at any time, on payment of fees for not less than five months, but those who have already paid fees for five months may remain until the end of the scholastic year on payment of a proportional fee for each month unexpired up to the 31st July in each year. The months of August and September are not counted as part of the five months paid for. The months of August and September, one week at Christmas, and one week at Easter and Whitsuntide are vacations. The School is open every day, *except Saturday.* Hours of study—Day, 9 to 3.30; Evening, 7 to 9. Evening Classes for Females, on Tuesdays, Thursdays, and Fridays.

Classes for Schoolmasters, Schoolmistresses, and Pupil-teachers of Elementary Schools meet on two evenings in each week. Fee, 5*s.* for the session.

Students properly qualified have full access to the collections of the Museum and Library, either for consultation or copying, as well as to all the School Lectures of the Department.

The reader will find much useful information respecting Scholarships and the Courses of Study in the National Art Training School in the 'Art Directory' published by the Science and Art Department, which may be obtained on application to the Secretary, price Eightpence.

The Fine-Art School (Slade School) of University College offers instruction of a higher kind to women as well as men in Drawing, Painting and Sculpture. The accommodation at present is limited, and it is necessary that applications from Students for admission should be made before or as soon as possible after the beginning of each Term. The Fees for the General Course are as follows:—For the Session 19*l.* 19*s.*; for each Term 7*l.* 7*s.* All students (except those specially exempted by the Slade Professor *) on entering the Schools are required to draw from the Antique until judged sufficiently advanced to draw from the

* Mr. A. Legros.

Life. They are allowed to paint from the Antique or the Life according to their proficiency. Subjects for Composition are given by the Professor from time to time. The Students pursue such other studies as the Professor may direct, and are required to work under his direction from the Antique, from the Nude, or from the Draped Model as he may think best for them, according to their degrees of proficiency.

The general Regulations of the Slade School are as follows:—

The studios are open for the Students from 9.30 A.M. to 5 P.M. except on Saturdays, when all the Schools are closed at 2 P.M.

Two models sit in the Life-Schools for five hours every day from 10 A.M.

The male and the female Students work together in the Antique School and from the Draped Model.

The College provides seats and easels; but the Students must furnish themselves with all the materials and with the other appliances that they may require.

A Refreshment Room and other accommodation, as well as a female attendant, are provided for the exclusive use of Ladies.

No fees less than that for a whole Term will be received.

Students entered to the General Course are entitled to work every day from the Nude or the Draped Model for five hours from 10 A.M., and from the Antique, or at other studies up to 5 P.M., except on Saturdays. Instruction in Etching is given by the Professor. A printer attends every Friday to prepare the plates and take proofs of the Students' works.

Additional Courses of instruction are provided in the school by means of Lectures on (1) Anatomy, (2) Perspective, (3) Archæology. The Fees for attendance at these are 1*l.* 11*s.* 6*d.* and 1*l.* 1*s.*

Under the Will of the late Mr. Felix Slade, six Scholarships of 50*l.* per annum each, and tenable for three years, have been founded in University College, to be awarded to Students in Fine Arts not more than nineteen years of age at the time of the award, for proficiency in Drawing,

Painting, and Sculpture. Two of these Scholarships may be awarded every year. Ladies as well as gentlemen are eligible. Election is made in June of each year. Following are the Regulations for the Competition:—

Competitors must produce certificates of birth, showing that they will not be more than nineteen years of age at the date of the election.

They must attend the day-classes in the Fine-Art School of the College during the Session preceding the date of election; and no one will be admissible to the competition who does not enter those Classes before the 16th of November in each year.

Competitors must also produce evidence of having passed an examination in general knowledge, such as the Matriculation Examination in the University of London, or some other equivalent examination that may be deemed satisfactory by the Council; or in default, must pass an examination of an elementary kind in the following subjects:—

(i) The English Language.
(ii) English History.
(iii) Greek and Roman History.
(iv) Ancient and Modern Geography.
(v) The elementary processes of Arithmetic.
(vi) One Foreign Language, to be chosen by the Candidate, or one Book of Euclid.

This Examination is held at the College in the month of January in each year.

The competition for the Scholarships will consist in various works of drawing and painting, or drawing and sculpture, including composition, to be prescribed by the Slade Professor from time to time; and the exact period during which the competition works must be executed will be announced every year.

The following conditions are attached to the tenure of the Scholarships:—

(i) The successful works in the competition for the Scholarships are to become the property of the College.

(ii) The taking out of Tickets for, and attendance on, the General Course of Instruction in the Fine-Art Schools during the tenure of the Scholarships.

(iii) Attendance on Courses of Lectures at the College on Anatomy and Perspective, or in any other subjects relating to Art, as may be required by the Slade Professor.

(iv) The giving of assistance to the Slade Professor in the maintenance of order in the Schools, in superintending, under his direction, the younger students, and in taking charge of any Library and Collection of Works of Art which may be formed for the use of the Fine-Art Schools.

It would be well for ladies who desire to become students in the Slade School to bear in mind the recommendation already given, namely, that they should make application well in advance of the date at which they may wish to join the classes. At the beginning of last Term (October 1878), it was necessary to reject ten applications for want of sufficient accommodation.

The schools of the Royal Academy may be said to hold in relation to the study of the Fine-Arts a position analogous to that which the schools of the Universities occupy in regard to the acquirement of classical and other knowledge. Admission to the Academy schools is open only to those who have already received a considerable education in art. Following are the general regulations applicable to students who may desire to enter the schools:—

It is required that applicants for admission as Students in the departments of Painting, Sculpture, and Engraving should have already attained such proficiency as will enable them to draw or model well. An acquaintance with Anatomy (comprehending a knowledge of the skeleton, and the names, origins, insertions, and uses of at least the external layer of muscles) is indispensable.

A Painter is required to produce as a specimen of ability a finished drawing in chalk about two feet high, of an Undraped Antique Statue; or if of the Theseus or of the Ilyssus (the only mutilated figures admissible) it must be accompanied by drawings of a Head, Hand, and Foot. Similar specimens are required from engravers.

A Sculptor must send a model either in the Round or in Relief about two feet high of an Undraped Antique Statue, accompanied by a drawing in outline of a similar figure.

Prior to the delivery of the specimens referred to, the applicant must obtain from the Registrar, through the written request of any Member of the Academy, or other artist or person of known respectability, a printed form, the blanks of which may be filled up and delivered, with the drawings or model, at the Royal Academy, on or before the 28th of June or the 28th of December, to be submitted to the first Council held after those dates. If approved of, the applicant will be entitled to admission as a Probationer, and three months are allowed in which to prepare, within the Academy, a set of Drawings or a Model and Drawings. The time of attendance is from 10 A.M. to 3 P.M.

A Painter or Engraver is required, during his probation, to make a finished drawing, in Chalk, not less than two feet high, from an Undraped Antique Statue, together with an Outline Drawing or Drawings of the same figure anatomised, showing the bones and muscles, in one or two drawings, with references to the several muscles, tendons, and bones contained therein.

A Sculptor is required, during his probation, to produce a model, in the Round or in High Relief, not less than two feet high, from a similar figure, together with an Outline Drawing or Drawings of the same figure anatomised, showing the bones and muscles, in one or two Drawings, with references to the several muscles, tendons, and bones contained therein.

These Drawings and Models will be submitted to the Council, together with the Drawings, or Models originally presented by the Applicant for admission as a Probationer. Should they be considered satisfactory by the Council, the Probationer will then be admitted as a Student of the Royal Academy for seven years, and receive a ticket of admission from the Keeper.

Each Candidate to be a Student in Architecture must submit to the

Council four Drawings (not necessarily made for the occasion), viz., a Plan, Elevation, and Section or details of some existing building, or a sufficiently important portion of a building or other monumental structure, together with a tinted or shaded Drawing from a cast or in the round; such Drawings being declared by him in writing to have been wholly executed by him, and the same being attested by the person recommending him to the best of his knowledge and belief. The Drawings are to be accompanied by a certificate (on a printed form to be obtained at the Academy) from an Architect Member of the Royal Academy, of the Royal Institute of British Architects, or of any other public Institution for teaching Art and Science, certifying that the Applicant has followed up the study of Architecture and Architectural Drawing, and has acquired a reasonable degree of proficiency in the same. If such drawings and certificates are approved by the Council, the Candidate will be required to make, in the Academy, further Drawings of a similar nature to those sent in, at least one original complete Design, and a Sketch Design and Drawing from the cast, executed each in one day, in the Architectural Class Room, which Drawings, together with those originally submitted, will be laid before the Council; and if approved, the Candidate will be admitted as Student for seven years, in like manner as other Students.

Those who have been unsuccessful in their first endeavours, may renew their application at any subsequent period, by again going through the prescribed forms; but the Drawings or Models submitted must be different from those sent in on any previous occasion.

If any Candidate is found endeavouring to impose on the Academy, by presenting, as specimens of his talents, Drawings or Models not of his own performance, he will be declared incapable of being admitted a Student of the Royal Academy.

It should be remarked that all instruction in the Academy is gratuitous, the Student finding her or his own materials. Once admitted to the schools of this august assembly, there would seem to be nothing to hinder a woman from earning a fairly large income.

Music.

In no Profession does there seem to be less opportunity presented to ladies for acquiring, even a moderate independence in the way of income, than in that of Music.

The advantage of possessing interest in the profession, or of belonging to a family already known to the public, appears to be so great, that persons less fortunate have small chance of success, unless unusually gifted.* Musical instruction can now be procured so cheaply as practically to make the position of teacher in the profession of no avail in a remunerative point of view. Still, there is no reason why thoroughness and industry in this department of knowledge should not prove at least as valuable as the exercise of the same judicious qualities in other branches of work. The essential qualification for success in Music is a distinct and earnest love for the art. Nothing else can possibly serve the student who looks forward to practising it as a profession. In fact without the ambition to excel in Music, as a person might hope to excel in Painting, or Sculpture, or any other art, it would be well if the student were to turn her attention to some other occupation presenting fewer chances of disappointment and failure.

Higher professional training in Music is afforded by the Royal Academy of Music (Tenterden Street, Hanover Square), which gives systematic instruction in all branches of the art.† Students are admitted on examination at the commencement of each term and half-term. The terms are as follows: Michaelmas Term commencing on the fourth Monday in September; Lent Term on the third Monday in January; Easter Term on the Fourth Monday in April. The Annual Fee for the entire course of study is 31*l.* 10*s.*, or 10*l.* 10*s.* per term, with an entrance fee of 5*l.* 5*s.*, which charge, when a student has remained in the Institution for

* 'The Year Book of Women's Work,' by Louisa M. Hubbard.

† Since the reformation of the Academy in 1868 by Sir Sterndale Bennett, it has steadily increased in numbers. At present there are 369 pupils attending its classes.

three consecutive years, is deducted from the fee for the tenth Term.

The Course of Instruction includes Two Weekly Lessons in a Principal Study, one in Harmony, one in a Second Study when deemed desirable, one in Elocution for Singers, and the advantages of attending the Sight-Singing Class and Violin Quartet Class, and the Orchestral and Choral practices.

Students may choose any one branch of Music as a Principal Study. Should the branch for which a male Student enters be Composition, Organ, Pianoforte, or Harp, he may be required to learn, in addition, any orchestral instrument the Committee may choose for him.

All Students * are required to learn Harmony and Pianoforte; and all are required to attend the Sight-Singing Class; and, when competent, to take part in the Orchestral and Choral practices, and in all public performances of the Academy.

Should the branch for which a Student enters be Singing, he or she is required to attend the Elocution Class.

The classes for the English, Italian, French, and German languages, and for the Science of Acoustics, may be attended by any of the Students on payment of an additional fee of 1*l.* 1*s.* per term for either class.

On leaving the Academy, Students may undergo an examination. Should the examination prove satisfactory, they will receive a Certificate; and, in special cases, the additional distinction of being made an Associate of the Institution. There are several Scholarships and Exhibitions open to female Students of the Academy.

The Classes and Lectures, held and given at TRINITY COLLEGE, LONDON (61, Weymouth Street, Portland Place),

* Except Orchestral Students, competent to take part upon any instrument in the orchestral practice.

seem to be organized principally with the view of promoting Musical Education. The scheme of these includes every subject connected with the Science and Art of Music, viz. Choir Management, Harmony, Counterpoint, Form in Musical Composition, Vocal Music, Organ (with opportunities for Practice), Pianoforte, Stringed Instruments, Vocal and Instrumental Practice, &c.

Higher Musical Examinations for Women have been instituted at the College to provide a system of Certificates for Governesses and other Female Teachers. Separate or combined Certificates may be taken in any of the following subjects :—Harmony, Counterpoint, General Musical Knowledge, Pianoforte (or Organ), Solo Singing, &c.

CHAPTER XV.

HIGHER EMPLOYMENT—*continued.* THE PRACTICE OF MEDICINE: THE LONDON SCHOOL OF MEDICINE FOR WOMEN—COURSE OF INSTRUCTION AND FEES. THE EXAMINATIONS OF THE PHARMACEUTICAL SOCIETY.

WOMEN have now (at 30, Henrietta Street, Brunswick Square, London) a MEDICAL SCHOOL * of their own, which enables them to obtain a complete and qualifying course of medical study. The lecturers in the school are well-known medical practitioners, and, with one or two exceptions, recognized teachers in the schools attached to the metropolitan hospitals. Since its opening in October, 1874, forty-three women have been admitted, a number not small, when it is considered that until the year 1877 no hospital for the qualifying course of clinical instruction was open to female students, and no medical examination awaited them wherein they might demonstrate their knowledge. In the latter year these discouragements were removed, first by the action of the governors of the Royal Free Hospital in admitting women to the hospital practice, and the clinical lectures of the medical staff for an experimental period of five years; and, next, by the passage of the Act of 1876 (commonly known as Mr. Russell Gurney's Act), which enabled any recognized medical examining body to open its doors to women as well

* The formal sanction of the Secretary of State for the Home Department has been given to the resolution of the Senate of the University of London, recognizing the London School of Medicine for Women as one of the institutions from which certificates of attendance are accepted. Students of the school can therefore now be admitted to the examinations for the Medical Degree of the University of London.

as to men. In virtue of the power conferred by this Act, the King's and Queen's College of Physicians in Ireland admits women to examination for its Diploma, and recent proceedings by the Senate of the University of London have placed within their reach all the degrees which it confers, including, of course, those in medicine. No hindrance, therefore, now exists in the way of women becoming, if they so desire, duly qualified medical practitioners.

Ladies who may wish to prepare for the Medical Profession must pass one of the Examinations in Arts recognized by the General Medical Council, such an examination being compulsory before registration as a Medical Student. Among these examinations are :—I. The Oxford and Cambridge Local Examinations, Senior and Junior. II. The Senior Local Examinations for Honorary Certificates of the University of Edinburgh. III. The Local Examination for Honours Certificates of the University of St. Andrews. IV. The Examination in Arts of the Society of Apothecaries in London.* V. The Examinations for a first-class Certificate of the Royal College of Preceptors. VI. The Local Examinations of the Queen's University in Ireland. Certificates must in all cases include English Literature, Latin, Arithmetic, Algebra, Geometry, and also one of the following optional subjects: — Greek, French, German, Natural Philosophy. With a single exception, all these Examinations have been treated at length in this book. The exception is, the examination of the Apothecaries' Society, which need not engage the attention of the reader if she feels qualified to pass such an educational test as the following scheme of examination provides, viz. :—

(1) Writing from Dictation.
(2) English Grammar.

* Held on the last Friday and Saturday in January, April, and September.

(3) Writing a short English Composition, such as a description of a place, an account of some useful or natural product, or the like.
(4) Arithmetic. A competent knowledge of the first four rules (simple and compound), of Vulgar Fractions and Decimals.
(5) Questions on the Geography of Europe, and particularly of the British Isles.
(6) Questions on the outlines of English History, that is, the succession of the Sovereigns, and the leading events of each reign.
(7) Mathematics. Euclid (Books I. and II.), or the subjects thereof; Algebra to Simple Equations inclusive.
(8) Translation of a passage from an easy Latin author (the second book of Cæsar's Commentaries, 'De Bello Gallico,' for instance).

And to show a fair degree of proficiency in one, at least, but not more than four of the following subjects, viz. :—

(1) Translation of a passage from an easy Greek author (the first Book of the 'Anabasis' of Xenophon, for instance).
(2) Translation of a passage from X. B. Saintine's 'Picciola.'
(3) Translation of a passage from Schiller's 'Wilhelm Tell.'
(With questions on the Grammar of each subject.)
(4) Mechanics. Questions of an elementary character.
(5) Chemistry. Questions on the elementary facts of Chemistry.
(6) Botany and Zoology. Questions on the classification of Plants and Animals.

But doubtless it would be far more convenient for a lady intending to enter the London School of Medicine for Women, to at once offer herself for examination at one of the "Local Examinations" centres of the Universities.

Courses of Lectures are given at the School on Chemistry, Anatomy, Physiology, Practice of Surgery, and Practice of Medicine, and a course of Practical Anatomy with Demonstrations, Lectures on Clinical Medicine and Clinical Surgery are delivered at the Royal Free Hospital, where daily clinical instruction is given to the students.

Intending students should apply to the Dean (Mr. A. T.

Norton, F.R.C.S.) for a form of application for admission. No student is admitted to the study of Medicine who has not completed her eighteenth year; and every student on being admitted is required to sign an undertaking to conform to the regulations of the School, for the time being.

Following is the table of Fees:—

ORDINARY COMPOUNDER'S FEE:—The fee for the ordinary curriculum of non-clinical Lectures is 80*l.* if paid in one sum, or if paid in instalments, 40*l.* for the first year, 30*l.* for the second, and 15*l.* for the third. The courses of Lectures included in this fee are as follows:—Two courses each of Anatomy, Practical Anatomy, and Practice of Medicine, and one course each of Physiology, Chemistry, Practical Chemistry, Botany, Materia Medica, Surgery, Pathology, Midwifery and Forensic Medicine.

GENERAL COMPOUNDER'S FEE:—The fee of 90*l.* if paid in one sum (or the annual fees of 45*l.*, 35*l.*, and 15*l.*, if in instalments) entitle a student to attend, in addition to the classes mentioned above, one course each of Practical Physiology, Comparative Anatomy, Ophthalmic Surgery, Mental Pathology and Hygiene.

PERPETUAL TICKET:—Any student having paid either of the above Compounding fees is, on a further payment of 6*l.* 6*s.* entitled to attend, at pleasure, additional courses of the Classes respectively mentioned above. Materials for the practical classes are charged extra when additional courses are taken.

FEES FOR SEPARATE CLASSES:—The fee for separate courses of the non-clinical lectures is 8*l.* 8*s.* for each subject in the winter course, and 5*l.* 5*s.* for each in the summer course.

Students who do not hold a perpetual ticket, and who have attended regularly, may repeat any course on payment of 2*l.* 2*s.* for each course. Materials for the practical classes will in such cases be charged according to a fixed scale. The fee for each course of twelve lectures on Mental Pathology, Ophthalmic Surgery, and Hygiene, respectively, is 2*l.* 2*s.*

HOSPITAL FEES:—The fee for Hospital instruction extending over four years, and including annual courses of Lectures on Clinical Medicine and Clinical Surgery, is 45*l.* if paid in one sum, or if paid in instalments, 20*l.* for the first year, and 15*l.* for each of the second and third years, the fourth year being free. No student is admitted to the Hospital for less than one year.

Preparation for the Medical Profession occupies at least four years, during three of which the student must attend lectures at the School. The fourth year should be employed in Hospital work and in Practical Midwifery, Practical Pharmacy, and Vaccination, the fees for which are paid to the respective Institutions at which these subjects are studied. Until the resources of the school are more fully developed, it is proposed to have a partial rotation of classes, the curriculum being repeated as far as possible biennially, and the lectures for first-year's students being given annually. Clinical Clerks, Surgical Dressers, a Pathological Registrar, and a Prosector for the class of Anatomy are chosen from among the senior students without further fee.

Ladies not desiring to study Medicine with a view to practise, may, by permission of the Executive Council, attend the classes on payment of the fees, without passing the Examination in Arts, but such students will not receive certificates of attendance. All persons requiring information on subjects connected with the medical education of women, or with the residence of students in the neighbourhood of the School, should communicate with Mrs. Thorne, Hon. Sec., 30, Henrietta Street, Brunswick Square, W.C.

It may be mentioned that the London School of Medicine for Women has acquired by purchase a valuable Museum belonging to the late Dr. Blundell, which was formerly at Guy's Hospital, and there is also a large Museum at the Royal Free Hospital for the instruction of students. The nucleus of a standard library for the use of lady students has been formed since the foundation of the School, and has recently been considerably enlarged under the superintendence of Mrs. Garrett Anderson, M.D., who undertakes the duties of Hon. Librarian.

Without venturing to express an opinion as to the appropriateness of women engaging in the practice of Medicine, I may be permitted to quote the following remarks bearing on the subject, made by one who has had every opportunity of judging of the success likely to attend ladies who look forward to adopting that practice as a profession. Mrs. Garrett Anderson, M.D., in the Inaugural Address which she delivered * to the students of the London School of Medicine for Women, at its close said:—"Every woman who undertakes the study of medicine, in at all the right spirit, gains at once this solid advantage—she puts aside frivolity and accepts for herself a serious aim in life. But this, precious as it is, and underlying, as it does, all other gains, is not all. She accepts also freedom, not from parental control so long as she is young enough to need it, but from ennui and from an unnatural prolongation of the restraints of childhood. In the important question of marriage she is free, no longer forced to marry as the only way of entering upon adult life. She is also free from the fear of poverty. Once having mastered her profession, she is assured at least against want, probably even she is certain of being able to gain a respectable competence. And if, as I believe, these gains flow to the individual, surely society shares them. It is no trifling good to society to have, even here and there, frivolity displaced by seriousness, unnatural childishness by experience and the discipline which results from responsibility, and idle poverty by industrious competence."

As collateral to the matter which has just been discussed, it might seem not inappropriate to direct attention to PHARMACY as likely to open up employment of a higher kind to women. "There is nothing," remarked the 'Lancet,' in an article calling attention to this special subject, "in the process of education, or in the business of a pharmaceutical chemist, that would be unbecoming in a woman. For pur-

* October 1st, 1877.

poses of neat compounding she would be a serious rival. The success of a pharmaceutical chemist turns very largely upon the way in which dispensing is conducted, and the natural handiness and neatness of a woman would find ample field in it. Doctors are only waiting until dispensing can be done at reasonable prices by chemists to hand over the whole of their prescriptions to them. Perhaps the introduction of women into the trade may hasten this most desirable arrangement." By the Pharmacy Act of 1868, women were admitted to the examination, the passing of which legally qualifies them to practise Pharmacy, and the Pharmaceutical Society admits ladies, as we have already mentioned in a preceding chapter, as students to the lectures given daily at their rooms, 17, Bloomsbury Square, W.C. Admission to the Laboratory is, as we have also previously noted, denied to women, so that they must gain the requisite knowledge of Practical Chemistry elsewhere. This, however, should not be very difficult to obtain.

Ladies who desire to obtain Registration as qualified Pharmaceutical Chemists and Druggists must conform to the following regulations. They must first pass a Preliminary Examination * in the following subjects, viz. :—

Latin. Translation into English of a paragraph from the first book of Cæsar 'De Bello Gallico'; Latin Grammar.

Arithmetic. The first four rules—Simple and Compound; Vulgar Fractions, and Decimals; Simple and Compound Proportion; a thorough knowledge of the British and Metrical systems of Weights and Measures.

---

* Certificates of having passed the Local Examinations of the Universities of Oxford, Cambridge, Durham, or Edinburgh, the Examination of the College of Preceptors, or those of any legally constituted Examining Body previously approved by the Council, *provided Latin and Arithmetic be included in the subjects*, are accepted in lieu of this examination, and must be forwarded to the Registrar, with the fee of Two Guineas, for the approval of the Board of Examiners.

English. Grammar and Composition.

The quality of the Handwriting is taken into account in awarding marks.

The Fee for this examination is *2l. 2s.*, and persons are admitted to examination at the following centres, throughout Great Britain, at 12 noon, on the first Tuesdays in January, April, July, and October in every year:—

Aberdeen.	Cheltenham.	Inverness.	Norwich.
Birmingham.	Darlington.	Jersey.	Nottingham.
Brighton.	Douglas, I. of Man.	Lancaster.	Oxford.
Bristol.	Dundee.	Leeds.	Peterborough.
Cambridge.	Edinburgh.	Lincoln.	Sheffield.
Canterbury.	Exeter.	Liverpool.	Shrewsbury.
Cardiff.	Glasgow.	London.	Southampton.
Carlisle.	Guernsey.	Manchester.	Truro.
Carmarthen.	Hull.	Newcastle.	Worcester.
Carnarvon.		Northampton.	York.

Candidates must give notice to the Registrar of the Pharmaceutical Society (17, Bloomsbury Square, W.C.), on a printed form of application, to be obtained from him, and pay the fee not less than *fourteen* days prior to that on which the examination is to be held. Each candidate must state at which of the centres she desires to present herself.

The Board of Examiners in London meets for conducting the Qualifying Examinations in February, April, June, July, October, and December. Candidates must give notice to the Registrar, and pay the fee, on or before the first day of the month in which the examinations are to be held, and they will receive due notice of the date on which they will be required to present themselves. Each candidate for the Qualifying Examination must, at the time of giving notice, produce a Registrar's Certificate of Birth, and a certified declaration that for three years she has been registered and employed as an Apprentice or Student, or has otherwise for three years been practically engaged in the translation and dispensing of prescriptions. Printed forms on which this declaration is to be made may be obtained from the Registrar.

Having passed the Preliminary Examination, and conformed to all the foregoing regulations, the candidate may present herself for the qualifying examinations known as the Minor and Major Examination.

THE MINOR EXAMINATION.

(For Registration under the Pharmacy Act, 1868, as Chemists and Druggists.)

FEE THREE GUINEAS.

Candidates must have attained the full age of twenty-one years.

The following form the subjects of examination :—

PRESCRIPTIONS.—The candidate is required to read without abbreviation autograph prescriptions; translate them into English; and render a literal as well as an appropriate translation of the directions for use. To detect errors, discover unusual doses, and have a general knowledge of Posology; also to render in good Latin ordinary prescriptions written in English.

PRACTICAL DISPENSING.—To weigh, measure, and compound medicines; write the directions in concise language in a *neat and distinct* hand; to finish and properly direct each package. [*In awarding marks in this subject the time taken by the candidate in doing the work is taken into account.*]

PHARMACY.—To recognize the Preparations of the Pharmacopœia which are not of a definite chemical nature, and have well-marked physical characters, such as extracts, tinctures, powders, &c.; to give the proportions of the active ingredients and possess a *practical* knowledge of the processes, and the principles of the processes, by which they are made, and of the best excipients and methods of manipulation for forming Emulsions, Pills, &c.

MATERIA MEDICA.—To recognize specimens of roots, barks, leaves, fruits, resins, gums, animal substances, &c., used in medicine; give the botanical and zoological names of the plants, &c., yielding them, and the Natural Families to which they belong; name the countries and sources from which they are obtained, the officinal preparations into which they enter, and judge the quality and freedom from adulteration or otherwise of the specimens.

BOTANY.—To recognize the more important indigenous plants used in medicine. To possess a general knowledge of the elementary structure of plants, and the structure and distinctive characters of roots, stems, leaves, and their parts. To name and describe the various parts of the flower.

CHEMISTRY.—To recognize the ordinary chemicals used in medicine. To possess a *practical* knowledge of the processes by which they are produced, the composition of such as are compound, and explain the decompositions that occur in their production and admixture, by equations or diagrams. To determine practically, by means of tests, the presence in solution of the chemicals in common use, and explain the reactions which occur in each case. To possess a general knowledge of the laws of chemical philosophy, and a *practical* knowledge of the means of determining specific gravities, densities, and temperature, and of the instruments appertaining thereto, and the physical and chemical constitution of the atmosphere.

THE MAJOR EXAMINATION.

(For Registration as Pharmaceutical Chemists under the Pharmacy Act, 1852.)

FEE FIVE GUINEAS.

Candidates for this Examination must have attained the full age of twenty-one years, and have passed the "Minor" Examination at least three months previously.

The following form the subjects of examination :—

MATERIA MEDICA.—This comprises a *practical* knowledge of the methods of estimating the value of important drugs, of obtaining their active proximate constituents in a separate state; of identifying them and ascertaining their purity or impurity by tests.

BOTANY.—This comprises an intimate acquaintance with the parts of the flower, fruit, and seed; the functions and mode of arrangement of the different organs of plants; a knowledge of the general principles of classification, and of the Linnæan and De Candolle's systems. The candidate must be able to distinguish practically between each of the following Natural Orders:—Ranunculaceæ, Papaveraceæ, Cruciferæ, Malvaceæ, Leguminosæ, Rosaceæ, Cucurbitaceæ, Umbelliferæ, Compositæ, Gentianaceæ, Convolvulaceæ, Solanaceæ, Atropaceæ, Labiatæ, Scrophulariaceæ, Polygonaceæ, Euphorbiaceæ, Orchidaceæ, Iridaceæ, Liliaceæ, Melanthaceæ, Graminaceæ; and refer to their respective orders such specimens as may be shown to him.

CHEMISTRY.—This comprehends an intimate knowledge of the laws of chemical philosophy, a *practical* knowledge of the nature and properties of the elements and their compounds, both organic and inorganic, especially those used in medicine or the arts. The different combinations and decompositions must be explained by equations; also the *qualitative* analysis of the more important chemicals, e. g. Nitrates, Chlorides, Carbonates, Sulphates, Phosphates, Oxalates, Tartrates, &c., and the detection of impurities in them, and the *volumetric* estimation of the strength of all Pharmacopœia preparations in which standard solutions are ordered to be used.

An elementary knowledge of the properties of light, heat, electricity, and magnetism is also required.

Books and Memoranda are permitted in the practical portion of this Examination.

CHAPTER XVI.

HIGHER EMPLOYMENT—*concluded:* THE POST OFFICE.

I AM not sure that I am altogether right in including under the head of "Higher Employment" the few situations of a better kind in the Post Office open to women. When I say "of a better kind," I refer more especially to the appointments in the Savings Bank Department, and Receiver and Accountant-General's Office. The salaries of Female Telegraph Clerks, Counterwomen, and Female Returners are much too low to make these situations acceptable to a lady of any considerable education. The highest rate of salary to be obtained by filling either of these offices is 30*s.* a week, and the hours of attendance average eight hours a day. The commencing pay for each is 14*s.* a week.

Of Female Clerks in the Savings Bank Department, there are at present employed, 119, and in the Receiver and Accountant-General's Office, 50. The vacancies caused by retirements during the past year were, in the first named, 7, and in the latter office, 11. Vacancies, as they occur, are filled up by competition, the nominations to compete resting with the Postmaster-General for the time being. The examination is conducted by the Civil Service Commissioners, and following are the prescribed subjects for the competition, viz. :—

(1) Handwriting and Orthography.
(2) English Grammar and Composition.
(3) Arithmetic (including vulgar and decimal fractions).
(4) Geography.

Candidates under seventeen or above twenty years of age are ineligible.

The Salary in each office is as follows:—

2nd Class	40*l.*,	rising by	7*l.* 10*s.*	yearly to	75*l.*
1st Class	80*l.*,	,,	7*l.* 10*s.*	,,	100*l.*
Principal Clerks	110*l.*,	,,	10*l.*	,,	150*l.*

It is to be hoped that, at no distant day, Government will see fit to open up further means of livelihood to women, by admitting them to other appointments besides those belonging to the Post Office. The position of a clerk is one which most women are well qualified to fill, and the experiment of employing them on official work has resulted satisfactorily both here and in the United States of America.

In writing "Finis" to this chapter, I am anxious to have it understood, that throughout this work I have had but one purpose in view, namely, to place before persons in the same rank of life with myself all the information I could collect bearing on the matter of the better education of women in this country. Added to which I have touched upon the subject of women's higher employment. I have endeavoured to avoid all partisanship, and have expressed no opinion as to whether it is in accordance with the fitness of things for ladies to take degrees in the Arts, Laws, Science, or Medicine. All that I have desired to plead for, and do most earnestly plead for, is that we should have a better system of education provided for girls of the Middle class, generally,—for girls whose parents have to pay, and, oftentimes, to pay dearly for their daughters' education. In the columns of the *Daily News* of January 17, 1879, just as I was sending this book to the printer's, my eye fell upon the following paragraph:—"The Birmingham School Board yesterday adopted a scheme for a higher education fund, towards which liberal donations have been given by various gentlemen. The objects of the fund are to remove the hindrances that may arise in the way of higher education in the case of children in Board Schools whose characters are good, whose attendance is regular, and who show a capacity for special and valuable work." Whereupon, I put to myself this question:—"If this state of things is to continue with respect to children in Board Schools, where will the children of Middle-class parents—against whom the doors of the Board Schools are closed—find themselves in the matter of education by and by?" At present, parents in the middle rank of life are in a far worse position with respect to the education of girls than parents in the rank of life below them. The one, in most cases, has to pay exorbitantly for teaching of, not unfrequently, a very indifferent kind; the other pays nothing, or next to nothing, for the best instruction it is in the power of the State to provide. Will no one in Parliament plead the cause of Female Middle-class Education?

LONDON: PRINTED BY WM. CLOWES & SONS, STAMFORD STREET & CHARING CROSS.

Advertisements.

See Advertisement, next page.

Blackheath and Greenwich Ladies' College,

DARTMOUTH HOUSE, BLACKHEATH.

PRINCIPAL—MISS BURTON.

FEES.

RESIDENT PUPILS UNDER 12 YEARS	70	GUINEAS PER ANNUM.
" " ABOVE 12 AND UNDER 15 YEARS ..	85	" "
" SENIOR PUPILS	100	" "
NON-RESIDENT PUPILS UNDER 12 YEARS	12	" "
" " ABOVE 12 AND UNDER 15 YEARS	16	" "
" SENIOR PUPILS	20	" "

ACCOMPLISHMENTS AT THE PROFESSORS' CHARGES.

THE education given is thorough in every respect. The curriculum is that laid down by the Cambridge Syndicate. All the pupils go through the same course, with such instigation as their respective ages require.

Many of them have passed the Cambridge University Examination with very good results for some years past.

Dartmouth House is situated on the west side of Blackheath, at about an equal distance from the Greenwich, Blackheath Hill, and the Lewisham Junction Railway Stations.

The Mansion is surrounded by 2½ acres of pleasure ground, reserved almost entirely for the recreation of the pupils; the grounds are quite secluded, and they open directly on to the Heath.

ST. MARGARET'S, WESTBOURNE, BOURNEMOUTH.

MISS WILLIAMS

Having had the advantage of many years' experience in Private Tuition, receives a limited number of PUPILS, for whose health and comfort every arrangement is made. The various accomplishments under eminent Professors. Languages taught by Foreign Governesses.

TERMS for Board and general Instruction, including French, German, and Arithmetic, for Pupils under 12 years of age, £60 per annum; above that age, £80. PROFESSORS' TERMS:—Pianoforte, 2 Guineas per Term; Singing, 2 Guineas; Drawing, 2 Guineas; Dancing, 2 Guineas.

The charge for Laundress is 2 Guineas a Term. The Seat in Church, 8s. a Term. Three months' notice is required before the removal of a Pupil. The year is divided into Three Terms.

PARKFIELD HOUSE, FOREST HILL, SYDENHAM, S.E.

MISS STRICKLAND

Receives young Ladies to educate under her personal superintendence, assisted by Certificated Resident English and Foreign Governesses. LANGUAGES: French, German, and Italian, by Resident Governesses. A Term's Notice required. TERMS: Board and Education in English and French, 60 guineas a year. Accomplishments extra.

PROFESSORS:—Science, Mr. Strange; English Literature, Dr. Speer, LL.D.; Pianoforte, Professor Von Kornatzki; Organ, Mr. Cellier; Harmonium, Mr. Cellier; Harp, Miss M. Beard; Singing, Miss Malraison; Class Singing, Miss Pemberton; Drawing, Mr. Rolfe, R.A.; Painting, Mr. Mudge, R.A.; Elocution, Mrs. Erskine; Dancing, Madame Rousseau; Latin, Dr. Speer; Shorthand, Mr. Rolfe; Arithmetic, Mr. Fincham.

Pupils received on (Moderate) Inclusive Terms.

QUEEN'S COLLEGE,

LONDON,

43 and 45, HARLEY STREET, W.

(ESTABLISHED 1848. INCORPORATED BY ROYAL CHARTER, 1853),

FOR THE GENERAL EDUCATION OF LADIES, AND FOR GRANTING CERTIFICATES OF KNOWLEDGE.

Patrons:

HER MAJESTY THE QUEEN.

H.R.H. THE PRINCESS OF WALES. H.R.H. THE PRINCESS LOUISE.

VISITOR—THE RIGHT HON. AND RIGHT REV. THE LORD BISHOP OF LONDON.

Principal—The Rev. J. LLEWELYN DAVIES, M.A.

Lady Resident—Miss GROVE.

BOARDERS ARE RECEIVED. PARTICULARS ON APPLICATION.

1. **Higher Course.**—For Students above Eighteen years of age. It is intended that this Course should give to Students engaged in preparing for the Degree Examinations in London University the assistance they require. The Compounding Fee for this Course is £4 4*s.*; for Four Courses of Lectures, £3 3*s.*; for each Course of Ten Lectures, £1 1*s.*; for a Single Lecture, 5*s.* The First Lecture of each Course is Free. Full details of the Lectures may be obtained on application to the Secretary.

2. **Ordinary Course.**—This consists of Four Years. The Course of Instruction and Text Books for each year will be found in the Prospectus. An Entrance Examination is held at the beginning of each Term.

3. **Preparatory Class.**—A Preparatory Class is organized for Pupils who do not reach the Standard required in the Entrance Examination.

COMPOUNDING FEES IN COLLEGE.

	£	s.	d.	
* *Compounders* under Fifteen	£8	8	0	a Term.
" above "	10	10	0	"
Non-Compounders, for Classes meeting twice a week (Drawing excepted)	2	2	0	"
Non-Compounders, for Classes meeting once a week	1	6	3	"
Drawing—Classes meeting once a week for 1½ hour	1	11	6	"
" " twice " "	2	12	6	"

The Fees for the Half-Term are two-thirds of the above.

If three or more Sisters attend as Compounders in the College at the same time, the youngest is received at half-fees.

* The attendance of *Compounders* is limited to *twenty-one* hours' of Class-teaching *per week.*

QUEEN'S COLLEGE SCHOOL,

For Children from Five to Fourteen Years of Age.

Lady Superintendent—Miss HAY. | *Assistant*—Miss WALKER.

FEES.

For Pupils under ten	£4	4*s.*	a Term.
" above ten and under twelve	5	5	"
" above twelve and under fourteen	6	6	"
" above fourteen	8	8	"

ELLERSLIE HIGH SCHOOL & COLLEGE, BLACKHEATH, LONDON.

(Established 30 years.)

A BOARDING *School,—but otherwise conducted similarly to the high* DAY *Schools—affording facilities for a thorough education in Classics, Modern Languages, Mathematics, Science, &c., meeting at the same time the most rigid requirements of parents in regard to accomplishments; but without the indiscriminate mixture of all grades as in the Public high Day Schools. The chief features are,—Modern Methods throughout,—*MASTERS *for majority of subjects.—Systematic attention to refinement and to musical and other accomplishments,—Rigidly systematic preparation for Art, Science, and the Cambridge Local Examinations. 42 ladies passed these in the three last years.*

The Principal avails herself of the privilege recently accorded to the Public Schools, and to Higher Schools and Colleges generally, of being examined by the Government authorities in Science and Art subjects, thus guaranteeing to parents and guardians a rigidly honest and reliable examination. In the last year's Cambridge Local, and also in the Science Examinations there was not a single failure, and several of the latter won Queen's Prizes. One lady passed the Senior "Cambridge." This year the Art Examination was added (in the College department) to those of the Science and Cambridge local, making three official examinations in all. The results were as follows:—Science examinations, sent up 15. Passed 14. Art examination, sent up 13. Passed 10. Cambridge Local, sent up 3. Passed 2, one in honours.

In the preparation for the examinations, no selection is made of pupils who may happen to show exceptional ability in order that special attention may be paid them to make a show of passes; but absolutely equal attention is paid to those of both moderate and superior powers. Without distinction or selection all the senior pupils are taken through the course prescribed by the Cambridge Syndicate (unless otherwise prescribed in certain cases by the parents), who determine whether their daughters shall sit for examination or not.

Amongst the professors are Herr Jules Jager,—Fred. W. Clark, (Queen's College, Oxford,)—Ralph Wilkinson,—Frank Elmore,—Charles Swinstead, Exhibitor, R.A., (Government School of Art, South Kensington,)—J. W. Wren, Esq., F.R.G.S., (Government School of Science, South Kensington.) A Parisienne (diplomée 1st class) is resident.

New School Rooms (16 feet high), new Dormitories (11 feet), were built recently (shown above, right-side of view) with every appliance for health. Auxiliary low pressure, warm (not hot) water pipes have been placed in the corridors and school rooms, but open fires are used also, to prevent stagnation of the air. For Ventilation there are Tobin's tubes, which supply continuous streams of air without draft.

The Junior Department is under guaranteed motherly care. In regard to comfort and exceptionable table—references to numerous parents. The terms are very moderate. Address Lady Principal, Loampit Hill, Blackheath, S.E.

There is in connection with the above, a superior School in Boulogne under a Parisienne diplomée (1st class), to which pupils may be sent (without extra charges) for perfecting their French; the Lady Principal of above being responsible. Full particulars sent.

Lightning Source UK Ltd.
Milton Keynes UK
UKHW012252121219
355304UK00001B/15/P